ANIMALS AND THE LAW IN ANTIQUITY

Program in Judaic Studies
Brown University
Box 1826
Providence, RI 02912

BROWN JUDAIC STUDIES

Edited by

David C. Jacobson
Saul M. Olyan
Rachel Rojanski
Michael L. Satlow
Adam Teller

Number 368
ANIMALS AND THE LAW IN ANTIQUITY

edited by
Saul M. Olyan and Jordan D. Rosenblum

ANIMALS AND THE LAW IN ANTIQUITY

Edited by
Saul M. Olyan
Jordan D. Rosenblum

Brown Judaic Studies
Providence, Rhode Island

© 2021 Brown University. All rights reserved.

No part of this work may be reproduced or transmitted in any form or by any means, electronic or mechanical, including photocopying and recording, or by means of any information storage or retrieval system, except as may be expressly permitted by the 1976 Copyright Act or in writing from the publisher. Requests for permission should be addressed in writing to the Rights and Permissions Office, Program in Judaic Studies, Brown University, Box 1826, Providence, RI 02912, USA.

Library of Congress Control Number: 2021941885

Contents

Contributors vii
Abbreviations ix

Introduction
  Saul M. Olyan and Jordan D. Rosenblum 1

"Mere" Things or Sentient Beings? The Legal Status of Animals
in Ancient Egyptian Society
  Rozenn Bailleul-LeSuer 13

Partial Persons, Unsafe Spaces: The Babylonian Production of Class
through Laws about Animals
  Seth Richardson 41

Symmetry or Asymmetry according to the Law? The Case of
Domesticated Animals and Human Beings
  Saul M. Olyan 69

Animals in Greek and Roman Criminal Law
  F. S. Naiden 83

Animal Acts: Diet and Law in the Acts of the Apostles and Early
Christian Practice
  Andrew McGowan 105

The Role of Laws in Porphyry's Arguments against Animal Sacrifice
  Miira Tuominen 121

Banning Animal Sacrifice ad Infinitum: Cui Bono?
  Daniel Ullucci 143

Dolphins Are Humans of the Sea (b. Bekhorot 8a): Animals and
Legal Categorization in Rabbinic Literature
Jordan D. Rosenblum 161

Response to Bailleul-LeSuer, Olyan, Richardson, and Tuominen
Andreas Schüle 177

Response to McGowan, Naiden, Ullucci, and Rosenblum
Beth Berkowitz 187

Indexes 199

Contributors

Rozenn Bailleul-LeSuer, SUNY Brockport
Beth Berkowitz, Barnard College
Andrew McGowan, Yale University
F. S. Naiden, University of North Carolina at Chapel Hill
Saul M. Olyan, Brown University
Seth Richardson, University of Chicago
Jordan D. Rosenblum, University of Wisconsin, Madison
Andreas Schüle, Universität Leipzig
Miira Tuominen, University of Stockholm
Daniel Ullucci, Stonehill College

Abbreviations

Classical Sources
Aelian
    Nat. an.   *De natura animalium*
Aristotle
    Ath. pol.   *Athenaion politeia*
    Eth. nic.   *Ethica nicomachea*
    Mir. ausc.   *De mirabilibus auscultationibus*
    Phys.   *Physica*
    Pol.   *Politica*
Cicero
    Tusc.   *Tusculanae disputationes*
Demosthenes
    Aristocr.   *In Aristocratem*
Diodorus Siculus
    Bib. hist.   *Biblioteca historica*
Herodotus
    Hist.   *Historiae*
I. Cret.   *Inscriptiones Creticae*
Iamblichus
    Myst.   *De mysteriis*
Pausanius
    Descr.   *Graeciae descriptio*
Plato
    Leg.   *Leges*
Pliny the Elder
    Nat.   *Naturalis historia*
Plotinus
    Enn.   *Enneads*
Plutarch
    De esu   *De esu carnium*
    Luc.   *Lucullus*
    Pel.   *Pelopidas*
    Quaest. conv.   *Quaestionum convivialum*
    Sol.   *Solon*
    Soll. an.   *De sollertia animalium*

Porphyry
    Abst.   *De abstinentia ab esu animalium*
Stobaeus
    Flor.   *Florilegium*

Rabbinic writings
    b.   Babylonian Talmud
    m.   Mishnah
    t.   Tosefta

Secondary Sources

AbB	Klaas R. Veenhof, ed., *Altbabylonische Briefe in Umschrift und Übersetzung*, 14 vols. (Leiden: Brill, 1964–2005).
AJP	*American Journal of Philology*
ANRW	Hildegard Temporini and Wolfgang Haase, eds., *Aufstieg und Niedergang der römischen Welt: Geschichte und Kultur Roms im Spiegel der neueren Forschung* (Berlin: de Gruyter, 1972–).
AOAT	Alter Orient und Altes Testament
AS	Assyriological Studies
BibInt	*Biblical Interpretation*
CAD	*The Assyrian Dictionary of the Oriental Institute of the University of Chicago*, 21 vols. (Chicago: Oriental Institute of the University of Chicago, 1956–2011).
ClQ	*Classical Quarterly*
CP	*Classical Philology*
CSEL	Corpus Scriptorum Ecclesiasticorum Latinorum
CT	*Cuneiform Texts from Babylonian Tablets in the British Museum*
CurBR	*Currents in Biblical Research*
CUSAS	Cornell University Studies in Assyriology and Sumerology
GRBS	*Greek, Roman, and Byzantine Studies*
HTR	*Harvard Theological Review*
IG	*Inscriptiones Graecae: Editio Minor* (Berlin: de Gruyter, 1924–).
IM	Iraq Museum
JCS	*Journal of Cuneiform Studies*
JECS	*Journal of Early Christian Studies*
JESHO	*Journal of the Economic and Social History of the Orient*
JRS	*Journal of Roman Studies*
JSQ	*Jewish Studies Quarterly*
JTS	*Journal of Theological Studies*
LSJ	Henry Liddell and Robert Scott, eds., *A Greek-English Lexicon*, rev. H. Stuart Jones (Oxford: Clarendon, 1968).
NovTSup	Supplements to Novum Testamentum
NTL	New Testament Library
OB	Old Babylonian

OLA	Orientalia Lovaniensia Analecta
OLD	P. G. W. Glare, ed., *The Oxford Latin Dictionary* (Oxford: Clarendon, 1982).
PBS	University of Pennsylvania, Publications of the Babylonian Section
RA	*Revue d'assyriologie et d'archéologie orientale*
RHR	*Revue de l'histoire des religions*
StPatr	Studia Patristica
VC	*Vigiliae Christianae*
WAW	Writings from the Ancient World
WGRW	Writings from the Greco-Roman World
TAPA	*Transactions of the American Philological Association*
TAPS	Transactions of the American Philosophical Society
TCL	Textes cunéiformes. Musée du Louvre
TLOB	Texts from the Late Old Babylonian Period
WUNT	Wissenschaftliche Untersuchungen zum Neuen Testament
YOS	Yale Oriental Series, Texts
ZAW	*Zeitschrift für die alttestamentliche Wissenschaft*

Introduction

SAUL M. OLYAN
Brown University

JORDAN D. ROSENBLUM
University of Wisconsin

A nimal law has become a topic of growing importance internationally, with animal welfare and animal rights often assuming center stage in contemporary debates about the legal status of animals. Not infrequently, nonspecialists marshal ancient texts in a decontextualized and ill-informed way to support or deny rights to animals, while specialists in fields such as Classics, Biblical Studies, Assyriology, Egyptology, Rabbinics, and Late Antique Christianity have only just begun to engage the topic of animals and the law in their respective areas.[1] The purpose of this volume is to bring together original studies by scholars from a range of ancient Mediterranean and West Asian fields on a variety of topics at the intersection of animals and the law in antiquity. These studies not only stake out new ground in their respective areas; they also allow us to begin to develop a comparative perspective on animals and the law in West Asian and Mediterranean antiquity, something that has never been done. Each of the two essays responding to the eight studies in the volume contributes directly to this comparative aim by bringing into relief continuities and discontinuities in the legal status and/or treatment of animals, as well as drawing attention to the most salient points in the essays from a comparative perspective. This introduction, for its part, brings the insights of the essays in this volume to bear on wider, contemporary discussion and debate about

---

1. For examples of the problematic use of ancient texts in arguments about animal rights, particularly the tendency to blame the Bible and, sometimes, other ancient texts for the history of animal oppression in the West, see "Nonspecialists' Engagement with Ancient Texts: A Critique" in this introduction.

animals and the law, including animal rights and animal welfare. In it, we introduce current international trends in animal law; offer a critique of some of the ways in which ancient Mediterranean and West Asian texts have been employed by contemporary nonspecialists; and suggest how such texts, as well as visual representations and other nonliterary material remains, read in a nuanced way by specialists, might contribute to current discussion and debate about animals and the law.

Current International Trends in Animal Law

Animal Law has come into its own in recent decades. Law schools throughout the world, from Hong Kong to India and from Russia to Mexico, teach courses in animal law and some offer specialization in the area; the annual Animal Law Conference, cosponsored by Lewis & Clark Law School's Center for Animal Studies and the Animal Legal Defense Fund, routinely draws hundreds of participants from around the world; peer reviewed scholarly journals specializing in animal law have been established in Finland, Spain, the United Kingdom, the United States, and Brazil, among other countries; organizations such as the Nonhuman Rights Project (nonhumanrights.org) in the United States, the Global Animal Law Project in Switzerland (globalanimallaw.org), One Voice in France (one-voice.fr) and the Asociación de Funcionarios y Abogados por los Derechos de los Animales in Argentina litigate and/or advocate and educate on behalf of animals. American federal and state law, and the laws of many other countries and subnational units, seek to protect animals from neglect and abuse (globalanimallaw.org/database/national/index.html). Several European countries have gone further than this: the Swiss, German, and Austrian constitutions themselves now enshrine the protection of animals (1992; 2002; 2004), and, since 2014, France's *Code civil* has recognized animals as "living beings endowed with sentience."[2] Although it remains unclear what kind of practical, quotidian impact recent European constitutional or legislative changes will have on animal lives, they are significant for their innovation, even if they do not unambiguously establish genuine legal rights for animals.[3] The fact is that even

---

2. "Les animaux sont des êtres vivants doués de sensibilité" (515-14 *Code civil*). For the constitutions of Switzerland, Germany, and Austria, and for the *Code civil* in France, see, conveniently, https://www.globalanimallaw.org/database/national/index.html.

3. Genuine rights, in the words of animal rights advocate and law professor Gary L. Francione, do "not evaporate in the face of consequential considerations" (*Animals, Property, and the Law*, Ethics and Action [Philadelphia: Temple University Press, 1995], 114). This means that genuine rights are not subject to the competing claims of others. Put another way, human interests do not trump the interests of animals with rights.

in countries that accord some form of legal recognition to animals and impose legal requirements for their care and treatment, animals can still be hunted; they are still slaughtered for food in considerable numbers; they are still displayed in zoos and made to perform in circuses; they are still subjected to scientific experimentation.[4] In short: Even in countries that have added the protection of animals to their constitutions or legal codes, animals lack genuine rights such as the right to life, the right to bodily integrity, and the right to bodily liberty; from the perspective of the law, full legal personhood continues to elude them.

The most noteworthy trend in contemporary international animal law is the fight to secure fundamental legal rights for animals. Focusing on apes, elephants, dolphins, and whales, the Nonhuman Rights Project, founded and led by Steven M. Wise, seeks to change the legal status of animals from "mere 'things,' which lack the capacity to possess any legal right, to 'legal persons,' who possess such fundamental rights as bodily liberty and bodily integrity." Furthermore, the organization aims to secure recognition for animals "as beings worthy of moral and legal consideration … with their own inherent interests in freedom from captivity, participation in a community of other members of their species, and the protection of their natural habitats" (nonhumanrights.org). Those working on behalf of the Nonhuman Rights Project pursue the organization's agenda partially through litigation at all levels, primarily by filing *habeas corpus* petitions on behalf of specific animals held in captivity with an eye to establishing legal personhood for these animals—at least with regard to *habeas corpus*—and as a result, their release to sanctuaries.[5] Although this tactic has yet to succeed in the United States, it found success in Argentina in 2015.[6]

One strategy used by activists to establish the legal personhood of animals, and thus legal rights such as the right to bodily integrity or bodily

---

4. Regarding the current situation in Germany, a country that has enshrined the protection of animals in its constitution, see, e.g., https://www.aerzte-gegen-tierversuche.de. On the Swiss situation, see Gieri Bolliger, who points out that even with protections enshrined in Swiss law and the Swiss constitution, animal interests are still routinely subordinated to those of human beings when the two come into conflict ("Legal Protection of Animal Dignity in Switzerland: Status Quo and Future Perspectives," *Animal Law Review* 22 [2016]: synopsis https://law.lclark.edu/law_reviews/animal_law_review/past_issues/volume_22_2.php.

5. A writ of *habeas corpus* is a court order demanding the delivery of an incarcerated or detained person to the court and justification for that person's imprisonment or detention (see further law.cornell.edu/wex/habeas_corpus). By utilizing *habeas corpus* petitions to pursue findings of legal personhood for captive animals, advocates implicitly assert that such animals are prisoners and that those who incarcerate them have no legal justification for doing so.

6. See https://www.animallaw.info/case/asociacion-de-funcionarios-y-abogados-por-los-derechos-de-los-animales-y-otros-contra-gcba.

liberty, is to draw an analogy between animals and very young children or adult persons who lack the ability to make and express rational choices or fulfill societal duties and responsibilities and who are not held legally accountable for their conduct. Although infants, persons with severe mental retardation or dementia, or persons who are in a coma are, with few exceptions, unable to bear social duties or responsibilities, or to make and express rational choices, they are not considered legally responsible for their actions but nonetheless possess fundamental legal rights such as the right to life and the right to bodily liberty. Given that this is the case, advocates for animal rights argue, why should animals continue to be denied such rights?[7] In the words of Steven M. Wise, "that very young humans and comatose humans are 'persons' with the capacity to possess legal rights, despite their inability to bear duties and responsibilities explodes the claim that the capacity to bear duties and responsibilities has any relevance to personhood and the capacity for legal rights."[8] Here, Wise is arguing against a commonplace counterargument undergirding decisions such as the 2014 New York State Appeals Court finding in *Lavery* that animals may be denied legal personhood and concomitant rights on account of their inability to fulfill legal duties and responsibilities.[9]

Another common approach deployed by advocates of animal rights such as the Nonhuman Rights Project is to focus initial efforts on a particular set of species (e.g., whales, elephants, dolphins, or apes) that possess autonomy (evidenced by intentional communication and an understanding of cause and effect, among other characteristics) and might be characterized as "cognitively complex," in the hope that advocacy for their legal rights might meet with more success than arguing on behalf of the legal personhood of all animals at once. According to Wise, after establishing legal rights for these highly intelligent animals, the effort will broaden to securing the rights of all animals. This approach privileges species that are most like human beings strategically in order eventually to attain rights for all animals; implicit is the assumption that courts will be more easily swayed by arguments in favor of the legal personhood of animals that

---

7. In fact, evidence suggests that animals with higher cognitive function might be more able to make and express rational choices than some human beings who lack cognitive abilities and, furthermore, that some cognitively complex animals may even be able to bear social duties and responsibilities in their own societies, as well as in human/animal contexts. On the latter point, see, e.g., Steven M. Wise, "A New York Appellate Court Takes A First Swing at Chimpanzee Personhood, and Misses," *Denver Law Review* 95 (2017): 265–87, here 280 and n. 104, which references affidavits presented to support a 2015 *habeas corpus* petition by the Nonhuman Rights Project to the New York State Supreme Court on behalf of Tommy, a chimpanzee held alone in captivity.

8. Wise, "New York Appellate Court," 286.

9. Ibid., 265.

most resemble human persons cognitively and otherwise.[10] It is worth noting that this strategy has found some initial success in court.[11]

A third contemporary strategy that is not infrequently evidenced is to adopt the argument that many human beings were once wholly or partially "legal things" but "attained personhood only after protracted struggles both inside and out of courtrooms," so why not animals, too?[12] The struggle to end and even criminalize slavery, to achieve full and equal rights for women, people of color, LGBTQ+ persons, and others subject to social and legal marginalization in any number of countries is held up by some contemporary advocates of animal rights as a model for present-day struggles to end "another intolerable wrong, the continuing rightlessness of nonhuman animals."[13]

These and other strategies to secure legal personhood and concomitant rights for animals are frequently paired with the argument that existing animal welfare laws and anticruelty statutes are deficient because they are often unenforced and even unenforceable and they typically privilege the interests of humans over those of animals in ways that genuine rights accorded to animals would not.[14] In the words of Wise, "these kinds of statutes and regulations are plainly inadequate and their inadequacy can never be remedied, for they were enacted not to protect the well-being of nonhuman animals, but rather to regulate the manner in which we humans exploit them. All history demonstrates that even the most fundamental interests of humans can never be adequately protected without legal rights. It is no different for nonhuman animals."[15] In contrast, there are those who argue that expanding, strengthening, and enforcing existing animal welfare laws would accord to animals the legal protections they deserve and thereby reduce their suffering; doing so would also be a more realistic goal for animal advocates.[16] In fact, since 1990, many state referenda in the

---

10. https://medium.com/@NonhumanRights/letter-1-from-the-front-lines-of-the-non-human-rights-projects-struggle-for-the-rights-of-nonhuman-b053b100af25.

11. See the 2018 opinion of New York Appeals Court Judge Eugene Fahey discussed by Wise (https://medium.com/@NonhumanRights/letter-2-from-the-front-lines-of-the-struggle-for-nonhuman-rights-january-2018-to-september-2018-c84f5e581d4f).

12. https://medium.com/@NonhumanRights/letter-1-from-the-front-lines-of-the-non-human-rights-projects-struggle-for-the-rights-of-nonhuman-b053b100af25.

13. Ibid.

14. On the characteristics of genuine rights, see the discussion in n. 3.

15. https://medium.com/@NonhumanRights/letter-1-from-the-front-lines-of-the-non-human-rights-projects-struggle-for-the-rights-of-nonhuman-b053b100af25. For a succinct and clear description of the animal welfare approach, see Sue Donaldson and Will Kymlicka, *Zoopolis: A Political Theory of Animal Rights* (New York: Oxford University Press, 2011), 3–4, which also includes a critique.

16. See, e.g., Cass R. Sunstein, "The Rights of Animals: A Very Short Primer," John M. Olin Program in Law and Economics Working Paper No. 157 (Chicago: University of Chicago Law School, 2002), 1–11.

United States that have sought to enhance animal welfare in some way have been successful, in contrast to previous efforts.[17] It remains to be seen which approach—securing genuine rights for animals or enhancing and enforcing animal welfare laws—ultimately wins the day, and results will likely differ from country to country.

Nonspecialists' Engagement with Ancient Texts: A Critique

Although biblical and, to a lesser degree, other ancient texts are frequently cited by contemporary nonspecialists who are engaged in debate about the status of animals in American law and the law of other countries, these writers—most often law professors or moral philosophers—typically depend on translations—often outdated or inaccurate—of the ancient texts they engage, so that they cannot speak of linguistic nuance or textual complexities. As a group, nonspecialists have demonstrated a tendency to privilege one biblical text in particular—Gen 1:28, in which humanity is told by God at creation to subdue the earth and rule over the animals—in their discussions, as if it were somehow normative or at minimum, representative, of biblical viewpoints on animals. Further, they not infrequently generalize about biblical and other ancient perspectives on the status of animals without any in-depth analysis.[18] An example is Lauren Magnotti, whose article "Pawing Open the Courthouse Door: Why Animals' Interests Should Matter When Courts Grant Standing" was published by *St. John's Law Review* in 2006. Regarding the Bible, the author, a law professor and practicing attorney, claims the following: "The theme of animal subjugation permeates the Bible. While there are some passages that teach that animals and humans share many similarities and that animals should be treated humanely, the Bible generally shows very little regard for the humane treatment of animals." Magnotti supports this generalization with little evidence, mentioning divinely ordained human rule over the animals in Gen 1:28, the practice of animal sacrifice, the story in Mark 5:1–13 about Jesus casting out demons, and Paul's nonliteral interpretation of Deut 25:4 in 1 Cor 9:9–10.[19] Her main purpose in treating biblical texts such as Gen 1:28 seems to be to demonstrate their direct

---

17. Donaldson and Kymlicka, *Zoopolis*, 1–2.

18. Genesis 1:28 reads: "Be fruitful, multiply, fill the earth and subdue it; and rule over the fish of the sea and the fowl of the heavens and all creatures that move on the earth" (trans. Saul M. Olyan).

19. Lauren Magnotti, "Pawing Open the Courthouse Door: Why Animals' Interests Should Matter When Courts Grant Standing," *St. John's Law Review* 80 (2006): 455–95, here 459–60. Magnotti's article was originally brought to our attention by Erin Evans, "Constitutional

influence on the Anglo-American legal tradition, which has viewed and continues to view animals as property, without legal personhood and rights.[20] Others, such as the moral philosopher Peter Singer, provide similarly superficial representations of the content of biblical texts that treat animals and, not unlike Magnotti, give pride of place to Gen 1:28. In fact, Singer's chapter title, "Man's Dominion ... a Short History of Speciesism," alludes directly and unmistakably to the verse, allowing it to shape his reading of other biblical texts.[21]

Yet nothing is said by these authors about the various laws in the Hebrew Bible that ascribe genuine rights to animals, rights that are evidently not subject to suspension or modification under any circumstances (e.g., the right to Sabbath rest according to Exod 23:12 and Deut 5:12–15).[22] That Deut 25:4—an ox threshing grain cannot be muzzled—read in its original context suggests that oxen have rights when they thresh goes unmentioned. Nor are the various texts that treat sacrifice as normative read by these authors alongside passages such as Isa 66:3, which takes a very different position, comparing the person who sacrifices an ox to one who strikes down and kills a human being. That humans and animals were created as vegetarians according to Gen 1:29–30 and that meat eating is not enshrined until after the flood (Gen 9:3–4) are not noticed by many contemporary nonspecialists; that animals, along with humans, are portrayed as treaty partners with God according to Gen 9:8–17 and are held legally liable for their actions according to texts such as Exod 21:28 is rarely referenced. In short, the reading of biblical law and narrative to be

---

Inclusion of Animal Rights in Germany and Switzerland: How Did Animal Protection Become an Issue of National Importance?" *Society and Animals* 18 (2010): 231–50, here 232.

20. Magnotti, "Pawing Open the Courthouse Door," 460–61, citing William Blackstone and James Kent. Steven M. Wise, argues that the laws of the Hebrew Bible and other ancient laws, mediated through Justinian, are responsible for the legal status of animals as property in later Anglo-American law ("The Legal Thinghood of Nonhuman Animals," *Boston College Environmental Affairs Law Review* 23 [1996]: 471–546, here 473).

21. Peter Singer, *Animal Liberation: The Definitive Classic of the Animal Movement* (1975; repr., New York: HarperCollins, 2009), 187–88. Another example of lack of engagement with and overgeneralization about the Bible is to be found in Donaldson and Kymlicka, *Zoopolis*, 266 n. 21. Here the authors speak of Gen 1:26–28 as if it represents a single biblical viewpoint on animals; furthermore, they imply that this viewpoint leads naturally to the conclusion that "only humans are entitled to inviolable rights." Yet another manifestation of this approach is Steven M. Wise, "Animal Rights, One Step at A Time," in *Animal Rights: Current Debates and New Directions*, ed. Cass R. Sunstein and Martha C. Nussbaum (New York: Oxford University Press, 2004), 22–23, where Gen 1:28 is quoted and 1:26–27 and 9:2–3 are alluded to. The content of these verses shapes the entire Judeo-Christian tradition, according to Wise, allowing "religion" "to obstruct animals' rights." See, similarly, Wise, "How Nonhuman Animals Were Trapped in a Nonexistent Universe," *Animal Law* 1 (1995): 15–45, here 31–32.

22. See Saul M. Olyan, "Are There Legal Texts in the Hebrew Bible That Evince a Concern for Animal Rights?," *BibInt* 27 (2019): 321–39.

found in the works of many contemporary nonspecialists ignores the complexity and nuance of biblical views of animals, including the views articulated in legal texts. Although Gen 1:28 has been foregrounded in the history of biblical interpretation on account of its presence in the first creation narrative, it is but one of many biblical texts that address the status of animals and is hardly representative of the Hebrew Bible as a whole. In fact, to privilege Gen 1:28 and ignore or play down the explicit or implicit meanings of other relevant biblical texts results in the effective suppression of the many distinct voices that may be found in the biblical anthology, voices that address the status of animals. Put differently, those who give Gen 1:28 pride of place read the biblical text as if it were speaking in one voice instead of many, embracing a conservative interpretive tradition that flattens the text and renders it far less interesting than it actually is.[23]

Such interpretive narratives involve acts of selective reading. For nonspecialists, this might not seem so obvious, as one text—which proves their desired point—might loom larger than all others. And unlike the specialist, nonspecialists likely have read only a handful of texts and have not gained, to use an animal metaphor, the eagle eye's view of the specialist. For example, nonspecialists will often point to the talmudic dictum "Humans are forbidden to eat before they feed their animals" as if it represents the monolithic rabbinic view of human–nonhuman relationships (b. Berakhot. 40a).[24] But the rabbinics specialist would note that the statement is attributed to Rav, a Babylonian authority who also said other things about animals.[25] For example, after a cat bit off the hand of an infant, Rav decreed four severe things regarding cats in general, including, "it is permitted to kill it" (b. Bava Qamma 80b).[26] Animals and animality are categories that the ancient rabbis use to think through various legal scenarios and regulations. Selectively choosing one text or another does a disservice to the wide range of attitudes that the rabbis represent.[27] We could multiply

---

23. For a nuanced analysis of the possible meanings of Gen 1:28 in its historical and literary settings, see particularly Jakob Wöhrle, "*Dominium terrae*: Exegetische und religionsgeschichtliche Überlegungen zum Herrschaftsauftrag in Gen. 1,26–28," ZAW 121 (2009): 171–88, with citations.

24. Trans. Jordan D. Rosenblum. This passage continues on to base this interpretation on the order of Deut 11:5, in which cattle are offered grass to eat and then, in regard to humans, it says "you shall eat and be satisfied." For an example of a nonspecialist who treats this text as if it is broadly representative of ancient rabbinic views on the subject, see Tamra Wright, "'Now We're Talking Pedagogy': Levinas, Animal Ethics, and Jewish Education," in *Face to Face with Animals: Levinas and the Animal Question*, ed. Peter Atterton and Tamra Wright (Albany: State University of New York Press, 2019), 203–23, here 215.

25. The dictum is introduced with the phrase "Rav Yehudah said that Rav said."

26. For the full context, see b. Bava Qamma 80a–b. On this passage, see Beth A. Berkowitz, *Animals and Animality in the Babylonian Talmud* (New York: Cambridge University Press, 2018), 138–43.

27. In general, see ibid.

examples of how nonspecialists (mis)use ancient texts to advance certain modern viewpoints—polemical or otherwise—about animals and the law. In fact, more than a few essays in this volume—usually in the opening sections—include a brief survey of how certain texts in the area of the author's specialty have been read, and then seek to offer a more nuanced view. These essays therefore serve to reflect on past and present wrong turns while, at the same time, suggesting possible future paths forward.

How Might Ancient Evidence Contribute to Contemporary Discussion and Debate?

Ancient Mediterranean and West Asian texts and nonliterary artifacts have much to contribute to the contemporary discussion and debate about animals and the law, including animal rights and animal welfare, as the essays in this volume reveal. First, aspects of the legal and social status of animals and their treatment today are evidenced in ancient sources as well, demonstrating that ideas and practices that we might be tempted to think of as distinct to our own societies and times are not ours alone. According to various texts, farm animals are personal property that may be bequeathed or rented out for service, and their care is motivated as often by their owner's financial interests as by concern for the animals themselves (Richardson), not unlike in various contexts at present. Violence toward and neglect of domesticated animals and captive wild animals are attested in a variety of ancient sources, including remains found in burials, visual depictions, and textual descriptions (Bailleul-LeSuer); sadly, these data parallel all too common contemporary practices. The hunting of lions is depicted in artistic representations and texts from Mesopotamia and Egypt as an elite and even royal activity (Bailleul-LeSuer), bringing to mind big game hunting for sport by the wealthy in contemporary African, Asian, and North American contexts. The use of wild animals in public games during the Roman imperial period (Naiden) is not unlike aspects of their display in circuses today. In ancient Egypt, rich and variegated evidence attests to the deep emotional bonds that some people had with their companion animals, which might be named and buried when they die (Bailleul-LeSuer), not altogether different from the treatment of some pets today. Mistreatment of animals under human care is sometimes condemned vociferously in ancient texts, just as it is by many today, as the angry reaction of the eighth-century BCE Nubian ruler Piye to his enemy the Pharaoh's neglect of his own horses demonstrates (Bailleul-LeSuer). Factory farming is evidenced in ancient Egypt, although its goal—to create new divinities to serve as messengers to the gods on behalf of petitioners—was quite different from its purpose in contemporary contexts (Bailleul-LeSuer). And forced feeding of waterfowl and cattle intended for sacrifice (Bailleul-LeSuer) is not unlike contemporary or recent practices in the Euro-North American food industry. Furthermore, it has been argued that ancient sources provide evidence of the legal personhood of animals, or at least their "partial personhood," to use Seth Richardson's term, and even of genuine animal rights. Such rights are extended, for example, by Exod 23:12, which mandates Sabbath rest for ox and donkey that may not be abridged or suspended due to contingencies.[28] At the same time, animal trials in ancient Greece suggest that defendants possessed some degree of legal personhood (Naiden). Thus, thinking about animal rights has a long history (Schüle) that includes thinking about "animal agency and intentionality" (Berkowitz).

Second, a number of the arguments commonly made in the present day in favor of legal rights for animals or, at minimum, the enforcement of existing animal welfare laws that seek to guarantee humane treatment of animals are adumbrated in ancient sources. Porphyry's arguments that those who aspire to genuine piety should not sacrifice harmless, domesticated animals because they feel pain, or that animals have speech of their own and therefore share in reason (Tuominen), are not unlike the claims made by present-day animal rights advocates who oppose the slaughter of animals for food or seek to establish animal autonomy on the basis of characteristics such as intentional communication or language. Similarly, the observation that some domesticated animals can modify their behavior as a result of experience, as exemplified by Egyptian horses that learn to avoid a beating according to P. Lansing 2.6–8 (Bailleul-LeSuer), is not unlike the claim often made in contemporary animal rights litigation that at least some animals understand cause and effect and are capable of learning new behaviors.[29]

But ancient West Asian and Mediterranean materials offer present-day readers more than simply the observation that characteristics of the treatment or the legal and social status of animals in contemporary contexts are paralleled in ancient materials, or the insight that many arguments made today on behalf of animals have a longer history than we might have assumed. They also provide evidence that might be used to construct novel legal arguments on behalf of animals, just as they have been used in the past to formulate justifications for denying animals legal personhood and rights (as in William Blackstone's use of Gen 1:28 in his influential *Commentaries on the Laws of England* [1765–69]).[30] For example, contemporary advocates for the legal personhood of animals could point to Greek animal trials, which implicitly ascribe some degree of legal personhood,

---

28. See n. 22.
29. See, e.g., Wise, "New York Appellate Court," 267.
30. See Magnotti, "Pawing Open the Courthouse Door," 460, for Blackstone.

holding animals responsible for their actions in a legal setting (Naiden). One might also mention the place of domesticated animals in—as opposed to outside of—the household along with slaves and free human household members according to some cuneiform texts (Richardson), or the implicit classification of farm animals with slaves and foreign residents in a law such as Exod 23:12, which ascribes to these distinct groups genuine rights.[31] In the latter two examples, the texts are telling us implicitly that animals and the human beings closely associated with them share important characteristics, for example, that their interests count and that they are worthy of legal protection or that they are equally members of the household, with all that that implies. Furthermore, some ancient texts assign to animals a value symmetrical to that of human beings, for example, a sacrificial animal may be used to substitute for a firstborn son according to Exod 13:13, 15; 34:20. Not ten or twenty or a hundred such animals, but one, suggesting a high valuation of the animal substitute, at least in the context of sacrifice (Olyan).

Although there is certainly ancient evidence that lends itself to contemporary use in advocacy for animal personhood and rights, we would be remiss were we to fail to mention the equally important data that have been used—or might be used—to construct arguments counter to those that seek to establish legal personhood and genuine rights for animals. Many ancient texts use animals to stake out the boundaries of what is properly human, implicitly dehumanizing or animalizing human outsiders and, in so doing, suggesting that the animal–human divide is not as ambiguous as other ancient texts might imply. Examples include rabbinic legal discourse, which sometimes dehumanizes gentiles by animalizing them (Rosenblum), or Greek and Roman laws, which pay no heed to neglect for and cruelty toward animals or slaves (Naiden). Furthermore, ancient Christian proscriptions of sacrifice were motivated not by concern for the animal victims themselves, as nonsacrificial slaughter continued to be practiced. Rather, banning sacrifice and stigmatizing it as impious and un-Roman, as in the Theodosian Code, functioned to demarcate Roman identity in a new way (Ullucci), just as the dietary choices envisioned by earlier Christian writers contributed to the establishment of the identities of their communities, at least in theory (McGowan). Thus, proscriptions of sacrifice such as those preserved in the Theodosian Code do not offer present-day animal advocates material of potential utility with which to construct arguments against contemporary practices of mass animal slaughter or meat consumption.

---

31. See n. 22.

Moving Forward

The essays in this volume tell us something about where the fields of their authors are at present with regard to the relationship of animals and the law and point toward productive ways forward for those particular fields. Taken together, these essays and the responses to them suggest that there is much more work to be done in order to understand how the perceived relationships of humans and nonhumans and the categories introduced to classify them affect ancient (and modern) law.

In *The Animal That Therefore I Am*, a collection of lectures that has become a classic in the field of Animal Studies, Jacques Derrida raises a series of questions with regard to the category "animal." In his first lecture, Derrida argues:

> *Animal* is a word that men have given themselves the right to give.... They have given themselves the word in order to corral a large number of living beings within a single concept: "The Animal," they say....
>
> Men would be first and foremost those living creatures who had given themselves the word that enables them to speak of the animal with a single voice and to designate it as the single being that remains without a response, without a word with which to respond.
>
> That wrong was committed long ago and with long-term consequences. It derives from this word, or rather it comes together in this word *animal*, which men have given themselves as at the origin of humanity, and which they have given themselves in order to be identified, in order to be recognized, with a view to being what they say they are, namely, men, capable of replying and responding in the name of men.[32]

While Derrida offers several paths forward (most famously is his neologism *animot*), his observations cited above have implications both for ancient legal texts and for those who study them. In fact, Derrida's mention of humans naming animals calls to mind Adam naming all of the animals in Gen 2:19-20.[33] Humans speak of—and for—animals. And when they do, we have much to learn. As we shall see, however, what we learn is often more about the human animal than about the nonhuman animal.

---

32. Jacques Derrida, *The Animal That Therefore I Am*, ed. Marie-Louise Mallet, trans. David Wills (New York: Fordham University Press, 2008), 32 (emphasis original).

33. Further, Adam names woman in Gen 2:23, which reminds us of the importance of considering gender when discussing human/nonhuman legal texts.

"Mere" Things or Sentient Beings?
The Legal Status of Animals in Ancient Egyptian Society

ROZENN BAILLEUL-LESUER
SUNY Brockport

Egyptologists who specialize in the study of ancient fauna should consider themselves extremely fortunate, as abundant documentation is at their disposal to further their research, not only textual and archaeological evidence, common to many other ancient civilizations, but also exquisite representations. Animals indeed feature extensively in the rich iconographic material that has survived from Pharaonic Egypt. They are part of the writing system;[1] they are depicted as participating in the daily life of both the farming community and members of the elite;[2] and their physical characteristics were adopted as symbols of royalty and the divine.[3] It is undeniable that the ancient Egyptian artists who painted and carved these scenes, the members of the ruling elite who devised the writing system, and the priests who borrowed from the animal world those abstract notions that they wished to associate with humankind and the

---

I would like to thank Saul Olyan and Jordan Rosenblum for inviting me to participate in the symposium "Animals and the Law in Antiquity," as well as Seth Richardson for his kind advice and support. I am also grateful to Solange Ashby, Linda Evans, and Foy Scalf for their help while researching and writing this paper.

1. Patrick F. Houlihan, "Animals in Egyptian Art and Hieroglyphs," in *A History of the Animal World in the Ancient Near East*, ed. Billie Jean Collins, HdO 1.64 (Leiden: Brill, 2002), 97–143; Pascal Vernus, "Les animaux dans l'écriture égyptienne," in *Bestiaire des pharaons*, ed. Pascal Vernus and Jean Yoyotte (Paris: A. Viénot, 2005), 62–75.

2. Patrick F. Houlihan, *The Animal World of the Pharaohs* (London: Thames & Hudson, 1996), 10–39; Douglas Brewer, "Hunting, Animal Husbandry and Diet in Ancient Egypt," in Collins, *History of the Animal World*, 427–56.

3. Emily Teeter, "Animals in Egyptian Literature," in Collins, *History of the Animal World*, 251–70; and in the same volume, Teeter, "Animals in Egyptian Religion," 335–60; See also Pascal Vernus, "Les animaux dans la religion égyptienne," in Vernus and Yoyotte, *Bestiaire des pharaons*, 20–49; and, in the same volume, Vernus, "Les animaux dans la littérature égyptienne," 50–61.

gods had very closely observed the creatures surrounding them. It remains harder for Egyptologists, however, to determine the type(s) of relationships ancient Egyptians maintained on a day-to-day basis with these animals. How did they treat the animals that shared their lives?

Because of the development of Animal Law and the growing impact of animal rights activists who are attempting to introduce a revised code of conduct regulating our own relationship with animals, it has become increasingly appealing to us, specialists of the animal world in antiquity, to establish how the ancients viewed the various kinds of animals in their surroundings—not so much at a symbolic and spiritual level, as this has been the focus of many studies,[4] but at a more mundane and pragmatic level. What categories of animals can we identify? How were they incorporated into people's lives? Can we tell if ancient Egyptians shared some emotional bonds with them? If so, how did they express them? And, ultimately, since our concern is the intersection of animals and the law in antiquity, can we ascertain the legal status of these different categories of animals? These questions will be addressed in turn in this essay. I will rely on the wide range of data at our disposal and adopt an interdisciplinary approach in order to bring us closer to drawing a realistic picture of the status of animals in ancient Egyptian society.

Animal Law

Before tackling the world of animals in ancient Egypt, I would like to review the principal objectives of the relatively new legal field that is Animal Law. As simply defined by the Animal Legal Defense Fund, Animal Law is a "combination of statutory and case law that relates to or has an impact on non-human animals."[5] Rather than focusing on the economic value of animals and how their loss affects their owners, this field strives to provide protection to animals and to ensure their welfare. Of special concern to Animal Law are the following four categories of animals:

---

4. For instance, Dimitri Meeks, "La hiérarchie des êtres vivants selon la conception égyptienne," in *Et in Ægypto et ad Ægyptum: Recueil d'études dédiées à Jean-Claude Grenier*, ed. Annie Gasse, Frédéric Servajean, and Christophe Thiers, Cahiers de l'ENIM 5 (Montpellier: Université Paul Valéry, 2012), 517–43; Cathie Spieser, "Animalité de l'homme, humanité de l'animal en Égypte ancienne," in *Apprivoiser le sauvage / Taming the Wild*, ed. M. Massiera, B. Mathieu, and Fr. Rouffet, CENiM (Montpellier: Université Paul Valéry, 2015), 307–20; Nadine Guilhou, "Entre hommes et dieux: Le statut de l'animal et la notion d'hybride dans l' Égypte ancienne," in *L'animal symbole*, ed. Marianne Besseyre, Pierre-Yves Le Pogam, and Florian Meunier (Paris: Editions du Comité des Travaux Historiques et Scientifiques, 2019), 223–32.

5. "Animal Law 101. An Overview of Animal Law," last consulted 31 May 2019, https://aldf.org/article/animal-law-101/. A more in-depth presentation of this field can be found in Jerrold Tannenbaum, "What Is Animal Law?," *Cleveland State Law Review* 61 (2013): 891–955.

companion animals; animals raised for food or research; animals used for entertainment, found in zoos, aquariums, and movies; and wildlife. As of today, in the United States, animals continue to be considered property as opposed to legal persons who are granted certain rights. During the past few decades, lawyers who specialize in the field of Animal Law have endeavored to prove that animals are not merely "legal things" but rather sentient beings, susceptible of feeling pain and distress.[6] It is now well established that animals should be considered "a distinctive subset of personal property with special protection."[7] A few countries have been successful in changing the legal status of their animals. In France, for example, since 2014, the *Code civil* no longer considers an animal solely as movable property but rather as a living being capable of feelings.[8] With this change in language, certain behaviors toward animals are no longer deemed acceptable. Instead, it becomes our responsibility as legal persons to ensure that these "living" creatures are not subjected to any cruel treatments that would cause pain and distress.

The various companion animals that share our homes have seen their conditions improve and their status rise significantly. In some contexts, such as divorces and separations, they are treated like dependents. Separated partners are given visitation rights to see their cat or dog. On the other hand, animal welfare groups are working tirelessly to improve the quality of life of farm animals. In the United Kingdom, the Farm Animal Welfare Committee is striving to grant all farm animals the Five Freedoms, which are currently listed as: "**Freedom from hunger or thirst** by ready access to fresh water and a diet to maintain full health and vigor; **Freedom from discomfort** by providing an appropriate environment including shelter and a comfortable resting area; **Freedom from pain, injury or disease** by prevention or rapid diagnosis and treatment; **Freedom to express (most) normal behavior** by providing sufficient space, proper facilities and company of the animal's own kind; **Freedom from fear and distress** by ensuring conditions and treatment which avoid mental suffering."[9] This relatively recent change in our perception of the animal world and the increased desire to improve the quality of life of the animals that inhabit our homes or contribute to our own welfare by working for us, by feeding us, or by entertaining us, are reflections of deep societal changes

---

6. Cara Feinberg, "Are Animals Things?," *Harvard Magazine*, March–April 2016, 1–9.

7. Richard L. Cupp Jr., "Animals as More Than 'Mere Things,' but Still Property: A Call for Continuing Evolution of the Animal Welfare Paradigm," *Legal Studies Research Paper Series* 19 (2016): 1–35, here 25.

8. Ibid., 19.

9. "Farm Animal Welfare Committee (FAWC)," last consulted 31 May 2019, https://www.gov.uk/government/groups/farm-animal-welfare-committee-fawc#assessment-of-farm-animal-welfare---five-freedoms-and-a-life-worth-living.

in a world where fewer and fewer people are in contact with animals raised solely for economic purposes.[10]

Categories of Animals in Ancient Egyptian Society

After briefly considering the current views regarding the legal status of animals in society, I would like to now turn my attention to the relationship that ancient Egyptians maintained with the environment and the animals living therein. Interestingly, no generic word for animal exists in the Egyptian language.[11] When describing the animal world, literary, religious, and funerary texts traditionally list the main faunal categories—mammals, birds, and fish—that were directly incorporated into the lives of ancient Egyptians.[12] It is not surprising that the main concerns of an agrarian society such as Egypt, whose population was primarily involved in food production, were focused on the animals that could improve their lives, whether as companions, beasts of burden, means of transport, or most importantly, as a source of protein.[13] As cited in the Instructions of Merikare (E 132–133): "it is (indeed) for them (i.e. human beings) that he (i.e. god) created plants and cattle, birds and fish, in order to feed them."[14]

As aptly stated by Sian Lewis, "Animal–human interactions are one of the few direct points of contact which we have with the ancient world."[15] Yet, deciphering the nature of these "ancient" interactions requires that we carefully consider side by side all sources of material evidence—texts,

---

10. Cupp, "Animals as More Than 'Mere Things,' but Still Property," 8.

11. Dimitri Meeks, "Zoomorphie et image des dieux dans l'Égypte ancienne," in *Corps des dieux*, ed. Charles Malamoud and Jean-Pierre Vernant (Paris: Gallimard, 1986), 171–91, here 174; Pascal Vernus, "Les animaux dans la langue égyptienne," in Vernus and Yoyotte, *Bestiaire des pharaons*, 76–93; Meeks,"La hiérarchie des êtres vivants," 523–43; Spieser, "Animalité de l'homme," 308.

12. Guilhou, "Entre hommes et dieux," 223.

13. For general presentations of the role of animals in ancient Egyptian society, see Joachim Boessneck, *Die Tierwelt des alten Ägypten: Untersucht anhand kulturgeschichtlicher und zoologischer Quellen* (Munich: Beck, 1988); Houlihan, *Animal World of the Pharaohs*; Philippe Germond and Jacques Livet, *An Egyptian Bestiary: Animals in Life and Religion in the Land of the Pharaohs* (New York: Thames & Hudson, 2001); Vernus and Yoyotte, *Bestiaire des pharaons*; Rozenn Bailleul-LeSuer, ed., *Between Heaven and Earth: Birds in Ancient Egypt*, Oriental Institute Museum Publications 35 (Chicago: Oriental Institute of the University of Chicago, 2012); Hélène Guichard, ed., *Des animaux et des Pharaons: Le règne animal dans l'Égypte ancienne* (Paris: Somogy éditions d'art, 2014).

14. Joachim F. Quack, *Studien zur Lehre für Merikare*, Göttinger Orientforschungen 4/23 (Wiesbaden: Harrassowitz, 1992), 78–79, 96.

15. Sian Lewis, "A Lifetime Together? Temporal Perspectives on Animal-Human Interactions," in *Interactions between Animals and Humans in Graeco-Roman Antiquity*, ed. Thorsten Fögen and Edmund Thomas (Berlin: de Gruyter, 2017), 19.

iconography, and archaeological and faunal remains. Specialists of the ancient Egyptian fauna have a wider range of material at their disposal than scholars researching other ancient cultures, since we have access to the actual mummified remains of some of these animals. In many instances, these remains are the most reliable and, theoretically, objective set of data we can consult to determine how certain species of animals were treated in antiquity.

Despite the potential danger of imposing a modern perspective on ancient material, I will use the pattern of faunal categorization defined within the framework of Animal Law as a model to identify the various categories of animals that came into contact with and shared the lives of ancient Egyptians.[16] Based on this model, the animals under consideration in this study can be organized in the following categories: companion animals; animals raised for utilitarian purposes (work, food, sacrifices); animals used for entertainment, gathered in hunting parks or menageries; and animals associated with the sacred animal cults.[17]

Companion Animals

Herodotus, in book 2 of *The Histories* dedicated to Egypt, considered it worthwhile to describe how ancient Egyptians handled the death of cats and dogs:

> What happens when a house catches on fire is most extraordinary: nobody takes the least trouble to put it out, for it is only the cats that matter ... all the inmates of a house where a cat has died of a natural death shave their eyebrows, and when a dog dies they shave their whole body including the head. Cats which have died are taken to Bubastis where they are embalmed and buried in sacred receptacles; dogs are buried also in sacred places, in the towns where they belong.[18] (*Hist.* 2.66–67)

Whether or not ancient Egyptians went to such extremes at the death of one of their household animals is hard to ascertain, as no evidence has

---

16. As demonstrated by Meeks ("La hiérarchie des êtres vivants," 539), Spieser ("Animalité de l'homme"), and Guilhou ("Entre hommes et dieux"), the ancient Egyptian system of classification is a reflection of the Egyptians' perception of the animals within their mythical conception of the world and only expresses the view of the literate, often religious, elite composing religious texts. It does not necessarily convey how animals were in fact perceived and treated by the large majority of the population.

17. Wildlife will also be considered, but only inasmuch as it can be incorporated into the four categories listed above.

18. Herodotus, *The Histories*, trans. Aubrey de Selincourt and A. R. Burns (New York: Penguin, 1972), 155.

survived to confirm it. Moreover, as I will discuss below, the animal burials listed in this account are those of sacred animals rather than pets. Notwithstanding this, we have ample evidence suggesting that some members of the upper classes developed strong emotional bonds with their companion animals—dogs, cats, baboons, and horses in particular (fig. 1).[19] For instance, the dog of an Old Kingdom ruler benefited from a funeral worthy of a human being of high status, as recorded in his funerary inscription:

> This is the guard dog of his majesty [and] Abwtiyw is his name. His majesty gave orders that he should be buried [and] gave him a coffin from the Royal Treasury, fine fabrics in abundance and incense. His majesty gave him perfumed oil [and] had a tomb built for him by a team of workmen. His majesty did this for him, in order that he [the dog] might be honored.[20]

FIGURE 1. Artist's sketch of Pharaoh spearing a lion (ca. 1186–1070 BCE). An unidentified king is represented as he is plunging his spear in the lion's neck. He is accompanied by his dog, whose position as companion animal is indicated by his collar. MMA 26.7.1453. Courtesy of The Metropolitan Museum of Art.

---

19. Boessneck, *Die Tierwelt*, 57–60; Houlihan, *Animal World of the Pharaohs*, 74-112; Florence Maruéjol, "Dans l'intimité des hommes," in Guichard, *Des animaux et des Pharaons*, 160-82.

20. George Reisner, "The Dog Which Was Honored by the King of Upper and Lower Egypt," *Bulletin of the Museum of Fine Arts* 34 (1936): 96–99.

In this case, this animal, during his life, was perceived by his owner not as a mere possession to be enjoyed but as a living being endowed with his own personality, worthy of being given a name. By having his name inscribed on his coffin, this dog had a better chance to join his master in the afterlife.[21] Similarly, on his Victory Stela found at Gebel Barkal (fig. 2), the Nubian ruler Piye (ca. 753–723 BCE) expressed his anger at seeing his Egyptian enemy neglecting the horses of the royal stables, which had been left to starve. Touched by such a despicable act, Piye cried out, "I swear by the love of Re … That my heart aches more for those starving horses than any of your evil deeds. I have no choice but to punish you for this."[22]

Figure 2. Lunette of the Victory Stela of Piye. From Auguste Mariette, *Monuments divers recueillis en Égypte et en Nubie* (Paris: A. Franck, 1872), plate 1. The depiction of a horse being presented to king Piye is a unique feature of this monument, otherwise unattested.

Several mummies of companion animals have also been recovered in the tombs of members of the ancient Egyptian elite.[23] Some of them, such as the female cat *Miw.t* of prince Thutmose (ca. 1400 BCE), were buried in exquisite limestone sarcophagi.[24] Others were deposited inside their owner's coffin.[25] It has been suggested, that "these animals were allowed to live out their natural lives."[26] It is also possible that some of them were dispatched at the time of their guardians' funeral, so as to be placed in their burial chamber. Needless to say, we can safely say that these ancient Egyptians showed great signs of affection toward their animal companions, an emotion they expressed by giving them names and providing

---

21. Germond and Livet, *Egyptian Bestiary*, 75.

22. Robert Kriech Ritner, *The Libyan Anarchy: Inscriptions from Egypt's Third Intermediate Period*, WAW 21 (Atlanta: Society of Biblical Literature, 2009), 465–92.

23. Salima Ikram, *Divine Creatures: Animal Mummies in Ancient Egypt* (Cairo: American University in Cairo Press, 2015), 1–4.

24. Cairo Museum CG 5003; Ikram, *Divine Creatures*, pl. 1.4.

25. Philadelphia University Museum E16220a and E16219, excavated by Petrie at Abydos.

26. Ikram, *Divine Creatures*, 4.

them with the proper burials and accompanying rituals that opened the door to the afterlife. Furthermore, King Piye's outrage at the sight of starving horses is a further indication that he considered these animals to be sentient beings, capable of pain and distress.

"Useful" Animals: Animals Hunted, Captured, and Raised for Work, Food, and Sacrifices

In ancient Egypt, animals were especially valued as an economic resource or for their ability to provide transport and work in fields.[27] Above all, fish were the most important and widespread source of protein available to all classes of society.[28] Birds could also be captured in the wetlands of the country and brought to farmyards, where they were kept in captivity until the need to dispatch them arose. They could then be consumed or sacrificed as funerary and religious offerings.[29] Domestic mammals, such as cattle and ovicaprids (sheep and goats), were prized possessions that tomb owners were proud to display as flourishing and working on their estates (fig. 3). Cattle were used for transport and fieldwork and provided the most sought after offerings.[30] Sheep and goats, while less prestigious, were nevertheless listed among the herds donated to temples by kings.[31] Pigs are seldom represented, yet they feature prominently in the kitchen midden of workmen's villages, such as Amarna.[32] Donkeys, just like today, were probably commonplace in the ancient Egyptian countryside, as they were a major mode of transportation for both people and goods.[33]

---

27. Brewer, "Hunting, Animal Husbandry and Diet," 427–56.
28. Douglas J. Brewer and Renée F. Friedman, *Fish and Fishing in Ancient Egypt*, Natural History of Egypt 2 (Warminster: Aris & Phillips, 1989).
29. Rozenn Bailleul-LeSuer, "The Exploitation of Live Avian Resources in Pharaonic Egypt: A Socio-Economic Study" (PhD diss., University of Chicago, 2016).
30. Salima Ikram, *Choice Cuts: Meat Production in Ancient Egypt*, OLA 69 (Leuven: Peeters, 1995).
31. Pascal Vernus, "Ovins," in Vernus and Yoyotte, *Bestiaire des pharaons*, 553–56, here 553.
32. "Zooarchaeology at Amarna, 2004-2005," last consulted 31 May 2019, http://www.amarnaproject.com/pages/recent_projects/faunal_human/zooarchaelogy.shtml; Louise Bertini, "Changes in Suid and Caprine Husbandry Practices throughout Dynastic Egypt Using Linear Enamel Hypoplasia (LEH)" (PhD diss., Durham University, 2011); Youri Volokhine, *Le porc en Égypte ancienne: Mythes et histoire à l'origine des interdits alimentaires*, Collection Religions 3 (Liège: Presses universitaires de Liège, 2014).
33. Pascal Vernus, "Âne domestique," in Vernus and Yoyotte, *Bestiaire des pharaons*, 459–70, here 459; Joseph Manning, "A Ptolemaic Agreement Concerning a Donkey with an Unusual Warranty Clause: The Strange Case of P. Dem. Princ. 1 (Inv. 7524)," *Enchoria* 28 (2002–2003): 46–61, here 47.

FIGURE 3. Inspection of cattle in the tomb of Ḏḥwty-ḥtp (Deir el-Bersheh, Twelfth Dynasty, ca. 1800 BCE). These herds were most likely partly owned by the king and placed under the responsibility of Ḏḥwty-ḥtp. In the second register are fattened oxen, or *iw3.w*. From Percy E. Newberry, *El Bersheh*, part 1, *The Tomb of Tehuti-Hetep* (London: Egypt Exploration Fund, 1893–1894), plate 18.

Most types of farm animals were viewed as costly investments that had to be protected from harm and from theft.[34] As written in the Instruction of 'Onchsheshonqy, no wise Egyptian "should despise a matter that pertains to a cow" (9/8). He should know that "all manner of beasts are welcome in the house. A thief is not welcome" (20/15). Archaeological excavations of settlements have indeed shown that many farm animals shared the same living spaces as their owners. At night, they were kept inside the house, in rooms that did not have a direct access to the street, thus minimizing any attempts of theft.[35] In some other instances, it was the herdsman who lived in the midst of the animals in his charge. In the Tale of the Two Brothers, the younger of the two brothers, Bata, was put in charge of the cattle, as it was also his responsibility to plow the fields. At the end of each day, "he would leave [his brother Anubis and his wife] to spend the night in his stable among the cattle" (1,5–7).[36] To thank Bata for taking such good care of them, for letting them graze in the fields and for allowing them to prosper, "the lead cow entered the stable and said to the herdsman [Bata], 'Look, your elder brother is standing in wait for you holding a spear to kill you. You must get away from him.' He heard what his lead cow said, and the next one entered and said the same" (Tale of the Two Brothers 5,9).[37] A meaningful and interdependent relationship had

---

34. For a comparative study of the price of commodities, including animals, in an ancient Egyptian community, see Jac. J. Janssen, *Commodity Prices from the Ramessid Period: An Economic Study of the Village of Necropolis Workmen at Thebes* (Leiden: Brill, 1975).

35. Bailleul-LeSuer, "Exploitation of Live Avian Resources," 389–400.

36. Translation by Edward F. Wente, "The Tale of the Two Brothers," in *The Literature of Ancient Egypt: An Anthology of Stories, Instructions, and Poetry*, ed. William Kelly Simpson (New Haven: Yale University Press, 2003), 80–90, here 81.

37. Translation by Wente, " Tale of the Two Brothers," 84. On the tradition of speaking animals in literary texts, see Teeter, "Animals in Egyptian Literature," 253–54.

obviously developed over time between the herdsman and the animals he guarded.[38] According to this tale, this strong animal–human connection benefited both parties: the cows had the opportunity to spend their day in the richest fields, and Bata, who had developed the ability to understand the animals in his charge, escaped the murder plot planned by his brother.[39]

Prior to the advent of bird domestication, captured wildfowl, for the most part ducks and geese, were kept in enclosures.[40] Aviaries were built around a body of water, and representations in tombs seem to imply that these birds were granted some freedom of movement. On the other hand, certain captive birds were selected to undergo force-feeding sessions: tomb scenes show birds being held by the neck and forced to swallow moist bread pellets. Similar treatment was inflicted on cattle, which became so fat as to barely be able to walk (fig. 4).[41] These animals were known as *iwȝ* and were destined to be sacrificed.[42]

FIGURE 4. Procession of fattened oxen (*iwȝ.w*), destined to be offered to the god Amun. Luxor Temple. Photo by Rozenn Bailleul-LeSuer.

---

38. For the concept of "meaningful relationships" developing between human beings and animals, see Lewis, "Lifetime Together?," 21.

39. This story is in itself interesting as it is the ancient Egyptian farming community that forged stronger bonds with the animals alongside whom they worked and for whom they cared. However, they are also those who are silent in the written record. The story of Bata and his cows may be a reflection of what could have been observed in the countryside. See Lewis, "Lifetime Together?," for a similar situation in classical Greece and Rome.

40. Bailleul-LeSuer, "Exploitation of Live Avian Resources," 251–55.

41. Brewer, "Hunting, Animal Husbandry and Diet," 436.

42. The term *iwȝ*, most commonly applied to cattle, could also be used with other ungulates of the desert, probably implying that these captured animals were to be confined, fattened, and ultimately destined for the slaughter house (Meeks, "La hiérarchie des êtres vivants," 525).

After the successful domestication of the goose, it became possible for gooseherds to lead flocks to the edge of the agricultural plain, where the domesticated birds were able to freely graze during the day.[43] The gaggle of free-range geese, presumably enjoying a better quality of life than enclosed birds, would return to the safety of the farm at the end of the day. These flocks were known as *mnmn.t ꜣpd.w*, the term *mnmn.t* referring to controlled flocks of farm animals, especially, but not exclusively, cattle.

Animals Used for Entertainment, Gathered in Hunting Parks or Menageries[44]

While hunting wild animals was at first the only option available for prehistoric Egyptians to have access to meat, it quickly became a prerogative of the elite after the introduction of the domestic mammalian quartet—cattle, sheep, goat, and pigs—in farmyards.[45] From the Old Kingdom onward, kings proudly recorded their hunting exploits on temple walls (fig. 5).[46] King Amenhotep III (ca. 1390–1353 BCE) went a step further and released a series of commemorative scarabs manufactured in large numbers, on which he is said to have killed more than one hundred lions during the first ten years of his reign, and slaughtered ninety-six wild bulls in his second regnal year.[47] Distributed throughout his empire, these texts proclaimed the king's power and mastery over the forces of nature, especially those fearsome creatures, the lion and the wild bull.[48]

A few desert hunting scenes encountered in tomb chapels show the fences that surrounded the areas where wild animals could be corralled (fig. 6).[49] Antelopes and gazelles, ostriches and hares are depicted as

---

43. Bailleul-LeSuer, "Exploitation of Live Avian Resources," 300-308.

44. For the distinction between menageries and zoological gardens, see Lloyd Llewellyn-Jones, "Keeping and Displaying Royal Tributes in Ancient Persia and the Near East," in Fögen and Thomas, *Interactions between Animals and Humans*, 305–38, here 324.

45. Linseele Veere and Wim Van Neer, "Exploitation of Desert and Other Wild Game in Ancient Egypt: The Archaeozoological Evidence from the Nile Valley," in *Desert Animals in the Eastern Sahara: Status, Economic Significance, and Cultural Reflection in Antiquity; Proceedings of an Interdisciplinary ACACIA Workshop Held at the University of Cologne, December 14–15, 2007*, ed. Heiko Riemer et al., Colloquium Africanum 4 (Cologne: Heinrich Barth Institut, 2009), 47–78; Stan Hendrickx, "L'iconographie de la chasse dans le contexte social prédynastique," *Archéo-Nil* 20 (2010): 106–33.

46. Houlihan, *Animal World of the Pharaohs*, 40–73.

47. Lawrence M. Berman, "Large Commemorative Scarabs," in *Egypt's Dazzling Sun: Amenhotep III and His World*, ed. Arielle P. Kozloff, Betsy M. Bryan and Lawrence M. Berman (Cleveland: Cleveland Museum of Art, 1992), 67–72.

48. Llewellyn-Jones, "Keeping and Displaying Royal Tributes," 318.

49. Houlihan, *Animal World of the Pharaohs*, 42–43.

FIGURE 5. Ramesses III (ca. 1187–1157 BCE) hunting wild bulls in the marshes, as carved on his mortuary temple of Medinet Habu, west bank of Thebes. Photo by Rozenn Bailleul-LeSuer.

FIGURE 6. Hunting park in the tomb of Ḏḥwty-ḥtp (Deir el-Bersheh, Twelfth Dynasty, ca. 1800 BCE). From Percy E. Newberry, *El Bersheh*, part 1, *The Tomb of Tehuti-Hetep* (London: Egypt Exploration Fund, 1893–1894), plate 7.

falling prey to the arrows shot by the tomb owner, often accompanied by his hunting dogs. In these situations, the human in the scene is actively trying to control the chaotic creatures, depicted as running in all directions in their attempts to avoid death. It is also this person who has the power to either harass these wild creatures by sending his dogs at them, or give them a "clean death" by killing them quickly with his weapons. Yet, while not as gruesome as some of the hunting friezes carved by Mesopotamian artists, it is still possible to see the animals, as described by Linda Kalof, as "frightened, cornered, and desperate."[50]

Kings also enjoyed surrounding themselves with exotic creatures brought as tribute and gifts from the foreign lands under their control. Syrian bears, leopards, giraffes, monkeys, and ostriches[51] are shown in processions moving toward Pharaoh (fig. 7).[52] Thutmose III (ca. 1479–1425 BCE) showed his interest in unusual plants and animals by incorporating them in the iconographic repertoire of his chapel known as the Akh-Menu in the Karnak temple complex. Akhenaten (ca. 1353–1336 BCE), in his North Palace at Amarna, may have kept some birds, antelopes, and other animals in several rooms of the palace.[53] For the wild animals that survived the journey from the site of their capture,[54] their existence, as they were maintained in captivity in royal compounds or temple grounds, was unlikely to be pleasant. As Lloyd Llewellyn-Jones remarks, "While the presentations of these auspicious animals is highlighted in the texts and iconography of the court, the sources are largely silent on the animals' fate. What happened to these creatures in the long term is difficult to

---

50. Linda Kalof, "Ancient Animals," in *A Cultural History of Animals in Antiquity*, ed. Linda Kalof and Brigitte Resl (Oxford: Berg, 2011), 6.

51. While ostriches were native to Egypt at the time, they often feature among the tributes brought by Nubian dignitaries.

52. Melinda K. Hartwig, *Tomb Painting and Identity in Ancient Thebes, 1419–1372 BCE* (Brussels: Fondation Égyptologique Reine Élisabeth, 2004), 73–76. For a description of the famous and decadent procession and display of animals during the reign of Ptolemy II (ca. 275 BCE), see Jo-Ann Shelton, "Beastly Spectacles in the Ancient Mediterranean World," in Kalof and Resl, *Cultural History of Animals*, 97–126, here 112–16. As described by Lloyd Llewellyn-Jones ("Keeping and Displaying Royal Tributes," 305), these animals were "breathing symbols of the Great King's power and his control of his vast dominions."

53. F. J. Weatherhead, *Amarna Palace Paintings*, ed. Alan B. Lloyd, Excavation Memoir 78 (London: Egypt Exploration Society, 2007), 143–82. Keeping wild animals in captivity may have been practiced in several of the king's palaces, as evidenced by the representations of enclosures filled with wild mammals on a fragmentary relief discovered at Karnak (Pierre Anus, "Un domaine thébain d'époque 'amarnienne' sur quelques blocs de remploi trouvés à Karnak," *Bulletin de l'Institut Français d'Archéologie Orientale* 69 [1969]: 69–88).

54. The animal death rate prior to arrival is likely to have been very high; see Michael MacKinnon, "Supplying Exotic Animals for the Roman Amphitheatre Games: New Reconstructions Combining Archaeological, Ancient Textual, Historical and Ethnographic Data," *Mouseion* series III 6 (2006): 147–50.

know."⁵⁵ Unless they had previously been tamed, their lives were probably spent in confinement, in cages, or tied with a rope. The analysis of faunal remains at the site of Hierakonpolis confirms this hypothesis: Wim Van Neer and his team discovered that a wide range of wild animals buried at the site—baboons, hippopotami, leopards, and aurochs—showed signs of having been kept in captivity for a period of time.⁵⁶ They also exhibited pathologies related to repeated beating and also prolonged tethering.

FIGURE 7. Tribute bearers from Nubia, bringing a baboon, a leopard, animal skins, elephant tusks, and ebony wood. Facsimile painting by Nina de Garis Davies from the tomb of Rekhmire (ca. 1479–1425 BCE). MMA 30.4.81. Courtesy of The Metropolitan Museum of Art.

Animals Associated with the Sacred Animal Cults

According to several ancient Egyptian cosmogonies, animals were created alongside gods and human beings.⁵⁷ Rather than being seen as inferior to humans, certain animals possessed unique abilities and knowledge that allowed them to communicate directly with the creator god. Baboons were in fact considered to be the "ideal and true performer of

---

55. Llewellyn-Jones, "Keeping and Displaying Royal Tributes," 329.

56. Wim Van Neer et al., "Traumatism in the Wild Animals Kept and Offered at Predynastic Hierakonpolis, Upper Egypt," *International Journal of Osteoarchaeology* 27.1 (2015): 86–105.

57. Guilhou, "Entre hommes et dieux," 224.

religion."⁵⁸ This communion between the animal world and the divine fully manifests itself in the phenomenon of sacred animal cults. In some instances, such as the cult of the Apis bull, a single member of a species was selected, based on distinct markings, to become the living manifestation of a deity—Ptah in the case of the Apis bull—during its lifetime. After a well-cared-for life within the temple precinct, the animal benefited in death from an elaborate burial in a specific necropolis, such as the Serapeum in Memphis for the mummies of Apis bulls.⁵⁹ The mummies of "single" sacred animals represent only a small percentage of all the mummies manufactured in conjunction with these cults. The large majority of the mummified animal remains belong to "sacralized" animals that acquired their divine status only after their deaths (see below).⁶⁰

One of the main characteristics of the religious phenomenon of sacred animal cults is indeed the quasi-industrial production of animal mummies, which have been found to contain the remains of a wide range of species, including cats, dogs, birds (ibises and birds of prey in particular), crocodiles, shrews, fish, rams, bulls, primates, snakes, and scarabs. Millions of mummies are known to have been manufactured during the many centuries of activity of the cult centers connected to animal cemeteries.⁶¹ At Saqqara, for instance, the ibis catacombs are said to have housed approximately four million mummies. As for the Anubeion, the galleries dedicated to the burial of dog mummies, more than seven million dogs were mummified and laid to rest within.⁶²

To provide the animals needed by the cult centers, we seem to see for the first time the concept of the factory farm emerging in animal husbandry. I thank my colleague Korshi Dosoo for bringing to my attention

---

58. H. te Velde, "Some Remarks on the Mysterious Language of the Baboons," in *Funerary Symbols and Religion: Essays Dedicated to Professor M. S. H. G. Heerm van Voss on the Occasion of His Retirement from the Chair of the History of Ancient Religions at the University of Amsterdam*, ed. J. H. Kamstra, H. Milde, and K. Wagtendonk (Kampen: Kok, 1988), 129–37, here 129.

59. Since much scholarship has been dedicated to the topic of sacred animal cults, the following list does not claim to be exhaustive but provides a starting point for an investigation into this religious phenomenon: Dieter Kessler, *Die heiligen Tiere und der König*, Ägypten und Altes Testament 16 (Wiesbaden: Harrassowitz, 1989); Foy Scalf, "The Role of Birds within the Religious Landscape of Ancient Egypt," in Bailleul-LeSuer, *Between Heaven and Earth*, 33–40, here 36–39; Edward Bleiberg, "Animal Mummies: The Souls of the Gods," in *Soulful Creatures: Animal Mummies in Ancient Egypt*, ed. Edward Bleiberg, Yekaterina Barbash, and Lisa Bruno (Brooklyn, NY: Brooklyn Museum, 2013), 63–106; Alain Charron, "Les animaux sacrés, du sauvage à l'élevage," in Massiera, Mathieu, and Rouffet, *Apprivoiser le sauvage / Taming the Wild*, 67–92; Ikram, *Divine Creatures*.

60. Bleiberg, *Animal Mummies*, 82.

61. Ikram, *Divine Creatures*, 9–15.

62. Salima Ikram, Paul T. Nicholson, Louise Bertini, and Delyth Hurley, "Killing Man's Best Friend?," *Archaeological Review from Cambridge* 28.2 (2013): 48–66, here 53.

the notion of "deading life," that is, life whose only purpose is death.[63] It appears that this was exactly the purpose of some of the animals raised in these "farms": it was only after their death that they became valuable to ancient Egyptian worshipers. After their demise, the animals were mummified and underwent the Opening of the Mouth ceremony, rituals that transformed these earthly creatures into divine beings. They could then act as messengers, delivering the prayers and requests that devotees wanted the gods to hear. Much evidence concerning these animal cults comes not only from texts written on ostraca and papyri or carved in stone but especially from the innumerable animal mummies that have been recovered near sacred spaces, such as temples and cemeteries, and have made their way into museums. Dogs and cats were often killed at a young age, sometimes a few months old.[64] The cause of death could be ascertained in some cases: the animals' necks had been broken (cats) or their skulls had been crushed (dogs and crocodiles).[65] In late Roman Egypt, several Greek and Demotic texts describe how to create divine beings by drowning animals in water or milk.[66]

While we can see signs of a violent death for many cats and dogs, mummified remains can also shed some light on the living conditions of some of these animals prior to their deaths. The examination of several mummies of baboons and other nonhuman primates collected in the animal necropolis of Tuna el-Gebel, Middle Egypt, has shown that they frequently suffered from chronic malnutrition, dental diseases, osteopathologies of the vertebral column, as well as fractures and other traumatic lesions. The animals were likely to have been kept in high walled enclosures, with limited access to the sun. Some of the more aggressive animals would have been confined to small cages. The zooarcheologists who worked on this material concluded their study as follows:

---

63. Korshi Dosoo, "Living Death and Deading Life: Animal Mummies in Graeco-Egyptian Ritual," in *Magikon Zoon: Animals in Magic* (conference, Paris, 6–7 June 2016), with reference to James Stanescu, "Beyond Biopolitics: Animal Studies, Factory Farms, and the Advent of Deading Life," *PhaenEx* 8.2 (2013): 135–60.

64. P. L. Armitage and J. Clutton-Brock, "A Radiological and Historical Investigation into the Mummification of Cats from Ancient Egypt," *Journal of Archaeological Science* 8.2 (1981): 185–96.

65. Lidija M. McKnight, "What Lies Beneath: Imaging Animal Mummies," in *Gifts for the Gods. Ancient Egyptian Mummies and the British*, ed. Lidija M. McKnight and Stephanie Atherton Woolham (Liverpool: Liverpool University Press, 2015), 72–79, here 74–76; Stéphanie Porcier, C. Berruyer, S. Pasquali, S. Ikram, D. Berthet, and P. Tafforeau, "Wild Crocodiles Hunted to Make Mummies in Roman Egypt: Evidence from Synchrotron Imaging," *Journal of Archaeological Science* 110 (2019): 1–8.

66. Dosoo, "Living Death and Deading Life."

It lies beyond the scope of this paper to reflect on the mental stress exerted on baboons, which were kept in enclosures and/or cages with limited or no possibility for interaction with the rest of the troop. Considering the fact, however, that baboons in the wild spend 45-50% of the day feeding and that the greatest part of baboon social interaction is social grooming, these observations cannot but indicate how deplorable the life of the temple baboons must have been, the reward of which was immortality.[67]

According to Greek and Roman literary sources, such as the work of Herodotus (*Hist.* 2.65), Diodorus Siculus (*Bib. Hist.* 1.83.8–9), and Cicero (*Tusc.* 5.27.78), anyone deliberately killing a sacred animal was not worthy of being tried but was automatically punished by death. P. Berlin P 23757 A recto, a fragmentary document from the Middle Egyptian site of Akhmim (ca. 245 BCE) provides some insight, albeit minimal, into the legal repercussions of mistreating certain types of sacred animals.[68] According to line 25 of this document,[69] anyone mistreating a sacred or "sacralized" animal might be sent to jail. Likewise, P. Ashm. 1984.77, a Demotic wisdom papyrus of the Roman period (late second or early third century CE) clearly states that one should not "beat any (sacred) animal with a stick, stone, or any (piece of wood)." One should "be careful with regard to the animals which are sacred."[70] Egyptian sources thus confirm the protected status of these sacred animals; yet it is impossible to conclude whether anyone intentionally killing a "sacralized" animal would be condemned to death. No evidence has surfaced to confirm or deny it. However, these cults benefited from royal protection and sponsorship: anyone attempting to defraud the various sanctuaries was most likely susceptible to suffer dire consequences.[71]

---

67. A. von den Driesch., D. Kessler, and J. Peters, "Mummified Baboons and Other Primates from the Saitic-Ptolemaic Animal Necropolis of Tuna El-Gebel, Middle Egypt," *Documenta Archaeobiologiae* 2 (2004): 231–78, here 261.

68. Sandra Lippert, *Ein demotische juristisches Lehrbuch: Untersuchungen zu Papyrus Berlin P 23757 rto*, Ägyptologische Abhandlungen 66 (Wiesbaden: Harrassowitz, 2004); Bernard Legras, "La répression des violences envers les animaux sacrés dans l'Égypte ptolémaïque," *Droits et Cultures* 71 (2016): 43–50.

69. "25: (In) «jail»: «if anyone mistreats (a "sacralized" animal), some (?) (cat), some (?)/ 26: some (?) ichneumon, (some) black *gm*-oxen, (some) cow, some (?) dog [...]/ 27: considering that 10 "sacralized" animals are expected" (Lippert, *Ein demotisches juristisches Lehrbuch*, 23–24 [my translation]; she comments on these lines on 45–48; see also Legras, "La répression des violences," 46).

70. P. Ashm. 1984.77.2/8-9. Richard Jasnow, "A Demotic Wisdom Papyrus in the Ashmolean Museum (P. Ashm. 1984.77 Verso)," *Enchoria* 11 (1991): 43–54, here 46, 49.

71. To gain insight into the abuses reported at the ibis catacombs of North Saqqara, see J. D. Ray, *The Archive of Hor*, Excavations at North Saqqâra Documentary Series 1 (London: Egypt Exploration Society, 1976).

The Place of Animals in the Ancient Egyptian Legal System

As guarantor of world order and justice, known as Maat (*Mꜣʿ.t*), in the country, Pharaoh was also theoretically in charge of establishing the sets of commands, rules, and rights that all citizens of the country had to follow. These rules were distributed in the form of royal decrees (*wḏ ny-sw.t*), on the one hand, and as laws of pharaoh (*hp.w n Pr ʿꜣ*), on the other.[72] A few examples of collections of laws have survived from the New Kingdom (ca. 1500 BCE) and later.[73] Yet no law code proper is known for most of ancient Egyptian history.[74] Hence, we have to turn to a variety of other sources to gain insight into the legal system of the country, sources such as royal decrees, administrative documents, private legal documents, personal letters, literary texts, and even religious texts. Animals frequently feature in legal contexts in these documents, in particular in inheritance documents, contracts, and even a few lawsuits, all of which would have been administered at the local court, or *ḳnb.t*, composed of members of the community (priests of the local temples, the town's mayor, and other members of the local administration).

Not surprisingly, since it is still the case in nearly every jurisdiction today, ancient Egyptian animals were considered to be a subset of personal property. They were listed in wills among "movables," coming after the listing of real estate (fields, houses, and farm buildings). As such, they could be inherited, sold, loaned, rented, shared in partnership and, like all valuables, they could also be subject to theft.[75] Thus, in private legal documents dated from the later periods of Egyptian history (664 BCE onward), farm animals were included in the possessions passed down from one generation to the next, as illustrated in the annuity contract written by *Pꜣ-ti-Wsir* to his wife ʿnḫ.t: "There belong to the children whom you will bear to me everything of all property which I possess and that which I shall acquire in house, field, courtyard, building plot, male servant, female

---

72. Brian Muhs, "Gender Relations and Inheritance in Legal Codes and Legal Practice in Ancient Egypt," in *Structures of Power: Law and Gender across the Ancient Near East and Beyond*, ed. Ilan Peled, University of Chicago Oriental Institute Seminars 12 (Chicago: Oriental Institute of the University of Chicago, 2017), 15–26, here 16.

73. Richard Jasnow, "The New Kingdom," in *A History of Ancient Near Eastern Law*, ed. Raymond Westbrook, HdO 1.72 (Leiden: Brill, 2003), 289–359, here 289.

74. Joseph Manning, "Demotic Law," in Westbrook, *History of Ancient Near Eastern Law*, 819–62, here 821.

75. Jasnow, "New Kingdom," 345.

servant, *cow, ass, every animal*, every office, every title deed, and every matter of a freeman whatsoever of mine."[76]

More written contracts and purchase agreements have survived from the New Kingdom onward. During the New Kingdom,[77] animals were part of the barter system: birds, for instance, could be exchanged for a goat.[78] Donkeys could be purchased[79] and were also available for hire: in a letter commenting on a possible donkey available for purchase, the scribe asks his colleague (or brother) to make sure that he treats the newly acquired animal well.[80] Cattle were a basic, yet crucial, component of the country's economy for the entire span of Egyptian history.[81] They were a prized and necessary possession of the upper and middle classes, just as they were essential "tools" for farmers as beasts of burden. In tombs, we see representations of herds of cattle being inspected before the tomb owner. This activity is recorded under the title *ir.t irw*, which can simply be translated as to "calculate the number of."[82] Herds of cattle belonging to the palace and to temples were scattered throughout the country and placed under the care of a small army of herdsmen. In exchange for allowing these men to make use of the animals, the owners of these cattle expected to receive fees, or rent, known under the terms *nḥb* and *bȝk.w*. Such arrangements did not always function smoothly. According to P. Cairo 57058, a certain institution, possibly a temple, had allowed a *ḥm*,

---

76. 331 BCE; Chicago Hawara Papyrus 2, 1–2 (emphasis added). Georges Hughes, Richard Jasnow, and James G. Keenan, *Oriental Institute Hawara Papyri. Demotic and Greek Texts from an Egyptian Family Archive in the Fayum (Fourth to Third Century B.C.)*, University of Chicago Oriental Institute Publications 113 (Chicago: Oriental Institute of the University of Chicago, 1997), 17.

77. A large majority of the evidence for this period was recovered at the site of Deir el-Medina, located at the desert margins on the west bank of the Nile, in Thebes. It housed the workers hired to build the royal tombs in the Valley of the Kings. See Janssen, *Commodity Prices*, 165–179, for a detailed list of the transactions that took place in the village of Deir el-Medina.

78. O. DeM 118 rt.; Bailleul-LeSuer, "Exploitation of Live Avian Resources," 389–91; Jasnow, "New Kingdom," 292, 338.

79. P. Turin 1976; Edward F. Wente, *Letters from Ancient Egypt*, WAW 1 (Atlanta: Scholars Press, 1990), 13; Jasnow, "New Kingdom," 292.

80. P. Cairo 58057; Wente, *Letters from Ancient Egypt*, 112–3; Jasnow, "New Kingdom," 340.

81. Brewer, "Hunting, Animal Husbandry and Diet," 445–46; Andrew H. Gordon, "The Observation and Use of Animals in the Development of Scientific Thought in the Ancient World with Especial Reference to Egypt," in Kalof and Resl, *Cultural History of Animals*, 127–50, here 135–37.

82. Jean-Marie Krutchen, *Le décret d'Horemheb: Traduction, commentaire épigraphique, philologique et institutionnel* (Brussels: Éditions de l'Université de Bruxelles, 1981), 85–88; Shafik Allam, "Taxe (?) sur le bétail dans l'Égypte ancienne," in *Stato, Economia, Lavoro nel Vicino Oriente Antico*, ed. Aldo Zanardo and Giovanni Pugliese Carratelli (Milan: Franco Angeli, 1988), 52–72.

"servant," to care for a few heads of cattle.[83] In return, this servant was expected to pay a *nḥb*. When asked to pay, this person claimed that he would not do so, since he no longer had the animals. A third party was asked to be involved, conduct a *ir.t irw*, and check that all the loaned cattle were accounted for.

The documentary evidence of the Saite and Persian periods (664–404 BCE) is far richer, with approximately 30 percent of all the extant sales contracts dealing with animal transactions. Donkeys and cows are the most frequent animals represented in these documents. Of special interest to our study are the sales involving cows.[84] In these sales agreements, the cows are almost invariably described in detail: their color, whether they are pregnant or not, and what their purpose was, e.g., plowing. We also learn their names and whether they had previously been branded. Finally, sales agreements record the prior ownership of the animal and whether it was purchased or born in the seller's corral.[85] Each animal is thus described as a specific individual, with distinguishing colors and marks;[86] yet, contrary to what Roger Bagnall has proposed for the Roman period,[87] cows could all the same be considered as fungible goods, which could be freely exchanged and replaced, as evidenced in P. Berlin 3130, dated to 486 BCE.[88] According to this document, a cow had been placed under the care of a herdsman, who was supposed to return his charge on a fixed date. In the meantime, however, it appears that the cow was slaughtered without the original owner's consent. Since this mishap had happened prior to the date when the herdsman was supposed to return the animal to the owner, a new contract was drawn, requesting that this herdsman supply a replacement animal before the deadline or pay five kite of silver ten days later. No mention is made whether the herdsman was penalized for being involved, directly or indirectly, with the death of the animal.

---

83. Allam, "Taxe (?) sur le bétail," 58.

84. Eugene Cruz-Uribe, *Saite and Persian Demotic Cattle Documents. A Study in Legal Forms and Principles in Ancient Egypt*, American Studies in Papyrology 26 (Chico, CA: Scholars Press, 1985).

85. Ibid., 47–52.

86. Lewis, "Lifetime Together?," 24: "This is not to say that the relationship between farmer and ox was necessarily sentimentalised.... An animal at the end of its useful life would be exploited for products such as hide, horn and tallow, but that does not devalue the close relationship between animal and owner during its life."

87. Roger S. Bagnall, "Sales of Movables," in *Law and Legal Practice in Egypt from Alexander to the Arab Conquest*, ed. James G. Keenan, Joseph Manning, and Uri Yiftach-Firanko (Cambridge: Cambridge University Press, 2014), 304–14, here 305: "The animals [in Roman sale contracts] are identifiable individuals with distinguishing colors and marks rather than fungible quantities."

88. Cruz-Uribe, *Saite and Persian Demotic Cattle Documents*, 25–27.

Cruelty against Animals in Ancient Egypt?

Roman citizens are renowned for their enjoyment at seeing arenas full of wild animals being slaughtered in the course of a festival.[89] Can we also find concrete evidence of deliberate animal cruelty in ancient Egypt? That some animals suffered the consequences of misunderstanding, ignorance, and indifference is certain, as evidenced by the various texts that record the death of animals placed in the care of certain guardians (see above in P. Berlin 3130). In chapter 125 of the Book of the Dead, the deceased is expected to claim: "I have not done crimes against people; I have not mistreated cattle."[90] Certain categories of animals also benefited from regional *bw.wt*, "abominations" or "interdictions," listed in several priestly encyclopedias.[91] As noted by Pierre Montet, it is important to keep in mind that the interdictions specific to each nome, or district, are not inspired by morality but are tied to a local cult or myth.[92] According to these documents, it was forbidden to approach a gazelle with malevolent intentions in the first nome of Upper Egypt. Likewise, certain violent behaviors against hippopotami, cattle (cows and oxen), wild and hunting dogs, rams, goats, birds (crane, vulture, and falcon), fish, and crocodiles were deemed as potentially harmful to the prosperity of several nomes, being injurious and disrespectful to the local deities.

A fable entitled The Lion in Search of Man, told by the god Thoth to the goddess Tefnut in the longer tale known as The Myth of the Eye of the Sun (Leiden Demotic Papyrus I 384), may reveal a darker aspect of the relationship ancient Egyptians maintained with the animal world.[93] The author(s) of this fable gave the animals a voice: they have the opportunity to describe how humans had mistreated them. A leopard had been flayed alive and left to die. The ox, cow, horse, and donkey had been mutilated and forced to work. A bear and a lion had also been cruelly tricked and

---

89. Shelton, "Beastly Spectacles," 116–26.
90. Miriam Lichtheim, *Ancient Egyptian Literature: A Book of Readings*, vol. 2, *The New Kingdom* (Berkeley: University of California Press, 1976), 125; J. Gwyn Griffiths, "The Accusing Animals," in *Religion und Philosophie im Alten Ägypten: Festgabe für Philippe Derchain zu seinem 65. Geburtstag am 24. Juli 1991*, ed. Ursula Verhoeven and Erhart Graefe, OLA 39 (Leuven: Peeters, 1991), 149–54, here 151. See also Sydney H. Aufrère, "Recherches sur les interdits religieux des régions de l'Égypte ancienne d'après les encyclopédies sacerdotales," *Droits et Cultures* 71 (2016): 15–41, here 18.
91. Aufrère, "Recherches sur les interdits religieux."
92. Pierre Montet, *Géographie de l'Égypte ancienne* (Paris: Imprimerie National, 1957), as cited by Aufrère, "Recherches sur les interdits religieux," 22.
93. Miriam Lichtheim, *Ancient Egyptian Literature: A Book of Readings*, vol. 3, *The Late Period* (Berkeley: University of California Press, 1980), 156–59.

injured. The abuse experienced by the animals of this fable is described in too realistic a fashion to not be a depiction of some witnessed animal cruelty.[94]

Likewise, certain representations clearly depict animals expressing severe distress and undoubtedly experiencing pain. I will use as illustrations the Book of the Dead vignette in which a live calf is shown having been mutilated (fig. 8),[95] and the relief that depicts King Akhenaten (ca. 1353–1336 BCE) sacrificing a pintail duck to the sun disk (fig. 9). As demonstrated by Linda Evans,[96] the protruding tongue of the animals shown in these two depictions is the artists' visual device to let the viewers know that these animals are "vocalizing." Thus, in the vignette from the Book of the Dead of Hunefer,[97] the artist depicted the cow as she is mooing, while witnessing her bleating calf being ritually mutilated. Its foreleg had just been cut and is being offered to the deceased. Likewise, in the offering scene carved on a talatat, or small block of stone, the duck may have been hissing, as Akhenaten grabbed its neck and lifted it, getting ready to sacrifice it to the Aten.

Figure 8. Vignette showing the ritual mutilation of a calf from the papyrus of Hunefer (Nineteenth Dynasty, ca. 1280 BCE). British Museum EA9901/5. © The Trustees of the British Museum. Used by permission of the British Museum.

---

94. Sian Lewis and Lloyd Llewellyn-Jones, *The Culture of Animals in Antiquity: A Sourcebook with Commentaries* (London: Routledge, 2018), 220–21.

95. Arthur Weigall, "An Ancient Egyptian Funeral Ceremony," *Journal of Egyptian Archaeology* 2 (1915): 10–12; Hermann Junker, *Giza III* (Vienna: Holder-Pichler-Tempsky, 1938), 229–31; Jacques Vandier, *Manuel d'archéologie égyptienne V:1* (Paris: A. & J. Picard, 1969), 136–38; Nadine Guilhou, "La mutilation rituelle du veau dans les scènes de funérailles au Nouvel Empire," *Bulletin de l'Institut Français d'Archéologie Orientale* 93 (1993): 227–98. N. Guilhou has been able to identify twenty versions of this scene, the majority of which date from the New Kingdom.

96. Linda Evans, *Animal Behaviour in Egyptian Art* (Oxford: Aris & Phillips, 2010), 193–94.

97. BM EA 9901/5.

In these contexts, these animals were no longer seen purely as a calf or a duck; rather, they had become living symbols of important concepts or actors in mythological reenactments. Whereas the cut foreleg of the calf was thought to represent the ḫpš, considered to be the choice cut of meat par excellence and an essential tool during the Opening of the Mouth ritual, Nadine Guilhou's close examination of all the surviving scenes including this tableau has led her to argue that this original hypothesis is erroneous. Instead, the scene of the calf being mutilated in the presence of his mother is the reenactment of an episode from the Contendings of Horus and Seth.[98] In this myth, Isis is said to cut the hands of her son Horus, hands that had been soiled by the semen of his uncle Seth. Being a magician, Isis restores Horus's hands, which can then hold the ḫpš used to perform the Opening of the Mouth ceremony on his father Osiris. In the scene discussed above, the calf has become the substitute for Horus, shown in the company of his mother Isis, in the guise of a cow. Guilhou further suggests that this short-lived ritual may have been performed using animal statuettes. Priests may also have pretended to perform the mutilation on living animals.[99] In either case, the animal lovers among us may breathe a sigh of relief as—if Guilhou is correct—no calf was hurt in the ceremony.

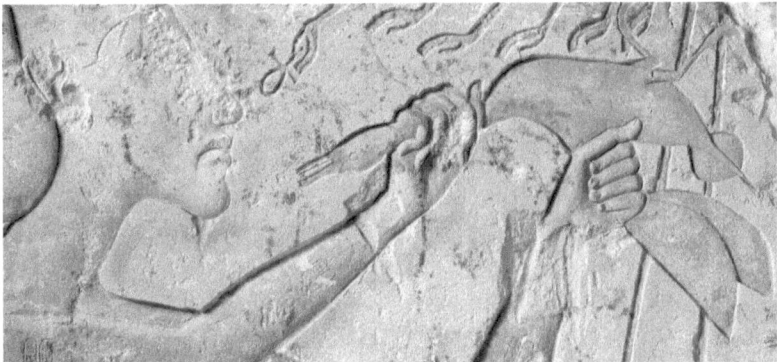

FIGURE 9. Block from a temple relief showing King Akhenaten sacrificing a pintail duck to the Aten (Eighteenth Dynasty, ca. 1353–1336 BCE). MMA 1985.328.2. Courtesy of The Metropolitan Museum of Art.

On the other hand, I doubt that a similar escape can be posited for the duck shown in the relief fragment. In literary and religious texts, wild birds of the marshes are often described as being the forces of chaos that

---

98. Guilhou, "La mutilation rituelle du veau," 285–95.
99. Ibid., 283 n. 17, 295.

needed to be exterminated, or the enemies that had to be kept at bay.[100] Thus, by sacrificing this duck, Akhenaten is not only providing food to the god, he is also maintaining Maat in the universe, one of the main responsibilities of the king, as explained above. These actions should undeniably be considered cruel, since they clearly caused pain and, ultimately, these animals' deaths. Yet, in ancient Egyptian society, the pain and distress caused to such animals seemed to have been justifiable since animal sacrifices were accepted as fulfilling specific functions. On the one hand, the sacrifices helped the deceased on their way to the afterlife, and, on the other hand, they guaranteed peace as well as moral and political order in Egypt by pacifying the gods. The pain and distress felt by animals was secondary—perhaps ignored—to the confirmation of the king's control over Maat, the promise of peace, and the guarantee of rebirth after death.

Finally, in the so-called daily life scenes covering the walls of elite tomb chapels, working animals are sometimes represented as about to be hit by agricultural workers, who are equipped with whips and staves. Sheep, goats, cattle, and especially donkeys could be subjected to serious beatings. The tomb of Iti, from Gebelein, includes a revealing detail: the artists did not fail to paint what appear to be open sores on the back side of a donkey, already loaded with baskets and followed by his driver (fig. 10).[101] Kim Taylor, manager of Animal Care in Egypt's Luxor center, states, "Here, in Luxor, donkeys are treated mainly as machines, not as living,

FIGURE 10. Scene from the tomb of Iti and Neferu in Gebelein showing a donkey transporting grain. Its rump is covered with open sores, probably the result of repeated beatings. (First Intermediate Period, ca. 2118–1980 BCE). S. 14354/15. Courtesy of the Museo Egizio, Turin.

---

100. Bailleul-LeSuer, " Exploitation of Live Avian Resources," 14–17.
101. Houlihan, *Animal World of the Pharaohs*, 29, pl. 13.

feeling creatures. There is no awareness that donkeys need 'maintenance' and not just attention when they break down.... They are routinely beaten, overworked, underfed." They also suffer treatment "that would result in prosecutions for cruelty in the UK and other countries."[102] We are left to wonder how often Taylor's comment regarding what she observes with Luxor's donkeys today could also apply to the ancient Egyptians' treatment of their working animals.

Conclusion

Attempting to ascertain the status of animals in ancient Egypt is certainly not a straightforward task, as the relationships the ancient Egyptians maintained with the animal world were complex, full of nuances, and often appear discordant to our modern eyes.[103] How can the cat be represented as the object of worship on stelae, whereas, simultaneously, thousands of kittens were deliberately killed in what could be compared to factory farms? While we would consider this situation unacceptable today,[104] ancient Egyptians may have seen these mass killings as benevolent gestures: thanks to the rituals performed on their remains, these animals were transformed into *nṯr.w*, "gods."

Ancient Egyptian farmers seemingly treated their farm animals just as many rural societies currently do. Animals were considered property that needed to be cared for in an appropriate fashion, in part to ensure the well-being of the animals, but especially to maximize the profitability of an investment. Certain animals were kept in confined spaces, with a limited range of movement, and were force-fed to increase their weight and ultimately improve the quality of their meat. Such treatment would be considered reprehensible by animal welfare groups, whose members are currently seeking to ban the force-feeding of ducks for the production of foie gras, and who are attempting to ensure that all animals are given sufficient space to move relatively freely. As for members of the elite, just like the denizens of our modern urban/suburban communities, they had the luxury of keeping animals solely for pleasure—some as companions, with which/whom they appeared to have shared some degree of emotional bond, and some as status symbols, which could be hunted or admired in parks.

---

102. www.ace-egypt.org.uk (last consulted 31 May 2019).

103. See the excellent introduction by Thorsten Fögen, and Edmund Thomas, in *Interactions between Animals and Humans*, on the challenges of tracing the animal–human relationships in the ancient world.

104. It continues to be "acceptable," however, to kill large numbers of animals bred specifically for their fur.

Finally, do we have enough evidence to say whether the ancient Egyptians considered animals as "mere things" or sentient beings? From the perspective of the literate elite, those who composed the texts quoted in this essay, I believe that animals were seen as sentient beings. Their distinct behaviors were utilized by scribes as metaphors to describe both humankind and the divine. For instance, the fearfulness of the lapwing came to represent the common Egyptian recoiling in awe before the might of Pharaoh, the living falcon. As recorded in P. Lansing 2, 6–8, even domestic animals had learned to behave so as to avoid a beating from their master, contrary to pupils, whose ears, said to be in their back, refused to listen. A teacher thus laments about his student:

> So also a cow is bought this year, and it plows the following year. It *learns to listen* to the herdsman; *it only lacks words*. Horses brought from the field, they *forget* their mothers. Yoked they go up and down on all of his majesty's errands. They become like those that bore them, that stand in the stable. They *do their utmost for fear* of a beating. But though I beat you with every kind of stick, you do not listen. If I knew another way of doing it, I would do it for you, that you might listen.[105]

Before the beating stick, animals and people appeared to have been equal (fig. 11).

FIGURE 11. Ostracon with the painted scene of a boy being beaten by a cat, perhaps his teacher, in front of a mouse dressed in the finely pleated kilt of a high official (Nineteenth Dynasty, ca. 1280 BCE). OIM E13951. Courtesy of the Oriental Institute of the University of Chicago.

---

105. Lichtheim, *Ancient Egyptian Literature*, 2:169 (emphasis added).

On the other hand, while they may not have been considered "mere" things by the farming community who used them extensively and reared them in their villages, animals remained a commodity that served a specific, utilitarian purpose. While we can safely assume that basic care was given to this valued "animate" property, it remains impossible to postulate how much energy was imparted to ensure the well-being of these tame and domesticated animals.

This essay does not claim to be an exhaustive review of the role of animals in the daily life and legal system of Pharaonic Egypt. Instead, I hope that it will challenge and motivate Egyptologists to pursue a more in-depth investigation into the lives of the animals that shared the Nile Valley with ancient Egyptians. Far from only being vehicles for the divine or metaphors in textual compositions, animals lived side by side with Egyptians of every social status. They served many crucial roles that allowed human beings to flourish by providing food for them, working in the fields, carrying heavy loads, or helping them win battles. Rules of conduct towards these animals existed, many of which were most likely orally conveyed or carried by tradition. Rather than only looking at the animals as symbols used by humans, let us focus on these animals for their own sakes. Finally, this study also reveals that, already in ancient Egypt, a class of citizens composed in part of educated, literate men was aware of the "inhumane" treatment suffered by some animals, as clearly described in the fable The Lion in Search of Man. Like the philosopher attempting to understand the nature of humankind, the educated man in the guise of the lion could not help but be disappointed by the cruel streak that he observed in humans. It appears that, even in antiquity, education was the key to a better understanding of nature, its intrinsic value, and the need to foster it.

Partial Persons, Unsafe Spaces:

The Babylonian Production of Class through Laws about Animals

SETH RICHARDSON
University of Chicago

> *Half a shekel is half a shekel wherever you go; discarded, it is a shekel belonging to the place of wild cattle and serpents.*
> —Sumerian Proverb (Collection 4:3)

This essay engages two overlapping questions about the legal treatments of animals in law collections from Mesopotamia's Old Babylonian period (ca. 2000–1600 BCE).[1] The first question focuses on the spaces in which animals were known according to law; the second looks at the principles of proportional value by which animals were positioned relative to people. I argue that the symbolic marginality and proportionality

---

1. Citations of Old Babylonian laws from law collections follow Martha T. Roth, *Law Collections from Mesopotamia and Asia Minor*, WAW 6 (Atlanta: Scholars Press, 1995): LL = Laws of Lipit-Ištar (of Isin, ca. 1930 BCE; LOx = "Laws about Rented Oxen," a scholastic exercise; SLEx = "A Sumerian Laws Exercise Tablet"; SLHF = "Sumerian Laws Handbook of Forms" (a practical compendium?); LE = Laws of Ešnunna (probably of Duduša, ca. 1780 BCE), and LH = Laws of Hammurabi (ca. 1750 BCE). No animal laws are preserved in the so-called "Laws of X" (ibid., 36–39). CUSAS = Cornell University Studies in Assyriology and Sumerology; ETCSL = J. A. Black et al., The Electronic Text Corpus of Sumerian Religion (Oxford, 1998–2006: http://etcsl.orinst.ox.ac.uk/). All other abbreviations follow the *CAD* (*The Assyrian Dictionary of the Oriental Institute of the University of Chicago,* 21 vols. [Chicago: Oriental Institute of the University of Chicago, 1956–2011]), and AbB for the fourteen-volume series *Altbabylonische Briefe in Umschrift und Übersetzung,* ed. Klaas R. Veenhof (Leiden: Brill, 1964–2005). I regret that 2020–2021 pandemic conditions prevented me from consulting Jim Ritter's (promisingly titled) article "Law and Order in Ancient Mesopotamia: Legal Codes and Mathematical Problems," in *The Normativity of Formal Orders and Procedures in Antiquity: A Comparison of Mathematical and Legal Systems,* ed. Daliah Bawanypeck, Annette Imhausen, and Guido Pfeifer (Münster: Ugarit-Verlag, 2020), 7–52.

of animals to people, in spatial and social terms, discursively grounded broader state claims about the scalarity of political subjectivity for all actors as "natural facts."

The first of my questions asks why such laws as there were concerning animals focused oversight on specifically nonurban spaces. Why did Mesopotamian law take such an interest in the damage done to animals in places that were liminal to state power? Why was it so vividly imagined what happened to cattle, not in city streets, villages, and pastures, but in deserts, swamps, and river-crossings—otherwise unregulated places that states did not substantially control?[2]

The second question asks how those same laws shaped and proposed the partial, relative, or imperfect legal personhood of both people and animals through metaphors of proportion. Various laws of the period awarded proportional financial damages for not only animal but also human death or injury, depending on social class, positioning animals as para-social beings. This relates directly to the limited sociality of animals depicted in letters, which illustrates that certain animals—mostly oxen, but sometimes donkeys, sheep, and goats[3]—counted as household members at the base of a scale that included slaves, servants, daughters, sons, wives, fathers, and even real estate.[4] All these counted as social beings and legal (if not always natural) persons to differing extents.[5] Slaves in particular were a complex arena for the working-out of questions of proportional class identity,[6] but animals as symbols had the clear advantage of being passive symbols, lacking agency. How were expressions of proportional value used to model social relations generally?

The two topics of bordering places and partial personhood are not so obviously related,[7] but they join up at a larger abstract issue of what law

---

2. See Seth Richardson, "Early Mesopotamia: The Presumptive State," *Past & Present* 215.1 (2012): 3–49.

3. The enumeration of oxen as part of the *bītum* ("household") is frequent (e.g., AbB I 37; III 11, 38, 54; IV 146; V 151, 218, 230; VI 179; IX 37, 48, 59; XII 9; XII 165; XIV 91; XIV 142); sheep and goats (e.g., AbB III 11; IX 37, 107; IX 256; XII 190; XIV 142) and donkeys (e.g., AbB II 177; III 36, 38; III 39; VII 143; IX 185) less so, but attested. No other animals are so mentioned. The character of these representations is very limited, mostly in fixed expressions reporting that various people and animals of the household are "well."

4. E.g., AbB X 186; cf. X 121. Compare Saul Olyan, "Are There Legal Texts in the Hebrew Bible That Evince a Concern for Animal Rights?," *BibInt* 27 (2019): 321–39, esp. 328–29.

5. For a different dimension of the question, see Gebhard Selz's analysis of classificatory and taxonomic features of the cuneiform writing system: "Reflections on the Pivotal Role of Animals in Early Mesopotamia," in *Animals and Their Relation to Gods, Humans and Things in the Ancient World*, ed. Raija Mattila, Sanae Ito, and Sebastian Fink, Studies in Universal and Cultural History (Wiesbaden: Springer, 2019), 23–56.

6. Seth Richardson, "Walking Capital: The Economic Function and Social Location of Babylonian Servitude," *Journal of Global Slavery* 4.3 (2019): 285–342.

7. Andreas Schüle, in this volume, poses the question of whether the "nearer/further" of liminality is really the same question as issues of proportion.

had to do with symbolic liminalities. Animals made possible the construction of degrees and kinds of legal personhood and jurisdiction because, like slaves, they could be positioned as simultaneously natural and marginal social beings. This strategy of ambivalence helped to fabricate state sovereignty by situating claims about the relative status, rights, and duties of state subjects in territorial and commercial terms through *Grundsymbolen* of the animal world, where the conceptual domains of nature and society were easily blurred. I will first outline the evidence for the theme of unregulated space; then examine the theme of proportional personhood; and then consider their relation in a conclusion.

Before diving into the particulars, I will reflect briefly on three types of previous work that prepare me to comment on animals and law. First, I have recently explored how and why animals were symbolically positioned so differently in Sumerian versus Akkadian literatures.[8] Sumerian works imagined talking animals as social and sentient persons who were, like humans, participants, revealers, and producers of "natural knowledge" immanent in the world. Later Akkadian literature, by contrast, depicted animals as mute and dangerous beasts, nonpersons who belonged to a world outside and opposite to the "divine knowledge" that was fundamentally textual, historical, and apprehensible exegetically. This comparison, while teaching me much about the symbolic potency of animals, had little to do with law. A second effort had to do with studying Mesopotamian legal history with a law-as-literature approach. Here, I explored ancient law not as a coherent system of practice but as a discursive arena in which states grounded claims to power over territory, membership, and identity.[9] This work about law, however, had little to do with animals. A third kind of work has been my edition and translation of practical cuneiform documents relating to the management and sale of animals, including their valuation—work that has little to do with either law or "knowledge." The present essay demands something of a synthesis of the three approaches, a triangulation of how literary, legal, and practical animals relate to one another in a particular historical context. I hope that, by the conclusion, I will have made it clear how questions of commercial value, relative personhood, and the state's use of law as a discourse of power were all settled on the bony, overworked frames of Babylonian sheep, donkeys, and oxen.

---

8. Seth Richardson, "Nature Engaged and Disengaged: The Case of Animals in Mesopotamian Literatures," in *Impious Dogs, Haughty Foxes and Exquisite Fish: Evaluative Perception and Interpretation of Animals in Ancient and Medieval Mediterranean Thought*, ed. Johannes Pahlitzsch and Tristan Schmidt (Berlin: de Gruyter, 2019), 11–40.

9. Seth Richardson, "Before Things Worked: A 'Low-Power' Model of Early Mesopotamia," in *Ancient States and Infrastructural Power: Europe, Asia, and America*, ed. Clifford Ando and Seth Richardson, Empire and After (Philadelphia: University of Pennsylvania Press, 2017), 17–62.

Legal Animals in Mesopotamia: A Word on Sources and Subjects

I begin by noting which animals were subject to law, either protected in themselves or as instruments to be regulated when causing damage to property, people, or other animals. The list is short: oxen are the subjects most of the time, and occasionally sheep, goats, and donkeys. These are exactly the same animals who show up as the household members worth reporting on in Old Babylonian letters (e.g., "The household is well, and the cattle are well," AbB V 151), and who, in estate inventories, are not listed with the *būšu* of the house, the mere "things" like chairs and beds and doors, but rather together with slaves, servants, children, and real property.[10] They could be owned and sold but were also afforded some degree of sociality.

One would not want to oversell the personhood of these "social animals." In the first place, every social being in a household (up to and including its head) could be given as a pledge for debt. But people alienated from their households, temporarily or permanently, for commercial debts should not therefore be understood as nonsocial beings; I only point out that we are looking at a culture in which all social beings were commercially valuable. In the second place, there is precious little affect or emotion expressed about animals, or expressions of care at all other than for their health in letters or literature (if, again, the same is largely true of humans).

Many other animals were depicted in Mesopotamian literature as natural to the urban environment and endowed with social identity and agency, such as foxes, pigs, pigeons, ravens, and mice, but these are absent from the laws and the letters. Dogs are mentioned only once by the laws (LE ¶56), and expressly as a potential danger;[11] dogs were thought of as street animals, and not part of a household per se. So, from the outset we can see that there was a conception of which animals were assimilated to

---

10. The same conceptual scope of the household is outlined in Exod 20:17, which prohibits the coveting not only of a neighbor's wife but also of his servants, oxen, donkeys, or "anything that belongs to your neighbor."

11. Cf. AbB XI 57: "There is a man (whom) a dog has bitten, and I am applying the bandages; send me the oil!"; AbB II 83: "If he comes to me empty-handed, the dogs will eat me!" For negative characterizations of dogs (including people as "dogs"), see also V 160; IX 39; XIII 70; cf. X 11. On dogs as street animals, see Seth Richardson "Getting Confident: The Assyrian Development of Elite Recognition Ethics," in *Cosmopolitanism and Empire: Universal Rulers, Local Elites, and Cultural Integration in the Ancient Near East and Mediterranean*, ed. Myles Lavan, Richard E. Payne, and John Weisweiler, Oxford Studies in Early Empires (Oxford: Oxford University Press, 2016), 29–64, here 50–51.

the social world of the household and law, and which belonged to the street or the wild (lions, elephants, snakes, fish, etc.). Legal attention to a few specific animals was thus predicated on their social relation to humans.

How, therefore, were these relations regulated? In six Old Babylonian law collections, there are sixty-six statutes mentioning these social animals.[12] Twenty-two have to do with the people who own or tend the animals, rather than the animals themselves: regulations for the rates to be paid to herdsmen, the use of common pastures, or against the sale of stolen animals.[13] Two laws are of uncertain content.[14] These twenty-four laws, then, are not examined here, as their attention is substantially focused on humans. The remaining forty-two laws attend to damages done to oxen, sheep, goats, or donkeys; to their health and care; or damages done by them, to people or other animals.[15] Only seven of these forty-two laws focus on the last type of situation—in which animals harm others—primarily and famously the ones about "goring oxen."[16] But these seven statutes have been the subject of the most sustained attention to "laws about animals," primarily for how they illuminate scholastic traditions.[17] Yet the problem of oxen goring people seems withal to have been a theoretical problem posed almost entirely in the laws and omens, and rarely found in practice documents—case law, letters, or lawsuits.[18] In sales and hires of

---

12. LL ¶¶a, 34–38; LOx ¶¶1–9; SLEx ¶¶9′–10′; SLHF iii 13–15, v 45, vi 11, 16, 23, 32; LE ¶¶3, 10, 40, 50, 53–57; LH ¶¶7–8, 35, 57–58, 224–25, 241–54, 256, 258, 261–71.

13. LL ¶a (ox rental rates); SLHF iii 13–15 (penalty for stealing a pig); LE ¶3 (hire rate for ox-drawn wagon), 10 (hire rate of donkey), 40 (sale of stolen slaves or oxen); LH ¶8 (stolen property), 35 (misappropriation of state-owned animals), 57–58 (rules for grazing), 241 (value of distrained oxen), 242/243 (ox rental rates), 255 (misuse of rented cattle), 256 (punishment for unsatisfied cattle hire is to be dragged around the field by the cattle), 258 (hire rates for ox drivers), 261 (hire rates for herdsmen), 264–265 (malpractice and theft by herdsman), 268–71 (hire rates for oxen, donkeys, goats, and cattle). Cf. Exod 22:1, 4, 9.

14. SLHF v 45 (in whole: "one ox for the rear of the team"); LH ¶262 ("If a man [gives] an ox or a sheep to a [herdsman …]." LL ¶38 almost certainly continues LL ¶¶34–37 and may be restored from LOx ¶5, which is also broken but clearly discusses damage to oxen. What part of the ox is at risk here?

15. LL ¶¶34–38 (LL ¶38 is arguably restorable from LOx ¶5); LOx ¶¶1–9; SLEx ¶¶9′–10′; SLHF vi 11, 16, 23, 32; LE ¶¶50, 53–57; LH ¶¶224–25, 244–54, 263, 266–67.

16. As Martha Roth has shown, these are really about *stray* oxen, unattended by people: "Errant Oxen, or: The Goring Ox Redux," in *Literature as Politics, Politics as Literature: Essays on the Ancient Near East in Honor of Peter Machinist*, ed. David S. Vanderhooft and Abraham Winitzer (Winona Lake, IN: Eisenbrauns, 2013), 397–404, here 400.

17. See esp. J. J. Finkelstein, *The Ox That Gored*, TAPS 71.2 (Philadelphia: American Philosophical Society, 1981); Martha Roth, "The Scholastic Exercise 'Laws about Rented Oxen,'" *JCS* 32 (1980): 127–46; and Roth, "Errant Oxen," including the relation of Mesopotamian laws to the compilations of Exod 21:28–36, e.g., "If [x], the man will die from being gored by a bull" (YOS X 23 r. 6).

18. See the examples in *CAD* N/1, s.v. *nakāpu* v. 1a ("to gore"), restricted to law provisions and omens. See further *CAD* Ḫ, s.v. *ḫalāqu/ḫalqu*, and R, s.v. *ragāmu*, which give no exempla for animals wandering off or claims raised about such. Raymond Westbrook, in his

oxen, such contractual provisions as existed protected the buyer against problems of animal health, not behavior,[19] for example, in representations by sellers that an animal was initially healthy,[20] or that someone hiring an ox would be responsible for damages caused to it, *ana īnī qarnī šuprī u zibbati*, "for eyes, horns, hooves, and tail."[21] In short, there is no evidence for "goring" as a problem in daily life, or even much for "wandering." That these legal provisions are primarily exercises in analogy cannot be in doubt; their symbolic potential did not primarily relate to the literal problems through which their allusive meanings were conveyed.

In light of this, it is remarkable that the forty-two laws whose subject is animals *being harmed* rather than harming (i.e., a 6:1 majority) have received so much less attention, though they, too, reflect a clear scribal tradition, at least within the various Mesopotamian law collections.[22] That various statutes within law collections reflect a scribal tradition, however, is not my focus, especially since the general idea is fairly well established. Instead, my interest has to do with the symbolic ways the laws deal with nonurban environments, on the one hand, and proportional value, on the other—different strategies of structuring legal and social marginality.

Legal Animals and Unregulated Space

I focus first on the subject of unregulated space and argue that laws about animals in borderlands not only reflected but produced ideas about territorial jurisdiction that metaphorically constructed the legal identity of

---

review of Old Babylonian law ("Old Babylonian Period," in *A History of Ancient Near Eastern Law*, ed. Raymond Westbrook, 2 vols., HdO 1.72 [Leiden: Brill, 2003], 1:415 §8.1.3.1) discusses only the evidence of law codes for animals injuring people. Note finally that "goring" oxen had a low profile in literary imagination as well, and mostly in proverbs as metaphors for royal authority ("The Instructions of Šuruppak" [line 94] and Sumerian Proverb Collection 2.154), e.g., "The palace is like a mighty river; its interior is a goring bull."

19. See pp. 64–65 below, on oxen as "known gorers."

20. For example, BM 87255 (edition forthcoming as TLOB 2.1.18) includes the rare stipulation of a warranty period to inspect an ox for epilepsy, a stipulation usually reserved for slave sales. References to animal health are rare beyond stating that they were either "well" or "dead" (see, e.g., AbB XIV 111); cf. TCL 1 4, fresh pastures to keep sheep "in good condition." Qualitative assessments of animals as "sick, diseased" (*marṣu*), "skinny" (*šīru maṭû*), or "healthy" (*namru*; see n. 61 below) are not used for animals until post-OB times, though such could be said of slaves in the OB.

21. PBS 8/2 196.

22. Esp. (with some variations): LL ¶34 ‖ LOx ¶3; LL ¶35 ‖ LOx ¶1, LH ¶247; LL ¶36 ‖ LOx ¶2; LL ¶37 ‖ LOx ¶4; LL ¶38 ‖ LOx ¶5; LOx ¶8 ‖ SLEx ¶9', SLHF vi 16 and 32, LH ¶244; SLHF vi 23 ‖ LOx ¶6 and ¶9; perhaps LH ¶246 ‖ LL ¶38/LOx ¶5; LH ¶248 ‖ LL ¶36/LOx ¶2 (horn), LL ¶37/ LOx ¶4 (tail), LL ¶34/LOx ¶3 (hoof). See also Exod 21:33–36. Roth covers some of these passages in "Scholastic Exercise."

persons living under state sovereignty. In at least thirteen of the laws in which animals are hurt or killed, the setting in which the damage occurs is a nonurban space. Either in combination or alone, three laws focus on the injury to an animal at a river crossing;[23] one specifies "open country";[24] six deal with the attack of a lion;[25] one imagines a canebrake or swamp;[26] and four deal with stray or wandering animals.[27] Less clearly, two statutes deal with injuries in "cattle pens" (*tarbaṣu*); such pens were commonly attested as attached to urban buildings, but the context dealing with the attack of a lion in at least one instance here (LH ¶266) also suggests a nonurban context (cf. LH ¶267, where the locale cannot necessarily be deduced).

Significantly, these landscapes and environments are nearly unique within the law collections. Out of nearly five hundred individual Old Babylonian law provisions, the only ones to mention river crossings, swamps, lion attacks, or wandering in open territory are these thirteen laws about animals, aside from two statutes (LH ¶17 ‖ LE ¶50) in which the subject of "wandering" in "open country" has to do with a fugitive slave.[28] In contrast, what happens in the narratives of other legal provisions to people—to merchants, farmers, soldiers, priestesses, or anyone else under the purview of the law—is virtually never conditioned by *where* they are when a problem occurs, because the laws took the urban environment to be a normal generic precondition for jurisdiction. The distinction of place that these animal laws make is, therefore, significant in its own right.[29]

One might assume that laws about animals were set in liminal environments because those were simply the kinds of places where animals were. But this is not so for human actors, whose activities often involved open countryside and caravan roads: yet no soldier in the laws is ever attacked by a lion, no herdsman is robbed in the steppe, no merchant loses his goods crossing a swamp. Human actors are not positioned by the laws in these places—only animals. Why should this be? It is clear that these legal provisions, which uniquely paired wild places and animals, meant to say as much about exceptional legal environments as they did about

---

23. LOx ¶6 and ¶9; SLHF vi 23.

24. LH ¶244; cf. LH ¶17.

25. LOx ¶7 and ¶8; SLEx ¶9´; SLHF vi 32; LH ¶¶244 and 266; see also Roth, "Scholastic Exercise": 137 re: FLP 1287 vi 16–22.

26. SLHF vi 16.

27. SLEx ¶¶9´–10´; LE ¶50; LH ¶263. Cf. Exod. 23:4. Cf. LH ¶250, where the setting is clearly urban; Finkelstein assumed that this goring ox was not "wandering" but was under the control of a non-negligent herder (*Ox That Gored*, 24).

28. LE ¶50 does not mention "open country," though I hold that in all cases to be understood where an animal or person is said to be *ḫalqu*, whether translated as "wandering," "stray," "fugitive," or "escaped."

29. As Roth aptly points out, laws about "goring" oxen are in fact about "*errant* oxen" ("Errant Oxen," 400).

animals per se; they intended something particular about the law and *place*. J. J. Finkelstein commented little about the function of place in his classic 1981 study *The Ox That Gored*; for Finkelstein, the heart of the matter in the animal laws was issues of property (especially about deodands). My point here has little implication about that treatment; I only emphasize another aspect, that the symbolic universe of the legal provisions suggests they spoke to issues of property and personality in the context of *jurisdiction*.

We must guard against the temptation to read law provisions in concrete terms. There are two types of theoretical problems in reading "laws" this way. In the first place, understanding the law collections as actionable statutes ignores their literary quality—that they are often metaphorical just-so stories belonging to the scribal rather than the juridical realm. Especially these animal laws found in multiple collections were (in Martha Roth's words) "primarily scholastic exercise[s] … and not in themselves to be viewed as expressions of Old Babylonian legal realities."[30] Secondarily, and as a corollary, evidence for the functional use of the legal provisions, as "laws" or "statutes," remains slight overall. Like the omen series to which they are literary twins, the laws offered symbols and model narratives whose most practical applications lay in their potential for legal reasoning by analogy, not as statutes anticipating specific cases. The passages invoking images of otherwise unregulated spaces have to be considered as models useful for a particular problem in judicial reasoning.

Therefore, the question becomes, What was it about animals that made them, of all symbols, ideal vehicles for making legal claims about bordering spaces? A starting point may lie in the clue that these laws drew a sharp difference between attacks by lions, for which owners were not protected, and river crossings and cases of wandering animals, for which renters and shepherds were generally liable for losses. One could infer that a distinction was being made about "nearer" and "farther" jurisdictions, and not only the liabilities therein, but (tacitly) the law's *ability* to adjudicate.[31]

Noting only this basic harmony with notions of jurisdiction, however, I move on to a second explanation proceeding from the *symbolic* potential of lions attacking oxen, and by extension of their habitat in the steppe-

---

30. Roth, "Scholastic Exercise," 142. Notwithstanding, this disclaimer follows several pages of relatively practical explanations of how such laws might have worked.

31. The setting of riverbanks, in particular, may relate to the deep-seated metaphorical investment that Mesopotamian culture made in distinguishing between nearer and farther river banks. This was a semantic and even deictic paradigm in which spatial expressions about riverbanks were among the most profound ways to distinguish between subjects and non-subjects, between "us" and "them," as suggested by the meaning-laden expressions *eber nāri/eberta/ebertān/ebertu* A, "(on) the far/other bank/side," which designated distinctions in property ownership, community membership, state territory, and even mantic states.

lands. Why should we think these laws did not reflect a real problem of lions attacking living oxen? Was this not a possibility? It certainly was: lions wandered the Syrian desert at this time, occasionally roaming into the lower alluvium. But to perform a reality check on the literary-legal depiction of the problem, consider the 2,762 documents published in the main Old Babylonian corpus of letters (i.e., AbB), roughly contemporary with the laws under discussion here. How are problems with cattle discussed there? Nine letters mention missing or stolen cattle;[32] six mention their grazing along river banks as problematic;[33] three discuss the movement of cattle across rivers or into marshes;[34] many mention hunger and/or theft of food allotments for cattle as the most common difficulty with oxen, of which I cite only a few of the most salient.[35]

Three more letters mention injuries to oxen, but only in ways that would confound anyone trying to find the application of statute law reflected in a real situation. In the first letter (AbB IX 71), an ox is simply said to have "sustained a wound," without any further detail. In a second (AbB XI 7), ox-drovers reported that an ox just "strayed away, and while he was eating grass, he fell down dead."[36] A third letter (AbB XII 177) relates that an angry farmer chased a loose ox out of his sesame field and broke its foot with an ax.[37] Even though two of these letters mention legal "investigations" of their situations, they do not reflect well any possibly relevant statutes.

But—most directly to the point—no letter out of almost three thousand mentions cattle or oxen in open country or being attacked by lions; in fact, lions are not mentioned in any of the letters, in any context.[38] The

---

32. AbB I 114 (cf. X 7); II 86; VI 9 and 10; VII 139; VIII 84?; XIII 41; and XIV 62 and 146.
33. AbB IV 150; VII 47, 49, and 50; IX 83; and XIV 132; the potential problems suggest vulnerability to theft.
34. AbB XI 58; XII 172; XIV 94; it is not clear, however, that these discuss problems, per se.
35. To cite only a few most salient examples: AbB III 11 and 46; VI 66; VIII 7; IX 67; X 15, 20, 41, and 96; XI 27 (reporting 49 of 189 cattle dead from starvation); XI 132; XI 160; XIV 54, 55, 94, 105, 164, and 174.
36. Cf. LH ¶249, a *force majeure* provision. Both the letter and the law require the renter to swear an oath; but the letter specifies that the plaintiff did not accept that verdict.
37. All of the statutes about injuries to oxen are specific to renters, which the farmer is not.
38. Neither do lion attacks show up in the 276 letters edited in Robert M. Whiting, *Old Babylonian Letters from Tell Asmar*, AS 22 (Chicago: Oriental Institute of the University of Chicago, 1987) and A. R. George, *Old Babylonian Texts in the Schøyen Collection*, part 1, *Selected Letters*, CUSAS 36 (Bethesda, MD: CDL Press, 2018). Cf. *CAD* N/2, s.v. *nēšu* s., "lion," 1b-1', which includes a few legal and administrative texts mentioning lion attacks against *people*. These include six OB contracts in which purchasers are (prospectively) indemnified for slaves killed by lions, and five other reports from Mari texts of (fatal) lion attacks (one, ironically, at a *tarbaṣum*, a "cattle-pen"). A twelfth document does report the killing of a cow by a lion, from Chagar Bazar, about five hundred miles north of Babylon.

contrast with literary texts could not be more stark: in omens, royal inscriptions, stories,[39] and proverbs, lions attack caravans, devour people leaving the city gate, and block the roads; they are especially cast as predators attacking sheepfolds and cowpens. They are consistently likened to thieves, enemies, and *ḫabbātū*, "robbers." *Ḫabbātū* appear in two ways: in literary contexts they were shadowy highwaymen, cut-throats, and brigands, the enemies of civilized life; but in administrative and economic documents, *ḫabbātū* show up as marginal encampments of workers and mercenaries who were tenuously associated with the state.[40] It is this metaphorical relationship of lions to nonurban and "lawless" people that I argue is the subtext of the lion-attack laws.

The attention paid by the law to lions attacking oxen was not answering some real and urgent everyday problem; were this the case, it ought at least to show up in the odd letter here and there. It is thus the literary and symbolic meaning of the motif we are after here. Consider the oracle query: "Will (the questioner) escape from an attack of the enemy, an attack of lions, an attack of robbers?"[41] Or the proverb, "A thief is a lion, but after he has been caught, he will be a slave."[42] Or the omen predicting that "either a lion or robbers will cause that man to abandon his expedition."[43] Paired in such imagery, lions and robbers were both said to "rampage" (*nadāru*) and "attack" (*šiḫṭu*, just as easily a "raid").[44]

In consideration of these associations, as well as the lawlike properties of omens and oracles, I suggest that the attack of a lion on an ox in a remote area in law modeled not only a principle of *force majeure*, an uncontrollable loss of property, but symbolized the limits of state jurisdiction over territories and people who lived beyond the reach of urban authority. If we know that Babylonian laws were the basis for reasoning by analogy, then a law about financial responsibility for a lion attacking an ox might be the basis for decisions about losses of property as acts of God; but that they

---

39. For example, the poem "The Three Ox-Drovers from Adab" (ETCSL 5.6.5), in which an owner cries, "What if my ox is devoured by a lion? I will not leave my ox!"

40. Seth Richardson, "By the Hand of a Robber: States, Mercenaries, and Bandits in Middle Bronze Age Mesopotamia," in *Piracy, Pillage, and Plunder in Antiquity: Appropriation and the Ancient World*, ed. Richard Evans and Martine De Marre (Oxford: Taylor & Francis, 2019), 9–26. The identity of *ḫabbātū*-robbers presents much the same tangle of interpretive problems as the *ḫāpiru*, so I avoid going into much detail here.

41. IM 67692, sub. *CAD* N/2, s.v. *nēšu* s.v. 1b-3'.

42. ETCSL 5.6.1: 30f.

43. *CT* 39 25 in *CAD* N/2, s.v. *nēšu* s. 1b-2'.

44. Also Aššurbanipal's hunting of wild lions causing damage, "… having fed on cattle, sheep and goats, and humans, (the lions) become fierce, and went on a rampage [*ēzizu*]" (*CAD* A/1, s.v. *alpu* s. 2b-3'). See further *CAD* Š/1, s.v. *šaḫāṭu* A 3, "to attack, to raid," said of enemies and nomads (a) and of animals (b), principally lions. Notwithstanding, the verbs used in the laws do not invoke this sense of raiding: gaz, "to kill" (LOx ¶¶7, 8 [restored], SLHF vi 32), gu₇ (*akālu*), "to devour" (SLEx ¶9'), and *dâku*, "to kill" (LH ¶¶244, 266).

happened out in distant locales, and implicitly at the hands of noncitizens (places and people where and who the state could not reach), acknowledged the limits of law altogether.

I will speculate further that the actors populating laws like Hammurabi ¶244, in which the lion and the ox meet in "open country," epitomize issues of personal as well as territorial jurisdiction. Significantly, the law collections otherwise avoid mention of people living in rural environments and non-state people as legal actors, and skirt the issue of "robbers" (ḫabbātū) as a class, covering only individual "thieves" (šarrāqū).[45] But if a lion, then, is like a "robber," the symbol of people unaffiliated with the state, then cattle are nothing if not preeminent symbols of state citizens, over whom the king is shepherd. What is tacitly recognized in these miniature narratives is that there were territories where state law did not operate, spaces not under sovereignty, and classes of people who were not (yet) made subject to it. State subjects who were owners of property were to assume that they risked it if and when they went to those places and among such people. This holds true as well for the canebrake or swamp (SLHF vi 16), where owners were not protected. The corollary point was that the indemnification of owners for animals lost in river crossings at full or partial value,[46] or where they had gone astray (i.e., from points of origin where they *were* initially safe),[47] marked the nearer limits of what the law was willing to police, since these places were liminal to state authority.

This all tracks well with an idea that the territorial and infrastructural footprint of state power in archaic times was substantially smaller and less comprehensive than we might think, and, correspondingly, that the size of non-state populations living outside those footprints was larger.[48] This may sound like a roundabout way of saying that there were simply limits to jurisdiction, which would be true as far as it goes but not particularly helpful; consider that there are limits to jurisdiction in modern legal systems as well. But the "footprint" idea is more specifically consistent with the metaphorical way in which law collections operated as ideological messages in Babylonian state society: states simultaneously claiming credit for generating justice at the conceptual level but often avoiding responsibility to adjudicate in fact.[49] In this respect, the laws about oxen and lions were an ideal way of addressing the limited reach of law over

---

45. An exception is LH ¶¶23–24, a passage dealing with ḫabbātū, but which, significantly, assigns liability for losses in those cases to the authorities who control the territory in which the robbery takes place. More typically, see the "thieves" (šarrāqī) mentioned in CUSAS 36 130, where sheep "have been stolen from inside your town"; cf. CUSAS 36 61.
46. Full value: LOx ¶6; replacement: SLHF vi 23; partial value: LOx ¶9.
47. SLEx ¶10' (replacement); LH ¶263 (replacement); cf. LE ¶50 (criminal charge).
48. Richardson, "Early Mesopotamia."
49. Richardson, "Before Things Worked," 37–39.

unregulated spaces and persons without openly specifying the state's lack of capacity, especially to police robbery in places it simply did not control, because the animals dropped into these vignettes could be positioned as proxies for state and non-state people. The bases for analogistic reasoning were clear: oxen were state subjects and goods, lions were non-state subjects; "open country" was not under jurisdiction, but closer ex-urban landscapes could be. The state thereby put daylight between itself and its *claims* of expansive power found in other royal literature—for example, where Hammurabi claims in the prologue to his laws that he "made justice prevail in the land" and "made the four regions obedient"—by quietly modeling the limits of its power in the natural and mantic world, using animals who could not, in literal terms, ever be mistaken for human subjects. The state "voice" used a complex of metaphors that permitted both types of reading, a convenient way to assert authority partly because it was unfalsifiable in any single construal.

Legal Animals and Proportionality

This brings me to my second subject: the endowment of legal animals with proportional legal personhood. The principle of proportional personhood, grounded in law, produced the relative social values that class structures require. Space does not permit a full history of class in Mesopotamia, but I want to make more than a mere distinction between "elites" and "non-elites," differences that had existed since Chalcolithic times. Rather, I refer to the openly denominated social classifications made by law. Importantly, these class names were not institutionally dependent: they did not derive from previously accepted temple, palace, or urban institutional titles but were developed within civil and commercial life. For OB Mesopotamia, such terms are famously enshrined in Hammurabi's laws' tripartite *awīlum-muškēnum-wardum*, conventionally understood to mean something like "free citizen," "commoner," and "slave."

But the three terms outside of Hammurabi's laws were almost never contrasted one to the other, and almost never denominated anyone's absolute status. A "slave" could mean an institutional inferior, a servant (somewhat colloquially, and often only temporarily), or many things in between;[50] its substantial legal implications were limited to sale and transfer. The word *muškēnum* (from a root meaning "to prostrate oneself") is quite simply poorly attested and therefore poorly understood. The word

---

50. Compare Olyan, "Are There Legal Texts," 337–38, for similar complications to simple understandings of slave status in biblical law.

in the Old Babylonian dialect almost exclusively referred to the liability of specific people for certain taxes.[51] Whatever larger meaning Hammurabi wanted to advance by suggesting *muškēnum* as a class of persons is simply not reflected in the broader culture. I understand the term to refer to an individual responsible for taxes or service through an institutional contract: a tenant, junior officer, concession holder, or prebendiary, not a broad class of "commoners." Meanwhile, with *awīlu*, we have the opposite problem: the word, which literally means only "man," had too many uses to possibly label one specific class.[52]

In any event, this emergent class structure had no real historical antecedents and was never really accomplished: relative class status was still being worked out over the whole Old Babylonian period, both outside of and in reference to other collective and institutional identities. While the fluidity of class structure is a fact of almost all historical times and places, it is important that these terms had no real historical antecedents and had heavily contextualized meanings outside of the law codes. As legal terms, these were really artifices. What is more, the class terms and structure erased what ought to have been a central feature of jurisprudence: no Old Babylonian laws paid respect to any *common* legal rights and duties of (all) "human beings"; the laws created legal subjectivity by creating protections through division and comparison rather than unities.[53] What we can see of class creation in Old Babylonian laws may not have been an entirely novel social sorting project, but it was a moment in which the criteria for sorting were brought to the forefront of the language.

Expressions of social proportionality were not entirely new; they had been in view at least since Ur-Namma's pledge in his twenty-first-century BCE law codes (LU Prologue A iv 162f.) that "I did not deliver the man of one shekel to the man of one mina; I did not deliver the man with one sheep to the man with one ox."[54] The concept governing the relativity of

---

51. See my "Before Things Worked," 47 n. 35, further arguing that the term does not mean a broad class of "commoners." On the particular and individual rather than general or collective nature of the tax liabilities of subjects to state, see my essay "Old Babylonian Taxation as Political Mechanism," in *Economic Complexity in the Ancient Near East: Management of Resources and Taxation (Third–Second Millennium BC)*, ed. Jana Mynářová and Sergio Alvernini (Prague: Charles University, 2020), 217–47.

52. For the *awīlū*, see my "Exercising Sympathy" (forthcoming), which frames the term's generation of class identity (as "gentleman") through expressions of sympathy in letters; for *wardum*, see my "Walking Capital," 296 and 331–36, for a look at the word's profoundly contingent nature.

53. See Saul Olyan, in this volume, with respect to Lev 27:2. It is remarkable, given the attention to the application of equivalence and parity in the Mesopotamian laws (or, to use Olyan's word, "symmetry"), that they contain no meta-commentary on it.

54. In this, both the animal and commercial bases of proportion are set forth, probably more clearly than anywhere else in the Mesopotamian evidence.

social position was a proportional scale of value. This scale not only included animals but depended on them as its foundation. It is not clear that this recognition much affected the ways in which animals were actually *treated*, or that it necessarily brought them into a social relationship with people; there is little other evidence for this. But it mattered much to the human social world that this scalarity was *conceived of* as proportional; that it was both rooted in the animal world and expressed as a matter of commercial value. The valuation of the para-social world that humans construct around animals first externalizes, then rationalizes, and finally naturalizes social relations that are, of course, entirely human-made.

I was initially brought to this observation in reading an article about nineteenth-century American slavery, in which it was demonstrated that it was the stable market prices of slaves that made it possible for courts to construct financial damages for insurance claims about them, which then "foreshadowed the evolution of law for free accident victims."[55] Only the fact that American slaves were so thoroughly commodified made it possible to not only put a price on their lives, but on their hands, feet, or legs; and this by extension still undergirds today the system of punitive legal damages that might be paid for *your* hand, *your* foot, *your* leg—or, indeed, for your life—codified in the accidental death and dismemberment schedules maintained today by employers and insurance companies.[56] Such a grammar of value for personal injury and death, like all systems of meaning, may make sense within its own rules but is ultimately constructed on arbitrary principles.

An analogous system of logic prevailed within and between Old Babylonian laws about slaves, where we find two structural principles about proportion in play in determining awards for damages: the proportional commercial value of body parts, and value expressed in proportion to other (nonslave) bodies, persons, or body parts. In the animal laws, for instance, LH ¶247 proposes that a renter who blinds the eye of an ox should pay half its value to the owner, whereas in LH ¶247 if he breaks its leg, he is liable to replace the ox with one of "comparable value." The two principles may overlap within a logical chain, as when, in LH ¶¶219–20, a physician who causes the death of a slave in surgery is responsible for replacing him/her with a slave "of comparable value" (*wardam kīma wardim*, lit., "slave like slave"); but if he only blinds the slave, he then delivers silver "equal to half his value" (*kaspam mišil šīmišu išaqqal*). Between these provi-

---

55. Jenny Bourne Wahl, "The Bondsman's Burden: An Economic Analysis of the Jurisprudence of Slaves and Common Carriers," *Journal of Economic History* 53 (1993): 495–526.

56. For example, according to the New York State Workers' Compensation Board, a lost arm is worth $124,800, while a thumb is worth $35,000; a fourth finger is worth only $6,000 (source: https://www.marketwatch.com/story/how-much-are-your-body-parts-worth).

sions, one finds a sense of the slave's market value as well as the proportional value of his life to his sight. Other Babylonian laws about damages to and by slaves employed a number of strategies to elaborate these two principles, based on value[57] and/or proportion.[58] These strategies, if extrapolated in literal terms across all the laws, imply that a slave's health was worth one-fifth of that of an *awīlu*, but his life was worth three-eighths; a fetus was worth one-tenth of a mother; a man's single blinded eye was the equivalent of a broken bone; a slave's freedom was worth twice the cost of his enslavement, and so on. The literal expression of abstract principles of course can easily produce grotesque effects and were not understood so literally;[59] they were primarily useful as analogies for judicial reasoning.[60] Notwithstanding, the application of proportional value to practical contexts can be seen in, for example, the designation of slaves as "2/3 healthy" (2/3 *namru*) in commercial contexts, suggesting an emerging sense of scalar values for human lives.[61]

Proportionalism was not exclusive of other strategies of liability: some provisions levied fines irrelevant to the price or value of a person or meted out bodily and other punishments unrelated to financial compensation. The laws also deferred to the original terms of specific contracts, or levied fines based on whatever a guilty party had on hand (e.g., LU ¶24 and SLHF viii 22), marginal values between costs and profits, or even more vaguely "claims." Proportionality was not therefore by any means the single rule that governed all judicial reasoning.

---

57. Damages based on value of slave: LU ¶24; LL ¶13; SLEx ¶4'; SLHF viii 11–15; LE ¶22; LH ¶¶114, 231, 278, 281.

58. Damages based on proportional value of slave: LU ¶5; LL ¶¶12, 14, 26; LE ¶¶23, 49(?), 55, 57; LH ¶¶116, 119, 214, 217, 220, 223. Sometimes the principle of proportion is expressed not within a cited provision but in comparison with a preceding one.

59. Proportion as an absolute basis for legal reasoning is parodied most famously in 1 Kgs 3:16–28.

60. The logic can be difficult for us to grasp when laws propose seemingly incommensurable proportions (see Beth Berkowitz, in this volume), for example, that the beating death of a man's son was punishable by the death of the attacker's son, but the beating death of a slave required a fine of twenty shekels (LH ¶116).

61. Francis Joannès, *Haradum II: Les textes de la période paléo-babylonienne (Samsu-iluna – Ammi-ṣaduqa)* (Paris: Éditions Recherche sur les Civilisations, 2006), 140–41, no. 99, the loan of a slave. The expression (appearing twice in the text) is, to my knowledge, a *hapax legomenon*, and a working system of proportional valuation otherwise unknown (ibid., 141: "... selon une échelle d'évaluation qui reste évidemment à déterminer."); one may further note that the value of the slave in this case, twenty shekels of silver, seems more or less a regular full price for a male slave. Having said that, this instance puts one in mind of the similarly unique expression used to describe Gilgameš, that he was "two-thirds god and one-third man."

But it was perhaps the most pervasive of principles throughout the laws as a whole. The proportionalism of the slave-damage statutes is especially clear where classifications of status come into play. This proportionality of punitive damages to infraction was embraced as far back as Ur III times: Ur-Namma's law code said that if a man cut off another man's foot, he would pay ten shekels of silver (LU ¶18); a shattered bone was worth sixty shekels (LU ¶19); a cut-off nose was worth forty (LU ¶20), and so forth.[62] But otherwise identical infractions committed against persons of different status merited damages on a gradient. A man who divorced his "equal-ranking wife" (gidlam/ḫirtu) was responsible for a sixty-shekel fine (LU ¶9), but if he divorced a "widow" (nukušu/almattu, i.e., widowed and remarried), he would pay only thirty (LU ¶10). A man who raped someone's wife would be killed (LU ¶6), but if he raped a slave woman, he would pay five shekels of silver. The principles of value and proportionality were not fully elaborated in this Ur III–period text, but were already present, rooted in the commercial valuative system by which human bodies could be priced in ownership.[63]

It is no surprise to discover that this logic extended further down into the animal world, where the proportionality of liability is expressed in at least twenty-nine Babylonian laws about damages to or by animals — wherein the hoof, neck, eye, horn, or tail of an ox was worth anywhere between one-fifth and one-half of its stated value, and full loss was valued at "comparable" or "equal" replacement.[64] Thus, I argue that when the Laws of Lipit-Ištar say that the broken horn of an ox is worth one-quarter of its value (LL ¶36), but its hoof is worth one-third (LL ¶34), it discursively informs the text's further claims of proportional value in representing that an injury fatal to the fetus of a free woman is worth thirty shekels of silver (LL ¶d), but the fetus of a slave is only worth five (LL ¶f). This differential class basis for punitive damages appears also in the Laws of Ešnunna (e.g., LE ¶¶54/55, 56/57) and Hammurabi (e.g., ¶LH 196f.), as does the valuation according to different body parts injured (e.g., LE ¶¶42–47, LH 196f.).[65] In contrast to proportional damages for injury to people, however, which were generally awarded in fixed prices (e.g., the 30/20/10 shekel damages of LH ¶¶207–9), those for animal injury were expressed in terms of (sale) "value" (šīmišu, lit., "its price"), reflecting the fact that prices for oxen as

---

62. People or their parts are also valued, irrespective of status, in LU ¶¶21–24. Perhaps the most fully elaborated system can be found in LE ¶¶42–48.

63. Babylonian slave prices probably influenced the system of legal fines for infractions against nonslaves, in, e.g., LH ¶¶198, 201, 203–4, 207–9 etc. — rather than slave-damage statutes (e.g., LH ¶¶199, 213–14) being an extension of settlement systems first developed between free persons.

64. LL ¶¶34–37; LOx ¶¶1–6, 9; SLEx ¶10'; SLHF vi 11, 16, 23, 32; LE ¶¶53–57; LH ¶¶224–25, 245–48, 251–52, 254, 263.

65. The latter feature is attested also in the earlier laws of Ur-Namma, LU ¶¶18–22.

expressed in sale contracts, while relatively stable in any given year, did vary over time.[66] In either sense, though, the determination of damages by proportion presupposes an objectively identifiable value.

Market value as the basis of damages for animal injury was explicit. Fractional values were typical, where proportions of one-fourth,[67] one-third,[68] one-half,[69] and others[70] appear, as well as equivalent 1:1 values, that is, "full price,"[71] with attention to the broad principles of parity that underlie many of the laws. In these passages about animals, market price (šám/šīmu) was specified. Only a few expressions of proportional damages were not linked to price per se, in-kind awards by "replacement"[72] or magnification (i.e., "twofold" by amount[73]). LE ¶53 offers this more elaborate notion of proportionality: "If an ox gores another ox and thus causes its death, the two ox-owners shall divide [i.e., in half] the value of the living ox and the carcass of the dead ox." The corollary is that remunerations for damages by/to animals were never set as fixed amounts or as corporal punishment for the guilty party, as they could be for damages to humans;[74] only with animals does the basis of the law's evaluation of proportional worth disappear entirely down into the market.

It is one thing to say that the topos of proportionality found in animal laws was part of a socio-legal discourse pervasive in many areas of Mesopotamian life—this is worth demonstrating, but not hard to do—and is a first claim to be explored below. But it is another claim beyond that to say that oxen (in particular) were foundational to a discursive system proposing to structure all social orders; that these particular expressions

---

66. On variations in prices for oxen and cows, see Howard Farber, "A Price and Wage Study for Northern Babylonia during the Old Babylonian Period," *JESHO* 21 (1978): 1–51, here 14–16, 37 (Graph 13); newer data support the idea, however, that, although prices could vary from one reign to the next, they were relatively consistent within specific markets. Stable prices are further reflected in the statutes in which replacement is envisioned as a remedy (esp. SLEx ¶10' ["ox for ox"]; but also SLHF vi 23; LH ¶¶245–46, 263 [all "ox for ox"], and 266–67; but also, in the negative ("he will not replace"), LOx ¶¶7–8; SLHF vi 32.

67. LL ¶¶36–37 (igi-4-gál šám); LOx ¶¶3, 5 (igi-4-gál šám); SLHF vi 11 (igi-4-gál); perhaps LH ¶¶225 and 248.

68. LL ¶34 (igi-3-gál šám); LOx ¶2 (igi-3-gál šám).

69. LL ¶35 (šu-ri-a šám); LOx ¶1 (šu-ri šám); LH ¶247 (1/2 šīmšu).

70. Two fractional values are broken and cannot be restored: LOx ¶¶4 and 9. Roth restores LH ¶¶225 and 248 as one-quarter (*Law Collections*, 124 and 127).

71. LOx ¶6 (šám til-la-bi).

72. Whether replacements are to be given or not. With the Sum. verb sug, "to repay, replace": LOx ¶¶7, 8; SLEx ¶10'; SLHF vi 16, 23, 32. LH ¶¶245–46, 263 give *alpam/immeram kīma alpim/immerim ... iriab*, "He will replace the ox/sheep with an ox/sheep of comparable value." SLHF vi 23 (alone) stipulates that the "replacement" animal should be "healthy" (gud silim-ma).

73. LH ¶254 (*tašna*).

74. The one exception might be LH ¶253, where the punishment for cattle weakened by the theft of fodder was to cut off the thief's hand; it could be debated whether this is fundamentally a law about animal injury or about theft.

of relative value were a bedrock on which other relations of status and property were subsequently constructed by law. This requires a theorization of evidence that does not make its logic explicit, a condition that discourse analysis considers virtual of profound social belief (i.e., in that that which is everywhere indicated but nowhere explained identifies truths so agreed-upon that they need not have been justified). What proportionality signals is that some important distinction was being made, and one not bounded by concerns purely at the level of bookkeeping. Rather, as Catherine Kingfisher, a scholar of modern cultures of inequality, has written, not only "binaries of personhood *versus* nonpersonhood" but also of "complete personhood *versus* incomplete personhood clearly describe systems of domination."[75]

The two claims must be taken in turn. First, I will comment on the extension of proportionality into other areas of law and social life. The broad lexicon of proportionality in the laws beyond animal statutes already suggests its importance at a theoretical level. Table 1 on the following page derives all of the proportional language found within *individual* Ur III and Old Babylonian legal provisions, in contexts of commercial, family, and criminal law. These examples do not include the vast number of provisions which in multifarious ways attempt to create parity (talionic or otherwise), restore equivalent damages for injury, or account for proportional awards between two or more statutes; nor does it include the many provisions that establish proportions of grain yields by acreage, builder's fees by square footage, interest rates on loans, and so on;[76] if we were to take these things on, we would be here all day (though they would only go to prove the point). Only specific and explicit statements of proportional value within individual decision statements are therefore schematized.

Despite excluding these other expressions of proportionality, the list of fractions is still long (see Table 1): we find fractions one-tenth, one-fourth, one-third, one-half, and two-thirds; and factors of two-, three-, five-, six-, ten-, twelve-, and thirtyfold. It is noteworthy not only how common proportional terms are, but also how their productivity is reflected outside of law provisions as well, in contracts and other economic documents. One need only skim over the Old Babylonian entries in the *CAD* for *mišlu*, *šaluštu* A, and so on, to see how often silver capital was halved, fields split in thirds, and so forth: proportionality inhered deeply in

---

75. Catherine Kingfisher, "Discourses of Personhood and Welfare Reform," in *Western Welfare in Decline: Globalization and Women's Poverty*, ed. Catherine Kingfisher (Philadelphia: University of Pennsylvania Press, 2002), 1–64, here 21. Similarly, see Colin Dayan, *The Law Is a White Dog* (Princeton: Princeton University Press, 2011), on the legal construction of incomplete/partial personhood.

76. E.g., LH ¶¶56–58, 63, 121, 228, 255.

TABLE 1. **Expressions of Proportion in Old Babylonian Legal Damages/Awards**[77]
(*animal laws appear in boldface and underlined*)

One-tenth	igi-10-gál	LL ¶7
One-fourth	igi-4-gál	LL ¶**36–37**; LOx ¶**3**, **5**; SLHF **vi 11**, viii 16, viii 26; LH ¶**225**, **248**
One-third	igi-3-gál	LL ¶**34**; LOx ¶**2**
	šaluštu A	LH ¶¶29, 46, 64, 181–182, 191; Kraus Edikt §17':23
One-half	*bamtu* A	SLEx ¶3' (as Sum. ba-ma-ta?); Kraus Edikt §12:31
	mišlu/mišlānu	LL ¶**35**; LOx ¶**1**; SLHF v 12; LH ¶¶46, 176a–b, 199, 220, 238, **247**; Kraus Edikt §8':27, §17':23
	muttatu A	LH ¶¶127, 137
Two-thirds	*šinipu, šittīnu*	LH ¶64
Twofold[78]	a-rá 2-àm	LU ¶15; LL ¶14
	túm ... tab	LL ¶29
	šanû A	LE ¶25; LH ¶¶ gap w, 101, 120, 124, 126, 160–161, 254
	^{min}min$_6$ / min	SLHF ii 26, iii 10, iii 13
Threefold	*adi* 3-*šu*	LH ¶106
Fivefold	*ḫamšīšu*	LH ¶12
	adi 5-*šu*	LH ¶112
Sixfold	*adi* 6-*šu*	LH ¶107; also Kraus Verfügungen 172 §7:42
Tenfold	*adi* 10-*šu*	LH ¶8, 265
Twelvefold	*adi* 12-*šu*	LH ¶5
Thirtyfold	*adi* 30-*šu*	LH ¶8

---

77. This list cannot accommodate the number and range of expressions of parity for "equal (division)," "equivalent," "proportional," or "comparable" awards, though the variety is fascinating. I also exclude rates of interest, e.g., Laws of X ¶¶m–n, because rates have different proportional effects over time.

78. See also "two-for-one" replacements in LE ¶23.

concepts for the allocation of property shares, which shaped the ownership of family estates and commercial goods alike.[79] Concepts of proportionality were embedded at the discourse level, beyond juridical literature,[80] highly productive in domains as diverse as omens,[81] theology,[82] and mathematics: note especially the use of the terms *igitennu*, "fraction, proportion," and NIM/*našû*, "multiplication by proportionality" as exclusive operations of Old Babylonian mathematics,[83] and the extension of numeric proportional expressions into literature, royal inscriptions, and riddles. The laws (and other royal literature) endeavored to establish a structure of relative values in multiple arenas: in prices for goods[84] and wages,[85] rates of state service,[86] the standardization of weights and measures,[87] and so on. Such measures reflect not only an attempt to regulate economic matters through royal law in practical terms but were diverse enough to extend proportionality as a schematic basis for political subjectivity overall.

Structures of social proportionality were envisioned by the laws in at least three dimensions. The best known (since the first edition of LH in 1902), and requiring least explanation, was the "class" system that the law

---

79. Among OB letters, note, e.g., AbB I 56; III 11; IV 131; VIII 12; IX 30, 195, 243; XI 102; XII 52, 54, 58; XIII 23, 104; XIV 74, 140.

80. Other common expressions for fractions are nevertheless rare in the laws: e.g., in economic documents note *šittān*, "two-thirds"; for mathematical texts, *sebītu*, "one-seventh"; for ominous literature, *muttatu* A, "half."

81. See, e.g., CAD A/1, s.v. *adi* A prep. 4, where *adi* with {n} in liver divination was used to indicate the division of ominous features into *n*-parts, their multiplication *n*-fold, or their recurrence *n*-times.

82. Consider, for instance, the expression of divine names as numbers. $^{d}30$ was already a normal orthographic variant for the name of the moon-god Sîn in the OB period (otherwise ^{d}EN.ZU). The process by which other equivalences were developed is less clear, but by the end of the second millennium we have the writings $^{(d)}10$ for Adad, $^{(d)}15$ for Ištar, $^{(d)}20$ for Šamaš, $^{(d)}40$ for Ea, $^{(d)}50$ for Enlil, and $^{(d)}60$ for Anu. See A. R. George, "The Civilizing of Ea-Enkidu: An Unusual Tablet of the Babylonian Gilgameš Epic," *RA* 101 (2007): 59–80; and R. Stieglitz, "Numerical Structuralism and Cosmogony in the Ancient Near East," *Journal of Social and Biological Structures* 5 (1982): 260–63.

83. See Eleanor Robson, *Mesopotamian Mathematics 2100–1600 BC: Technical Constants in Bureaucracy and Education*, Oxford Editions of Cuneiform Texts 14 (Oxford: Clarendon, 1999), 90–91, and CAD I/J, s.v. *igitennu* (cf. ibid., for *igibû*, "reciprocal"). See also CAD N/2, s.v. *našû* A 1h, "to multiply"; cf. Jen Høyrup's specification of its OB meaning as "multiplication by proportion" ("Written Mathematical Traditions in Ancient Mesopotamia: Knowledge, Ignorance, and Reasonable Guesses," in *Traditions of Written Knowledge in Ancient Egypt and Mesopotamia: Proceedings of Two Workshops Held at Goethe-University, Frankfurt/Main in December 2011 and May 2012*, ed. Daliah Bawanypeck and Annette Imhausen, AOAT 403 [Münster: Ugarit-Verlag, 2015], 189–213).

84. LE ¶¶1–2, etc. See Richardson, "Early Mesopotamia," 36–44, for rates and rhetoric.

85. LL ¶a, LE ¶3ff., LH ¶¶273–74, etc.

86. E.g., LL Prologue ii 25–26, seventy days of service for a household with a living father, ten days for a household of dependent workers.

87. See, e.g., LU A iii 135f.

collections of Ešnunna and Hammurabi attempted to reify: the society of the *awīlum* ("gentleman"), *muškēnum* ("subordinate"),[88] and *wardum* ("slave"). In this, proportionality was not only being applied to the evaluation of individual social beings (that is, literally, *for his/her value*), but also to develop the class system *en tout*. This is not the place to rehearse the long scholarly conversation about the exclusivity or integrity, in either juridical or political terms, of the three classifications. Suffice it to say that these labels were important for the resolution of specific legal situations, and (as I note above) were always relative and not absolute denominations of status. Class identity was generated in the commercial and social contexts of civil society, and not institutionally determined. For royal laws to take credit for or pretend to *create* status was therefore chimerical: as real as class formation was, it was an unfinished process, and one being generated outside of state control. States nevertheless hoped to define class by reframing it in juridical terms and grounding its conceptual basis in proportional value, which, by extension, came to account for slaves, children, women, men — the class system in its entirety.

Roth recently hinted at the relationship of proportionality to class in her 2013 article on "Errant Oxen," positing that the "pattern of class hierarchy" in laws with proportional penalties was a literary device and "organizing principle" that reflected "the social positions of legal dependents."[89] I would keep the words and only flip that logic to argue that such laws attempted to *create and control* rather than reflect an already existing class system, with proportionality as its productive metaphor. Proportionality underlay the architecture of family life in the legal imagination, especially with regard to family property, where status and rank were primary concerns. For instance, the laws paid much attention to the rights and position of primary wives, denoted as "first-ranking" or of "equal" rank to their husbands, relative to secondary ones.[90] Proportions and shares of estate divisions for heirs were also a leading topical concern in the laws, where order was also established by ranking heirs as X *itti* Y *uštamaḫḫar*, "to make X equal to Y," or with the verb *manû*, to "reckon" someone as belonging to a ranked status. And the law proposed to evaluate the rank within the family of daughters who held cultic offices external to it, as *šugītu-* or *nadītu-*women, along these same lines. At stake was the

---

88. Cf. the *nisku* class of the Uru'inimgina laws, and the *miqtu*-persons in LL ¶¶15–16.
89. Roth, "Errant Oxen," 404.
90. Sumerian gidlam, Akkadian *ḫīrtu*. The meaning relies on context, whether the law discusses her in relation only to her husband (where the translation "equal rank" is appropriate), or also in relation to other wives, where in theory an idea of primacy may be inferred. But it must be noted that no term for "second-rank" or "lower-rank" is ever invoked in the laws, only contrasts of the "first-rank" wife to other women/wives: LL ¶24 and 28, LH ¶138, 141, to "other wives/women" (in LL ¶28, to a "healthy" one); LL ¶26, LH ¶¶170-71, to slave-women; LL ¶27, 30, to prostitutes. Rank was clearly at stake, but not denominated.

allocation of proportional shares of family estates, of unparalleled importance for the life chances of individuals. This is all suggested in the pervasive language associated with estate divisions, for example, *apšitû* ("allocation"), *bīt abim* ("paternal estate"), *izzuzu* ("to divide"), *šeriktu* ("dowry"), *terḫatu* ("bridewealth"), *zittu* ("share"), and so on; see esp. LH ¶¶158–184. Once again, it was an extension of the generic presumption of ordering ranks and proportions through law which enabled state claims to structure private family life.

Finally, and also famously, one could point to proportionality as structuring bodily punishments—the most invasive infrastructural claims of all—in the creation of docile bodies by the state's right to mortify portions or wholes. What is commonly obscured by understanding proportional corporal or capital punishment in Mesopotamia as "talionic," from Latin *tāliōnis*, a "(similar and equal punishment) in kind," is that many punishments had symbolic balance without being, in fact, "similar or equal"—the etymological root centering on the concept of "kind" rather than "equal," per se.[91] Consider, for instance, the punishment of an adopted child who verbally disavows his adoptive parents by saying, "You are not my mother/father": his tongue is cut out (LH ¶192).[92] But that same child, "repudiating" (from the verb *zêru*) the same adoptive parents, is to have his eyes plucked out (LH ¶193). It is hardly clear what the substantial difference is between a "disavowal" and a "repudiation"; the punishment on the tongue may allude to disavowal as a speech act, but *zêru* has no particularly visual semantics by which to connect it to a punishment on the eyes. There is a fairly ambivalent sense, then, in which they together illustrate punishments "equal" to crimes: just as important as the first statute's vague similarity to the crime it punishes, is the implicit claim of the second law to proportionally extrapolate from the first a bodily punishment that is in no way similar. It would profit us little to produce a *catalogue raisonné* of the horrific punishments of the law codes—bodies burned, heads shaved, ears cut off, and so on—except to point out that whatever claims to "similarity" they had were based largely on proportionality rather than identity; and that many other dissimilar punishments, though formally positioned in ways that suggest they were "extrapolated" from talionic ones, were in fact entirely arbitrary.[93] What we have here is the *simulation* of proportional logic in aid of state claims on the body.

---

91. Cf. Francesco Parisi ("The Genesis of Liability in Ancient Law," *American Law and Economics Review* 3.1 [2001]: 82–124), who argues that the biblical limitation of talionic of 1:1 retaliation was equilibrious, replacing the earlier (but unidentified) "unstable dynamics" introduced by unequal retributive damages; caveat emptor.

92. Cf. the punishment for the disobedient (~unhearing) slaves in LH ¶¶205, 282, whose ears are cut off.

93. For example, a woman who "is circumspect" (*naṣratma*) and repudiates her husband returns to her father's house (LH ¶142: proportional); a woman who "is not circum-

This brief survey should illustrate the first claim, namely, *that* proportionality was a major discursive strategy in law, society, and economy, beyond regulations about animals. I return now more closely and secondarily to the particular role of animals in this symbolic order. There are two subordinate points worth making. The first is that animals (and especially oxen) were openly positioned at the base of the proportional social order. The second is that their commodified bodies blurred the distinction between the natural and social world, discursively wicking or sublimating a quality of naturalness up into a constructed social system. In this, animals shared a special symbolic relationship to slaves, whose similarly commodified bodies "translated" this principle into the human realm;[94] as a most basic point, we may draw attention to how similar their contracts of sale were in formal terms.

To address the first point, there can be little question that certain animals were understood to belong to the social world of the household. As mentioned, oxen, sheep, and donkeys were distinguished in estate divisions from *possessions*; they were not *būšu*, "property." Like other members of the household, animals were not mere "things." Meanwhile, in the imaginative realm, the behaviors and bodies of animals populated the mantic world of omens; were cosmologically ordered by the identification of their "positions" (ki-gub) in the "divine order" (giš-ḫur) of the universe; and a few precious texts reveal that oxen, at least, were usually endowed with personal names, giving them a place in the social world.[95] These were the same "social animals" who were imagined to speak in proverbs and literature, and the same animals addressed by the laws.

But their place in the social order (like all beings) was bounded. Even literary works featured them only in set pieces with one animal or a few interacting—mimicking and parodying human behavior—but never *with* humans, as in *Winnie-the-Pooh* or *The Chronicles of Narnia*; and no Mesopotamian myth, proverb, or story conjured a whole story world of animals, such as we have in *Wind in the Willows* or *Animal Farm*. Their narrative role rarely rises above motif, and, among all the human qualities and abilities ascribed to them, they were never depicted as literate—for an audience

---

spect" (*lā naṣratma*) is cast into the river (LH ¶143: arbitrary). Or, in reverse, a man who strikes a pregnant woman and causes her to lose her fetus pays thirty shekels of silver (LL ¶d: arbitrary); if the woman also dies, he is killed (LL ¶e: proportional). Saul Olyan suggests that a similar arbitrariness is on display in various punishments of Lev 20.

94. See Olyan, "Are There Legal Texts," 333–34, 338, on a similar textual creation of common biblical legal classifications for slaves and animals.

95. On these points, see Richardson, "Nature Engaged and Disengaged," 28 n. 81, 27 n. 77, and 19 n. 42, respectively. Note the additional oxen names noted in *CAD* A/1, s.v. *alpu* s. 1a-2'b'. Cf. the radically different situation described by Ivan Kreilkamp, "The Emotional Extravagance of Victorian Pet-Keeping," *Victorian Review* 39 (2013): 71–74.

that knew that even some slaves were literate.[96] As mentioned above, even though oxen, donkeys, sheep, and goats were counted as household members,[97] they were accounted the least of them by their parallel position with or below slaves and servants in the standard greetings and a few stray expressions of concern in letters (e.g., "Do not neglect the animals").[98] The finite range of the "social animals" of letters, as against the wider tableau we find in literature, suggests conceptual distinctions between everyday animals belonging to the household, and then, in descending order of literary attention, the familiar animals of the city (e.g., dogs, foxes, ravens), more exotic animals of more remote ecosystems (e.g., turtles, elephants, aurochs, herons), and the nonsocial, nonspeaking vermin set entirely outside of the social realm (e.g., the unvoiced but otherwise literarily attested maggots, snakes,[99] scorpions, hyenas, etc.).

If the Mesopotamian laws modeled a certain proportional status of animals to people, either as commodified property being damaged or as instruments of damage, they never cast animals themselves as having liability, let alone as moral agents. The closest we come to the notion of intent comes in LH ¶251 (|| LE ¶54):

> If a man's ox is a known gorer, and the authorities of his city quarter notify him,[100] but he does not blunt(?) its horns or control his ox, and that ox gores to death a member of the *awīlu*-class, he (the owner) shall give 30 shekels of silver.

The Akkadian is awkward here, and the key term ("gorer," *nakkāpû*) is a *dis legomenon*, known only from LH ¶251, giving *nakkāpīma kīma nakkāpû*, literally, only "keeps goring like a gorer" and || LE ¶54, only *nakkāpīma*, "repeatedly goring." Awareness of the behavioral problem of "repeated goring" and responsibility for control belonged to the owner, and only after "notification" (*ušēdīšu*, "they make known to him") was he liable.[101] The ox was in no way culpable. As Marilyn Katz has argued regarding the differing provision of Exod 21:29, which calls for the offending ox to be stoned to death as well as for the owner to be executed, even in this more

---

96. Richardson, "Walking Capital," 311.
97. See n. 3 above.
98. Richardson, "Walking Capital," 327 n. 272.
99. Note esp. the "snake immune to incantations" in the poem "Gilgameš, Enkidu, and the Netherworld" (ETCSL 1.8.1.4).
100. I differ slightly from Roth's translation here (*Law Collections*, 128), insofar as she interpolates "that it is a known gorer" following "notify him." The phrase is logically consistent but not represented in the Akkadian; cf. n. 101 below.
101. Cf. Exod 21:29, where וְהוּעַד is a *hophal* (passive-causitive) verb form whose root (עוד) is derived from the noun "witness," meaning "to be warned," therefore differing from the sense "to (be made to) know," which would be from the verb ידע. My thanks to Nathaniel Levtow for parsing help.

extreme punishment, animal behavior was distinguished from agency: the stoning of the ox reflects the absolution of "the community as a whole" for communal pollution, an expiation of group blood-guilt, and not for the animal's liability.[102] In this respect, animals had a legal personhood inferior even to slaves, who had some legal liability (see, e.g., LH ¶¶205, 282) and capacity (e.g., to give testimony, but not to bring suit).[103]

But if animals had (very) diminished legal capacity, it was also the case that people shared with them a similarly limited personhood, since everyone was commodifiable.[104] As distant as the ox and the *awīlum* were on the socioeconomic spectrum, they and everyone in between were (at least) equally capable of being distrained for debt, commercially valuable in the marketplace and under the law. The boundaries of human distinctiveness that we take for granted in modern society are not inscribed in quite the same places in this ancient culture. To hold, therefore, that animals, lacking both rights and duties, were only legal objects because they were not quite legal persons to the same extent; or that animals, their value reckoned in the same ways as people, were legal persons because they were recognized in similar ways; ignores that salability and personhood were not distinctions or exclusions that Babylonian law made about anyone — only distinctions about *proportional* value and membership, with animals simply positioned as the least among others.

It is my second and last contention that the partial personhood found in the law formed the zone at which the structuration of class was accomplished by a blurring of major conceptual domains. Because certain animals had a borderline degree of social personhood, below humans but above other animals; because this was conceived of in literary terms, but to limited degrees; because the legal value of animals (as against humans) was determined *only* in the marketplace; because they were salable, like humans, but lacked their legal capacity and liability; because they had commodified bodies; and most of all because they belonged simultaneously or alternatively to the natural and social worlds: the regulation of animals grounded a discourse of social proportionality for all people in "natural" facts. They were provided with just enough recognition under

---

102. Marilyn A. Katz, "Ox-Slaughter and Goring Oxen: Homicide, Animal Sacrifice and Judicial Process," *Yale Journal of Law & the Humanities* 4.2 (1992): 249–72, here 264; the biblical passage itself, however, does not mention anything about "pollution." Cf. F. S. Naiden and Miira Tuominen, in this volume, on concepts of pollution.

103. Richardson, "Walking Capital," 312 with n. 137, 326, and 332.

104. See Jordan Rosenblum, in this volume, on the use of "animality" to dehumanize humans and behaviors. Compare the ambiguous legal status of animals and people in contemporary contexts: see Taimie L. Bryant, "Sacrificing the Sacrifice of Animals: Legal Personhood for Animals, the Status of Animals as Property, and the Presumed Primacy of Humans," *Rutgers Law Journal* 39.1 (2008): 247–330, here 330: "[D]irect legal standing for animals could be an important procedural means of seeking the substantive goal of decentering humans."

law to bring them within the orbit of a larger valuative system, thereby recoding valuation itself as a natural and normal social habit (as it had not been, in most ways, in earlier periods). This symbolic construct permitted the class order envisioned by Hammurabi's code to appear as a natural and accomplished fact.

Conclusion

I have put forward two arguments about animals that are thematically related to liminality, one spatial and one social. I posited that animals were topically ideal as the analogistic basis for legal reasoning about the territorial and personal limits of jurisdiction, metaphorizing the borders of state sovereignty over places and people. And I argued that the "partial personhood" of animals was ideally suited to a discourse of proportional value and the construction of class society. As a Sumerian proverb put it, "Let the ox be struck with a stick and let the sheep be given the whip. Where there is no toughness, no one can go about their business, not even a minister":[105] even the uppermost reaches of the social order were structured by the control of bodies down below.

Animals—especially oxen—were the ideal symbols with which to inscribe limiting discourses about social life because they were imagined to occupy its social and physical margins while still fundamentally accounted for in its central places: in households, markets, and law courts. In proverbs, the behavior of talking animals defined the boundaries of social mores, but for matters below the level of what the law could adjudicate: their parodic behavior instructed men on moral vices like vanity, greed, or hostility, but not crimes of theft, murder, or fornication. But, under law, animals populated the peripheries of the social landscape, where law faded out into the hinterlands and nonsubject peoples; they constituted the lowest level at which remediable injury was recognized. That it was not even the lowest-ranking people who were delegated to establish these imaginative boundaries, but rather the highest-ranking animals, gives us a clue about the basis for law itself, which must be discursively constructed to appear as an extension of natural and unquestioned orders.

I do not mean to be overly cynical about projects of subjectivity such as Hammurabi's laws meant to assert; probably no political discourse has ever existed without such naturalizing justifications. But because our attention has often been on positive articulations of rights and duties for

---

105. ETCSL, 6.1.28, SP (Sumerian Proverb) 28.7.

"full persons," there has been less comment on the definitions of insufficiency which inscribe the lower boundaries of personhood. We may think that people accept the premise of subjectivity—partly abridging but partly defending specified contours of personal sovereignty—because it satisfies a legal-rational set of relations, and because we assume a gradually emergent congruence of legal personhood with full social personhood. But that satisfaction is always in the background buttressed by a corollary arbitrary construction of other less perfected personhoods, of one's relations to "lower" social orders, all of which must entail moral compromise. The limited personhood of animals (and therefore slaves, servants, children, wives, and citizen-subjects) was the insufficiency by which Babylonians were encouraged to accept at the discourse level, as a natural and unalterable social fact, that all people were just another kind of legal animal, commodifiable and transferrable. And that is exploitation.

Symmetry or Asymmetry according to the Law?

The Case of Domesticated Animals and Human Beings

SAUL M. OLYAN
Brown University

Biblical legal collections privilege certain constituencies over others. Male heads of household are frequently addressed directly, while dependents are spoken of in the third person, suggesting their inferior status, as in Deut 5:21–22: "You shall not desire the wife of your neighbor, nor shall you desire the house of your neighbor, his field, his male slave, his female slave, his ox, his donkey, or anything else that belongs to your neighbor."[1] Priestly rank is realized through the ascription of priestly holiness and other markers of superior social standing to males of the Aaronid line, as in Num 17:5, part of P's postscript to the narrative of Korah's rebellion. In this text, the presentation of incense before Yhwh is cast as a prerogative of Aaronid priests alone, and non-Aaronids are threatened with death should they attempt to usurp this priestly privilege.[2] Priests with physical defects (*mûmîm*) are forbidden to offer sacrifice to Yhwh, in contrast to their whole-bodied peers (Lev 21:21, 23).[3] And, while women of childbearing age are disadvantaged for extended periods of time by

---

1. All translations in this essay are my own.
2. According to the hypothetical Priestly Writing (P), only male descendants of Aaron are priests. The P narrative in Num 16:1–17:5 seeks to realize this contested claim by having Yhwh condemn and kill Korah and the story's other non-Aaronid claimants to the priesthood. For the assignment of this narrative to P rather than H, see my argument in Saul M. Olyan, *Rites and Rank: Hierarchy in Biblical Representations of Cult* (Princeton: Princeton University Press, 2000), 27 and 136 n. 63. On its polemical aspects, as well as those of similar narratives about the priesthood in the Pentateuch, see, e.g., the classic treatment of Frank Moore Cross, "The Priestly Houses of Early Israel," in *Canaanite Myth and Hebrew Epic: Essays in the History of the Religion of Israel* (Cambridge: Harvard University Press, 1973), 195–215.
3. On such defects, see my discussion ahead.

impurity regulations (Lev 12:1–8; 15:19–24), males who have an emission of semen are polluting for only one day (Lev 15:16–18; Deut 23:10–12).[4]

Although asymmetrical treatment of classes of persons on the basis of distinctions grounded in gender, priestly status, wholeness of body, and life stage—among other axes of inequality—often characterizes biblical law, this is not always the case. Some legal materials are surprisingly egalitarian in their handling of persons who are often disadvantaged in other legal texts. An example of this is the Holiness School's frequently stated demand that resident aliens (*gērîm*) be treated in the same manner as natives of the land, as in Exod 12:48–49: "[The resident alien] shall be like the native of the land.... There shall be one teaching [*tôrâ*] for the native and for the resident alien who resides in your midst." This commandment differs from other legal texts that treat the resident alien asymmetrically vis-à-vis the native, as in Deut 14:21, a law that exempts the resident alien from the ritual requirement of avoiding the eating of carcasses, in contrast to native Israelites, who must not consume them. Other passages prescribe the same cultic obligations for all Israelites—apparently including women, children, and slaves—without exception, as in Exod 12:47, regarding the eating of the Passover offering: "All of the assembly [*ʿēdâ*] of Israel shall perform it." This text contrasts with many others that prescribe different ritual requirements for particular household members, as in Exod 23:17, which obligates only males to undertake the three yearly pilgrimages: "Three times a year, all of your males shall appear in the presence of the lord Yhwh."[5] Divergent legal requirements or statuses for classes of persons, sometimes within the same corpus of laws, likely reflect varying

---

4. These are only a few examples of the legal regulations, representations of ritual practice, or narratives depicting Israel's past that create and perpetuate a pervasive gender inequality among persons in biblical texts. They disadvantage women of childbearing age by stigmatizing them as subject to major impurities and separating them from cultic activity for extended periods of time. In addition, see other materials that ascribe a secondary social status to women, for example, the institution of a male only priesthood or the constitution of households under a male head or elder who is often addressed directly by the legal materials, in contrast to women and other dependents. In addition, note texts that assume that only males constitute "the people" of Israel (e.g., Exod 19:15). Finally, the second creation story, traditionally ascribed to the hypothetical source J, naturalizes superior male status in a variety of subtle and not so subtle ways (Gen 2:21–23; 3:9, 13, 16). Although dissenting voices may be discerned in the biblical text (e.g., Gen 1:27–28), the predominant viewpoint in the biblical anthology is that of gender inequality.

5. See similarly Deut 16:16, which reworks the older formulation in Exod 23:17, but preserves the male-only requirement. Deuteronomy 16:11, 14 provide a contrasting perspective, evidently obligating the whole community to make a pilgrimage on Shavuot and Sukkot, including the head of household's daughter, his male and female slaves, and the resident alien, widow and fatherless person, although these verses do not mention the head of household's wife explicitly, as is universally noted.

viewpoints in legal circles as well as the gradual growth of the biblical text through supplementation.[6]

Given the mix of asymmetrical and symmetrical treatment accorded to various classes of persons in biblical law, it is natural to ask how the handling of domesticated animals and that of human beings might compare in these same legal collections. Are such animals always dealt with differently from human beings, or are there texts that treat domesticated animals and human beings symmetrically? Furthermore, what does symmetrical handling of domesticated animals and human beings in legal texts suggest about the status or value of said animals and human beings vis-à-vis one another? And finally, do some of the same axes of inequality that pertain to human beings when they are dealt with asymmetrically—for example, on the basis of gender or physical wholeness—apply to domesticated animals as well? It is my purpose here to begin to explore the question of symmetry and asymmetry in the legal treatment of domesticated animals and human beings in the Hebrew Bible.[7] My focus will be domesticated animals because these are at issue in many biblical legal formulations, in contrast to wild animals.[8] I will consider a sampling of legal texts that address cultic issues specifically, as these laws are the most frequent context in which human beings and domesticated animals are considered together and implicitly compared.

I begin with Lev 27:1–13, the first section of an appendix to the Holiness Code, which speaks of assigning monetary valuations to various classes of human beings and animals for the purpose of fulfilling vows.[9]

---

6. On supplementation in legal texts, see recently the essays in *Supplementation and the Study of the Hebrew Bible*, ed. Saul M. Olyan and Jacob L. Wright, BJS 361 (Providence, RI: Brown Judaic Studies, 2018). For scholarly debate about the nature and function of biblical law, particularly the degree to which it reflects ancient communal practice, see, e.g., Bruce Wells, "What Is Biblical Law? A Look at Pentateuchal Rules and Near Eastern Practice," *CBQ* 70 (2008): 223–43.

7. Scholarship on the representation of animals in biblical, cuneiform, rabbinic, and other ancient texts, including legal materials, has recently multiplied exponentially. Examples include Saul M. Olyan, "Are There Legal Texts in the Hebrew Bible that Evince a Concern for Animal Rights?," *BibInt* 27 (2019): 321–39; Seth Richardson, "Nature Engaged and Disengaged: The Case of Animals in Mesopotamian Literatures," in *Impious Dogs, Haughty Foxes and Exquisite Fish: Evaluative Perception and Interpretation of Animals in Ancient and Medieval Mediterranean Thought*, ed. Johannes Pahlitzsch and Tristan Schmidt (Berlin: de Gruyter, 2019), 11–40; Beth A. Berkowitz, *Animals and Animality in the Babylonian Talmud* (New York: Cambridge University Press, 2018); Ken Stone, *Reading the Hebrew Bible with Animal Studies* (Stanford, CA: Stanford University Press, 2018); and Rachel Neis, "Reproduction of Species: Humans, Animals, and Hybrids in Early Rabbinic Science," *JSQ* 24 (2017): 1–29.

8. Note, however, that there are exceptions to this pattern, e.g., Exod 23:10–11, which reserves a part of what grows on its own during the sabbatical year for wild animals specifically.

9. See Jacob Milgrom, *Leviticus 23–27: A New Translation with Introduction and Commentary*,

Human beings are classified by this text and assessed monetarily according to age and gender: A male between twenty and sixty years old is valued at 50 shekels, a female at 30; a male between five and twenty years of age is assessed at 20 shekels, a female at 10 shekels. Similar differences characterize the valuations of males and females of one month to five years old (5 shekels versus 3) and of sixty years of age or older (15 shekels versus 10). Nothing is said in the text about physical condition (e.g., the presence or absence of "defects") or factors other than gender and age. In contrast, vowed animals are not assigned fixed values by the text and are classified according to a wholly different schema that ignores both gender and age: clean, sacrificial animals are dealt with as one category; unclean, nonsacrificial animals as a second. Clean, sacrificial animals vowed to Yhwh are sanctified according to 27:9, but nothing is said of their valuation or how it is to be determined. In contrast, unclean, nonsacrificial animals are not sanctified and are to be brought before the priest for ad hoc valuation based apparently on their physical condition.[10] Whether receiving sanctified status somehow confers an unstated fixed value on the clean, sacrificial animals remains unclear; perhaps more likely, the text assumes that the clean, sanctified sacrificial animals will also be brought before the priest for ad hoc assessment. Although this is not stated explicitly, Lev 27:14 suggests it, since it calls for the priest to assign a monetary value to sanctified houses and uses the same idiom. At all events, whether the animals in question are clean or unclean, their valuation does not appear to be based on age or gender and, in the case of unclean animals and likely clean, sacrificial animals as well, it is not fixed in advance as it is for persons. Thus, although both human beings and animals can be vowed and assessed monetarily according to Lev 27:1–13, there is evidence for asymmetrical handling both among human beings and among animals, as well as an asymmetry of treatment between animals and human beings.

In contrast to Lev 27:1–13, a passage from the same chapter of Leviticus that concerns the voluntary consignment of persons, domesticated animals, and fields to what may be termed "eradication" (*ḥērem*) (27:28–29), evidences a consistently symmetrical treatment for human beings and animals:

AB 3B (New York: Doubleday, 2000), 2407–9, for discussion of the origin and function of the chapter.

10. The main evidence in support of this is to be found in Lev 27:10, which uses the adjectives *ṭôb* and *raʿ* to refer to the condition of the animal in question. See Milgrom, *Leviticus 23–27*, 2377, on two possible ways to interpret *ṭôb* and *raʿ* in verse 10 (defective/whole or healthy/emaciated). In verse 12, the expression *bên ṭôb ûbên raʿ* may refer to the assessment itself rather than the condition of the animal, given the masculine gender of the adjectives; Milgrom (*Leviticus 23–27*, 2378) follows E. A. Speiser on this, rendering "whether high or low." In any case, the physical condition of the animal is nonetheless the most likely criterion for the valuation.

Anything consigned to eradication [ḥērem], which a man consigns to eradication for Yhwh, of all that belongs to him, including human beings, four legged beasts, and fields that are his possession, may not be sold and may not be redeemed [gʾl]; everything consigned to eradication is most holy; it belongs to Yhwh. Anyone consigned to eradication ... among human beings may not be ransomed [pdh]; he shall surely be put to death.

In this text's distinct version of the eradication ideology, persons may consign other human beings, domesticated animals, or fields under their power to eradication; in no case can any of these be sold, redeemed, or ransomed.[11] Thus, domesticated animals and human beings consigned to eradication, along with fields, are treated symmetrically in a number of respects: all possess the same ritual status (they are "most holy"); all "belong to Yhwh." In the case of human beings and, implicitly, domesticated animals, all are to be slaughtered without the possibility of redemption or ransoming.[12] As for the fields, they are evidently taken over by the sanctuary for the benefit of its priestly staff, as Lev 27:21 suggests.[13] Thus, in contrast to persons and domesticated animals consigned to eradication, nonliving things are not actually destroyed.[14] If there is asymmetry in this text, it is to be found in the divergent handling of fields, on the one hand, and domesticated animals and human beings, on the other; in contrast,

---

11. The verbs $gʾl$ and pdh are apparently used interchangeably here. Contrast the possibility of redemption for items that a person voluntarily sanctifies according to verses 14–21. Although this version of the eradication ideology finds its context in the sacrificial cult and it is clearly nonpunitive, other, better-attested forms of the ideology—what I call "mass eradication"—are very frequently punitive and find their context in war and conquest rather than the rites of the sanctuary (e.g., Deut 13:13–19; Joshua 6–7; 1 Sam 15:4–35). On eradication, see my treatment in *Violent Rituals of the Hebrew Bible* (New York: Oxford University Press, 2019), 29–35. Some have assumed that the persons assigned to eradication in Lev 27:28 must be slaves because they "belong to" the man who consigns them, in contrast to family members and other free dependents, who do not "belong to" him (e.g., Milgrom, *Leviticus 23–27*, 2393). But this does not necessarily follow, as a number of texts suggest. These include Exod 20:17, regarding a man who might desire that which "belongs to" his neighbor, including the neighbor's wife; Exod 21:7, regarding a father who sells his daughter as a slave; or Josh 7:24, regarding Achan's household members who die along with Achan for Achan's sacrilege. In my view, we cannot be sure of whom Lev 27:28 speaks when it refers to persons a man might consign to eradication. These might include members of the household who are not slaves, as the texts cited above suggest.

12. The text is explicit about the requirement to slaughter the human beings consigned to eradication. Although the requirement to slaughter the consigned domesticated animals is not stated explicitly, it is implied by the statement that nothing consigned to eradication may be redeemed.

13. Leviticus 21:21 compares the treatment of sanctified fields to that of fields consigned to eradication, stating that it is the same: "When the field goes out in the Jubilee, it shall be holy to Yhwh, like a field consigned to eradication; it shall be the priest's."

14. See similarly Josh 6:19, 24, part of a paradigmatic narrative of mass eradication, according to which precious metals seized during the conquest of Jericho are to be consigned to Yhwh's treasury rather than destroyed.

human beings and domesticated animals share a consistently symmetrical treatment here.

Various versions of the so-called law of the firstborn make up my third example of interest. Some formulations of the law of the firstborn treat animals and persons with consistent symmetry while others are in the main asymmetrical in their treatment. Exodus 34:19-20 is an example of the law of the firstborn that handles sacrificial animals, unclean animals that cannot be sacrificed and human beings for the most part asymmetrically:

> Everything that opens the womb [*peṭer reḥem*] belongs to me: the male [*hazzākār][15] of all your livestock [*miqnəkā*], the firstborn [*peṭer*] of cattle and sheep.[16] But the firstborn of the donkey [*peṭer ḥămôr*] you shall ransom [*pdh*] with a sheep, and if you do not ransom it, you shall break its neck. Every firstborn [*bəkôr*] of your sons you shall ransom [*pdh*].[17]

Although Yhwh claims all male firstborn animals and human beings as his own possession according to this law, only the firstborn of clean, sacrificial animals are to be sacrificed; the firstborn of an unclean domestic animal such as the donkey may be ransomed with a sheep and allowed to live or be killed in a nonsacrificial manner if the owner does not choose to ransom it.[18] In contrast to the handling of both clean, sacrificial animals and unclean, nonsacrificial animals, firstborn sons, called *bəkôr* rather than *peṭer reḥem* in this text, are to be ransomed without exception, presumably with a sheep, although this is not stated explicitly.[19] Thus, this formulation of the law of the firstborn handles firstborn sons, the male firstborn of sacrificial animals, and the firstborn of unclean, nonsacrificial animals

---

15. The MT reading *tizzākār* is a classic crux. Inner-biblical interpreters who recast this text render *hazzəkārîm* (Exod 13:12). Following LXX (*ta arsenika*), moderns typically reconstruct *hazzəkārîm* or *hazzākār* (e.g., Otto Eißfeldt, *Molk als Opferbegriff im Punischen und Hebräischen und das Ende des Gottes Moloch*, Beiträge zur religionsgeschichte des altertums 3 [Halle: Niemeyer, 1935], 54 n. 2; Brevard S. Childs, *The Book of Exodus: A Critical, Theological Commentary*, OTL [Philadelphia: Westminster, 1974], 604; Rainer Albertz, *Exodus*, vol. 2, *Ex 19–40*, Zürcher Bibelkommentare 2.2 [Zurich: Theologischer Verlag, 2015], 302 n. 1). I reconstruct a singular *hazzākār*, given the use of singular nouns (*peṭer reḥem, miqneh, peṭer šôr wāśeh*) throughout this verse. It is difficult to explain what might have led to the form *tzkr* in the MT.

16. MT's *wəkol miqnəkā* is awkward and likely a gloss; it is missing from LXX[B].

17. The use of *bəkôr* for the human firstborn and *peṭer reḥem* for that of animals is one of a number of cruxes in this text.

18. The requirement that the firstborn of the donkey or other unclean animals be ransomed with a sheep or killed indicates clearly that sacrifice is indeed at issue in these formulations, even if it is not mentioned explicitly with regard to clean sacrificial animals or human beings.

19. It is stated explicitly for the donkey firstborn's ransoming, which suggests that the same applies to a human being. The narrative of Gen 22:13 suggests substitution with a sheep as well.

differently, understanding each as a separate category of firstborn with its own, distinct ritual requirements and, in the case of the firstborn sons, its own distinct technical term for the firstborn (bəkôr). Yet, at the same time, Yhwh makes the same claim on all three categories of firstborn—they all belong to him—and evidently it is males that are the focus of Yhwh's interest in each case.[20] Thus, the largely asymmetrical handling of the firstborn in Exod 34:19–20 is balanced to some extent by some symmetrical dimensions such as Yhwh's claim on all types of firstborn and their male gender.[21] To this we might compare Lev 27:1–13, which has a symmetrical dimension—animals and human beings may both be assessed monetarily to fulfill vows—although the assessments of animals and human beings respectively are based on very different considerations (age and gender vs. purity status and physical condition) and determined differently (set amounts vs. ad hoc valuation).

In contrast to Exod 34:19–20, Exod 22:28b–29 is a formulation of the law of the firstborn that accords a consistently symmetrical treatment to both animals and human beings: "The firstborn [bəkôr] of your sons you shall give to me. Thus you shall do with your ox and your sheep. Seven days he shall remain with his mother, but on the eighth day, you shall give him to me." According to this law, Yhwh makes a claim on both firstborn sons and the firstborn of sacrificial animals, and each is referred to as bəkôr; in contrast to Exod 34:19–20, unclean, nonsacrificial animals are evidently not of interest and, therefore, are not mentioned. Furthermore, no explicit reference is made to males specifically, although other formulations of the law of the firstborn refer to males (e.g., Exod 13:12; 34:19; Deut 15:19). Males are therefore likely of interest in this passage as well, although we cannot be certain that females are excluded from consideration. In Exod 22:28b–29, both the newborn sacrificial animal and the human infant are to remain with their respective mothers for seven days and be given to Yhwh on the eighth day. Because even the possibility of substitution is not mentioned, most critical scholars assume that according to this formulation, the firstborn son is to be sacrificed after seven days, not unlike the firstborn sacrificial animal.[22] Thus, like Lev 27:28–29,

---

20. It is difficult to reconcile the firstborn requirement with the claim on only males. What if the firstborn is female? Furthermore, in the case of human beings, is the text speaking of the mother's firstborn—that which opens the womb—as with animals, when it uses the term bəkôr, or is the text speaking of a father's firstborn, a meaning bəkôr often has in other biblical passages (e.g., Exod 4:22; 11:5; 12:29; Deut 21:15–17; 1 Kgs 16:34; Jer 31:9; and Mic 6:7)? This remains unclear.

21. Exodus 13:11–13 recasts 34:19–20, addressing a number of difficulties in the text. It does, however, preserve the three distinct categories of firstborn evidenced in 34:19–20.

22. E.g., Heath D. Dewrell, *Child Sacrifice in Ancient Israel*, Explorations in Ancient Near Eastern Civilizations 5 (Winona Lake, IN: Eisenbrauns, 2017), 72–90, 129, 145–46; William H. C. Propp, *Exodus 19–40: A New Translation with Introduction and Commentary*, AB 2A (New

which concerns the voluntary consignment of domesticated animals, human beings, and fields to eradication, this formulation of the law of the firstborn is entirely symmetrical in its handling of sacrificial animals and human beings.[23]

My final focus is the legal treatment of priests and sacrificial animals understood to possess a "defect" (*mûm*). Defects include blindness, lameness, genital damage, broken limbs, a missing eye or tooth, and certain skin afflictions, among other physical conditions.[24] Some texts characterize defects as "ugly" (Deut 15:21; 17:1), others associate them with "destruction" (*mošḥâ*) (Lev 22:25; Mal 1:14); an animal with a defect is even designated an "abomination of Yhwh" (Deut 17:1). Holiness legal texts place limits on the cultic activity of a priest or high priest with a defect. The priest with a defect may not approach the altar to offer sacrifice to Yhwh, nor may the defective high priest enter the innermost area of the sanctuary to perform high priestly rites; to do either would profane the holiness of Yhwh's cult place (Lev 21:17, 21, 23).[25] Yet priests with defects may nonetheless eat of the most holy and holy foods—the sanctified offerings assigned to them—like priests without defects (Lev 21:22). The fact that defective priests may eat holy and most holy foods demonstrates clearly that their defects profane holiness only when they perform cultic acts forbidden to them, not when they undertake other priestly responsibilities or are simply present in the sanctuary. This suggests that priests do not lose their priestly sanctification on account of their defects and that their stigmatization and marginalization are not complete.[26]

York: Doubleday, 2006), 264–71; Jon D. Levenson, *The Death and Resurrection of the Beloved Son: The Transformation of Child Sacrifice in Judaism and Christianity* (New Haven: Yale University Press, 1993), 3–17; Hartmut Gese, "Ezechiel 20,25f. und die Erstgeburtsopfer," in *Beiträge zur Alttestamentlichen Theologie: Festschrift für Walther Zimmerli zum 70. Geburtstag*, ed. Herbert Donner, Robert Hanhart, and Rudolf Smend (Göttingen: Vandenhoeck & Ruprecht, 1977), 140–51, here 143–47; Otto Kaiser, "Den Erstgeborenen deiner Söhne sollst du mir geben: Erwägungen zum Kinderopfer im Alten Testament," in *Denkender Glaube: Festschrift Carl Heinz Ratschow zur Vollendung seines 65. Lebensjahres am 22. Juli 1976 gewidmet von Kollegen, Schülern und Freunden*, ed. Otto Kaiser (Berlin: de Gruyter, 1976), 24–48; Eißfeldt, *Molk als Opferbegriff*, 52–54.

23. Another formulation, in Num 3:11–13, 41, is also entirely symmetrical in its treatment of animals and human beings, except that, in this case, all are to be ransomed, with the Levites substituting for the human firstborn and their animals substituting for the Israelites' animals.

24. See, e.g., Lev 21:18–20; 22:22–23; 24:19–20; Deut 15:21–23; 17:1; Mal 1:8.

25. On the area of the sanctuary behind the veil and the manner in which it is to be entered by the high priest, see Lev 16:1–4.

26. On the most holy foods, reserved for males of the priestly line alone, see further Num 18:9–10; for the holy foods, which may also be eaten by others residing in priestly households (e.g., women and slaves), see Num 18:11 and Lev 22:11–13. If, according to Lev 21, priests with defects had lost their priestly sanctification, it seems quite unlikely that they would still have access to the most holy foods. For priestly sanctification according to Lev 21,

When we compare the handling of sacrificial animals with defects to that of defective priests, we notice both differences and similarities. While Lev 21:22 suggests that priests with defects continue to possess their sanctified status, defective firstborn sacrificial animals may not be sanctified by the worshiper, according to Deut 15:21–22, and therefore they are never set apart as holy.[27] In addition, although, according to Lev 21:17–23, all defects without exception apparently disqualify priests from offering sacrifice or performing high priestly duties, Lev 22:23 allows the offering of animals described as *śārûaᶜ wəqālûṭ* ("having a limb too long or short") as voluntary sacrifices, although not to fulfill vows.[28] Finally, the offering of defective sacrificial animals is described as wrong (Mal 1:8) and is said to be forbidden (Lev 21:17; Deut 15:21); the animals themselves are described as "ugly" (Deut 15:21; 17:1), said to have "their destruction" in them (Lev 22:25), called "destroyed things" (Mal 1:14) and abominations (Deut 17:1). They are even characterized as "polluted food" (uniquely, in Mal 1:7), but the rhetoric of the profanation of holiness (*ḥll*) is not used of such animals or the act of sacrificing them in any text, in contrast to Lev 21:23, which speaks of the defective priest who offers sacrifice or carries out high priestly rites as profaning Yhwh's holy sanctuaries.

Yet, at the same time, there is a considerable degree of symmetrical treatment as well. The same vocabulary of defect (*mûm*) is used of both human beings and animals, and many of the same defects (e.g., blindness, lameness) are associated with both. Furthermore, just as priests with defects may not approach the altar to present sacrifices to Yhwh (Lev 21:17, 21, 23), so, according to a number of texts, defective sacrificial animals may not be offered as sacrifices to Yhwh on the altar.[29] Thus, the handling of sacrificial animals and priests with defects is in some ways symmetrical, in others asymmetrical. In each case, the vocabulary of defect

---

see verses 6–9. Verse 9, which concerns the untoward behavior of a priest's daughter, suggests that priestly sanctification may potentially be lost.

27. That such animals are not sanctified is made clear in verse 22, where it is said that they may be eaten outside of the sanctuary by both the clean and the unclean alike. Were they sanctified like nondefective firstborn animals, the unclean would not be permitted to eat them. Other texts speak of the holiness of sacrifices (e.g., Lev 22:3, 15; Num 18:9–19).

28. Contrast Lev 22:20–22, 24, 25, which assert that all animals with defects are unacceptable for sacrifice. I have argued previously that verse 23 is likely a modifying gloss on the text (*Rites and Rank*, 170 n. 11). For the meaning of *śārûaᶜ wəqālûṭ*, see Milgrom, *Leviticus 17–22: A New Translation with Introduction and Commentary*, AB 3A (New York: Doubleday, 2000), 1878.

29. Deuteronomy 17:1 interdicts all such animal offerings, while Deut 15:21 bans the defective firstborn of sacrificial animals specifically; Lev 22:20–22, 24, 25, for their part, proscribe the offering of defective sacrificial animals to fulfill a vow or as a voluntary offering. The one exception to the well-attested proscription of defective sacrificial animals as offerings is to be found in Lev 22:23, which allows an animal with a limb too long or short (*śārûaᶜ wəqālûṭ*) as a voluntary offering.

(*mûm*) is shared in common, and the presence of defects disqualifies, marginalizes, and stigmatizes. Yet the precise ways in which it does so and the particular associations of that which is deemed defective can vary considerably.

To what extent do the axes of inequality that frequently create asymmetry among human beings—for example, wholeness of body or gender—apply to domesticated animals as well? As I have sought to demonstrate, the whole/defective contrast often creates asymmetries among both human beings and sacrificial animals.[30] The manner in which the whole/defective dyad realizes and communicates inequality often differs among sacrificial animals, among human beings, or between animals and human beings.[31] Nonetheless, devaluing, exclusion, and/or marginalization of some kind are recurrently the result of being cast as defective. Domesticated animals and human beings can both be described as having a "defect" (*mûm*), and many of the same defects are associated with both. Furthermore, sacrificial animals with defects are almost without exception excluded from sacrifice, just as priests with defects are forbidden to perform sacrifices.[32] Thus, the whole/defective distinction is an axis of inequality closely paralleled between domesticated animals and human beings in many respects.

In contrast, gender, richly evidenced in biblical texts as a primary axis of inequality among persons, creates asymmetry much less frequently among sacrificial animals. Although whole-bodied male animals are often required by the Priestly Writing for higher-ranked sacrifices such as the whole offering (ʿôlâ; Lev 1:3, 10; 16:5), the purification offering (*ḥaṭṭāʾt*; Lev 4:3, 14, 23; 16:5), or the reparation offering (*ʾāšām*; Lev 5:15), this is not consistently the case. In Lev 4:28, 32, it is a whole-bodied female animal that is obligatory for the purification offering; similarly, in Lev 5:6, a female without defect from the flock is required for the reparation offering. Perhaps most striking, the red cow of Num 19:1–10, whose ashes are to be used to purify those polluted by corpse contact, is obviously a female animal, not a male. Yet there is some evidence that male animals are privileged over female animals in some sacrificial contexts. Versions of the law of the firstborn that require the sacrifice of "everything that opens the womb" (*peṭer reḥem*) or "the firstborn" (*bəkôr*) either mention the male gender

---

30. Although priests were my primary human focus, according to several texts, defects also disadvantage nonpriestly persons, leading to forms of exclusion or marginalization from community and cult (e.g., Deut 23:2; 2 Sam 5:8b).

31. For example, Deut 17:1 classifies defective sacrificial animals as ugly abominations; in contrast, Mal 1:7 refers to them as polluted food, and Mal 1:14 calls them "destroyed" things.

32. As mentioned, Lev 22:23 is the one exception, and it concerns one particular defect (*śārûaʿ wəqālûṭ*) and one particular type of sacrifice (the voluntary offering), which is of lower rank than others (compare the treatment of the vow in the same verse).

of the required animal specifically, as in Exod 13:12, 15; 34:19; and Deut 15:19, or seem to imply that males are the focus of the law's interest, as in Exod 22:28b–29. Thus, among sacrificial animals, gender distinctions are attested in the legal materials that are extant, but these writings do not consistently create a hierarchy of value that ranks male animals over female animals. For some types of sacrifice, one is hard-pressed to find evidence of male privilege; for other types, male privilege is clearly evident.

Conclusions

A number of conclusions emerge from this investigation. First, there are indeed legal materials in which domesticated animals and human beings receive a consistently symmetrical treatment. Examples of this include Exod 22:28b–29, a version of the law of the firstborn, and Lev 27:28–29, which concerns the voluntary consignment of domesticated animals or human beings to eradication. In the former, the eight-day-old young of sacrificial animals and the eight-day-old child are to be given to Yhwh, almost certainly meaning they are to be sacrificed; in the latter, both domesticated animals and human beings consigned to eradication are deemed "most holy" and may not be sold, redeemed, or ransomed. Yet, in contrast, other legal materials deal with domesticated animals differently from human beings, although strikingly, in each case of divergent handling that I examined, there was nonetheless an element of symmetry present. This element of symmetry creates the foundation for implicit comparison—which generates asymmetry—to take place.[33] Thus, as with laws pertaining only to classes of human beings, a mix of asymmetrical and symmetrical treatment is evidenced when one considers the handling of domesticated animals and persons in extant biblical legal texts. Just as some legal texts draw a legally meaningful distinction between resident aliens and native-born Israelites while others do not, so some laws deal

---

33. An example of this is Exod 34:19–20, in which firstborn male sacrificial animals are to be sacrificed to Yhwh, the firstborn male young of unclean domesticated animals are to be ransomed with a sheep or killed in a noncultic manner, and firstborn sons are to be ransomed. Although the text creates three distinct classes of firstborn, each with its own cultic requirements, Yhwh nonetheless makes the same claim on all males that open the womb (*peṭer reḥem*)—they belong to Yhwh says the text—whether they are sacrificial animals, unclean domesticated animals, or human beings. In short, all firstborn males of the domicile—human or animal—share a common distinction setting them apart from non-firstborn males and all females of their particular class, whatever the specific ritual requirements mandated for them. This shared distinction establishes the basis for implicit comparison and the resulting creation of asymmetry among firstborn males of the domicile, according to Exod 34:19–20.

with human beings and domesticated animals differently while others treat them symmetrically.[34] The reasons for such varying legal handling of domesticated animals and human beings in biblical materials are probably the same as those that explain the different ways in which groups of persons are treated: extant texts likely reflect competing legal positions in conjunction with the growth of the biblical text through supplementation.[35]

What might symmetrical treatment of domesticated animals and human beings in some legal texts suggest about the relative status or value of those animals and human beings? The fact that Yhwh claims both the male firstborn young of sacrificial animals and firstborn sons after eight days (Exod 22:28b–29) and that this almost certainly means that they are to be sacrificed suggests that they share a symmetrical cultic status and are subject to common ritual requirements. The same holds true for persons and domesticated animals consigned to eradication in Lev 27:28–29, a text according to which such animals and human beings are classified as "most holy," the highest cultic status known to biblical authors, and may not be redeemed or ransomed. But does symmetrical treatment (e.g., killing on the eighth day; not being subject to redemption or ransoming) or shared cultic status (e.g., "most holy") imply a comparable value?[36] The fact that the life of one sacrificial animal can potentially substitute for the life of one human being, according to a number of legal texts, does indeed suggest some kind of symmetry in terms of value, even if only for the purposes of sacrifice (Exod 13:13, 15; 34:20 by implication; see also Gen 22:13). Were this not the case, the life of one sacrificial animal would not be sufficient to substitute for the life of a human being.[37] The same assumption—comparable value for the purposes of sacrifice—might also be implied by texts such as Exod 22:28b–29 and Lev 27:28–29, even if it is not stated explicitly. Thus, according to some legal texts, domesticated animals and human beings might be assigned a common—that is, elite—cultic status, might be subject to symmetrical ritual requirements, and perhaps might even share

---

34. E.g., Deut 14:21 versus Exod 12:48–49 for the resident alien and the native-born Israelite, and Exod 34:19–20 versus 22:28b–29 regarding the firstborn.

35. On this, see n. 6.

36. A valuation might be expressed through a monetary figure (the equivalent of X in silver is Y), an implicit hierarchy of value (X is worth more than Y), or an equivalence in kind (X may substitute for Y). Examples of monetary valuations of sacrificial animals include Lev 5:15; 27:3–7. For an implicit hierarchy of value with respect to animals required to address unknowing transgressions that result in guilt, see, e.g., Lev 4:3, 13–14, 22–23, 27–28. (This text implies that a bull without a defect is most valuable, followed by a male goat without a defect, followed by a female goat without a defect.) For equivalence in kind, see the examples that follow regarding sacrificial substitution.

37. Note, however, Mic 6:6–7, a nonlegal, poetic text that seems implicitly to equate the sacrifice of the firstborn son (*bəkôr*) with that of thousands of sacrificial animals, suggesting a significant asymmetry of value between such animals and persons in the eyes of the text's author.

a comparable valuation, at least for the purposes of sacrifice. Needless to say, to assign an equivalent value to a domesticated animal and a human being—even if only for the purposes of sacrifice—is a striking and noteworthy thing, with important implications for our understanding of the status and value of domesticated animals according to biblical law, particularly for those who seek to ground contemporary arguments in favor of animal rights in biblical texts.[38] Although there are certainly biblical legal texts that clearly assign a greater value to a human life than to the life of a domesticated animal (e.g., Lev 24:21), other biblical laws suggest some kind of symmetry of value, at least in particular contexts (e.g., that of sacrifice).

Finally, it is worth noting that the extent to which distinctions of gender and physical wholeness—the axes of inequality that often realize social hierarchy among human beings—also have significance for the ranking of domesticated animals in biblical legal texts is uneven. Although the absence of physical wholeness very frequently produces asymmetry among both human beings and sacrificial animals, gender functions less consistently as an axis of inequality among domesticated animals. On the one hand, the Priestly Writing sometimes requires female whole-bodied animals for higher ranked sacrifices such as the purification or reparation offerings, just as it requires whole-bodied male animals for these sacrifices; female animals also play a prominent role in other vital sacrifices (e.g., the red cow). Yet, at the same time, according to any number of formulations, Yhwh's claim on the firstborn of animals is a claim on males specifically, suggesting their higher status. Thus, gender functions less often to create asymmetry among sacrificial animals than it does to establish hierarchy among human beings.

---

38. For an argument that Exod 23:10–11, 12; Lev 25:2–7; and Deut 5:12–15 ascribe rights to animals and a critique of the handling of relevant biblical texts by nonspecialists engaged in animal rights advocacy, see my article "Are There Legal Texts in the Hebrew Bible That Evince a Concern for Animal Rights?"

Animals in Greek and Roman Criminal Law

F. S. NAIDEN
University of North Carolina at Chapel Hill

> He prayeth best, who loveth best
> All things great and small;
> For the dear God who loveth us,
> He made and loveth all.
> —Coleridge, *Rime of the Ancient Mariner*[1]

The subject of animals in ancient criminal law emerged among early modern jurists like Lord Coke, who realized that the status of animals under the law of their own times owed something to the Roman law of noxal surrender. If the jurists did not know of similarities between their own law and Greek law, they did know about the putative influence of Genesis and Leviticus on the Common Law of England and on the provincial or national law codes on the Continent. Coke and his contemporaries acknowledged religious influences on the legal status of animals.[2]

Then, in the mid-nineteenth century, anthropological and sociological explanations for ancient law came into vogue, as in Sir Henry Maine and Sir James Frazer, who thought that laws about animals reflected superstitions that the ancients struggled to outgrow. Douglas MacDowell provides a recent example of an evolutionary explanation for Greek law about

---

1. Samuel Taylor Coleridge, *The Complete Poetical Works of Samuel Taylor Coleridge: Including Poems and Versions of Poems Now Published for the First Time*, vol. 1, *Poems*, ed. Ernest Hartley Coleridge (Oxford: Oxford University Press, 1912), 1:209.

2. Regarding Coke and other British authorities on criminal proceedings against animals, see Henry de Bracton, *On the Laws and Customs of England*, trans. Samuel E. Thorne, 4 vols. (Cambridge: Belknap Press of Harvard University Press, 1968), 1:3, c. 5; Edward Coke, *First Part of the Institutes of the Laws of England, Or, a Commentary upon Littleton* (Philadelphia: Robert H. Small, 1853), 1:38–40, 79–80; Matthew Hale with George Wilson, *Historia Placitorum Coronae* (Philadelphia: Robert H. Small, 1847), 419–24. The most recent reference in federal jurisprudence is Calero-Toledo v. Pearson Yacht Leasing Co., 416 U.S. 663 (1974) 663 (W. Brennan).

animals. Outside of Classics, recent historians have proposed cultural explanations for legal peculiarities such as the English deodand, an animal held responsible for human deaths or injuries.[3] Explanations of this kind describe how legal terms or practices reflect the literature and society from which they come. This essay proposes such an explanation for Greek and Roman laws about animals. It deals with just one subject, grave harm done by animals to human beings: first, homicide; and, second, battery and property damage.[4]

Greek and Roman law tended to put animals committing these crimes in the same category as slaves, and sometimes in the same category as certain objects. Animals, slaves, and implements were all appurtenances of the owner, who was often the head of a household, the Greek *kyrios* and Roman *paterfamilias*. Women might well be the owners, but men owned, bought, and sold more, and monopolized the law courts. The law was for men's benefit, not that of the slaves or animals, any more than it was for the benefit of mere objects. Religious beliefs justified the law, and these

---

3. Oliver Finkelstein, "The Goring Ox: Some Historical Perspectives on Deodands, Forfeitures, Wrongful Death and the Western Notion of Sovereignty," *Temple Law Quarterly* 46 (1973): 169–220, here 169, 182; Nicholas Humphreys, "Introduction" to Edward Evans, *The Criminal Prosecution and Capital Punishment of Animals* (New York: E. P. Dutton, 1906; repr., London, 1987); Joseph Lynch, "Harrison and Hick on God and Animal Pain," *Sophia* 33 (1994): 63–73; Paul Harrison, "God and Animal Minds: A Response to Lynch," *Sophia* 35 (1996): 67–78; Leonard Levy, *License to Steal: The Forfeiture of Property* (Chapel Hill: University of North Carolina Press, 1996), chapter 1; Thomas Sutton, "The Deodand and the Responsibility for Death," *Journal of Legal History* 18 (1997): 44–55. On trials of objects, see F. S. Naiden, "The Sword Did It: A Greek Explanation for Suicide," *ClQ* 65 (2015): 75–85.

For evolutionists in respect to Greek law, see Douglas M. MacDowell, *The Law in Classical Athens*, Aspects of Greek and Roman Life (London: Thames & Hudson, 1978), 117–18, describing a ritual pointing the way toward medieval and modern coroners' courts. William Hyde expressly follows J. G. Frazer (*The Golden Bough: A Study in Comparative Religion* [London: Macmillan, 1912]) and W. Robertson Smith (*Lectures on the Religion of the Semites: The Fundamental Institutions; First series*, 2nd ed. [London: Adam & Charles Black, 1894]) in "The Prosecution of Lifeless Things and Animals in Greek Law," parts 1 and 2, *American Journal of Philology* 38 (1917): 152–75, 285–303. Part 2 provides a conspectus of relevant classical sources. An early evolutionist with respect to Roman law was Marcel Mauss, "La religion et les origines du droit penal," *RHR* 35 (1897): 31–60, here 49.

4. Standard works include Karl von Amira, *Thierstrafen und Thierprocesse*, Mittheilungen des Instituts für österreichische Geschichtsforschung 12.4 (Innsbruck, 1891), 545–606; Evans, *Criminal Prosecution*. Von Amira held that Indo-European *noxae deditio* evolved into medieval animal trials. For another evolutionary view, see F. W. Maitland and Frederick Pollock, *The History of English Law before the Time of Edward I*, 2nd ed. (Cambridge: Cambridge University Press, 1911), 470–71: "Law which demands a 'noxal surrender' of the peccant slave or ox is already a mitigation of older law which would not have let the master off so easily." At this missing, earlier stage, the owner himself stood trial for murder. Contrasting with evolutionary histories are explanations for the law's retaining obsolete terms like *deodand*, as Oliver Wendell Holmes Jr., complains in *The Common Law* (Boston: Little, Brown, 1881), 5.

beliefs brought with them ontological assumptions, in other words, assumptions about the way in which animals have their being, as opposed to humans, assumptions similar to those made about slaves as opposed to free persons.

* * *

In Greece (which is to say, in classical Athenian sources, since animals are scarcely mentioned elsewhere), all homicide law featured pollution, even when the doer of the deed was an animal. For this reason, the community responded to a homicidal animal as it did to a human killer—with a trial followed by punishments meant to isolate the perpetrator from the community. If an animal only wounded a human being, an altogether different and simpler procedure resulted: the *kyrios* or other owner of the animal surrendered it to the victim or to the victim's relatives, who could then do what they liked, and presumably slaughter it. In each case, the animal served as a substitute for its master, but, in the case of murder, the substitute was removed, whereas in the case of battery it was forfeited. In Roman law (which is to say, in the *Digest* and *Institutes*, since animals are scarcely mentioned in other legal sources) pollution did not affect homicide proceedings, so in the case of murder, the same kind of surrender of the animal, the "noxal surrender" of Gaius and Justinian, took place as in the Greek instances in which an animal was forfeited. The animal again served as a substitute for the owner.

How did the Athenians go about putting animals on trial for homicide? Plato explains:

> If a beast of burden or some other living creature murders someone, except when this happens at public games, the relatives of the victim should prosecute the killer. Whichever magistrates (and however many magistrates) the relatives pick must hear the case. If they condemn the creature, they must kill it and remove it beyond the borders of the community. (*Leg.* 9.873e)

Although Plato is describing the new community projected in his *Laws*, Aristotle and Demosthenes show that Athenian law was the same, save that the judges were the King Archon and the four tribal kings—all of them important priests—and the court was the Prytaneion. Aristotle and Demosthenes also report that the law was the same for deaths supposedly caused by objects such as falling branches.[5]

The requirements of denouncing the animal and expelling its corpse reveal the concern about pollution. An animal that killed a human being polluted the community in which the killing occurred, and so, like a

---

5. Demosthenes, *Aristocr.* 23.80; Aristotle, *Ath. pol.* 54.7. All translations are my own.

86   *Animals and the Law in Antiquity*

human killer, the animal had to be isolated and then expelled. If it were not, the ghost of the victim would be angry and would punish the community. Similarly, an object causing a human death and acting independently, since no person was involved, counted as a source of pollution. Once again, the ghost of the victim would be angry. As Aristotle and Demosthenes say, these objects were put on trial, isolated, and disposed of.

No case law for animal homicide survives, but Pausanias reports proceedings against objects. On the island of Thasos, a statue of the late Olympic victor Theagenes fell and killed one man in a crowd of people who would often come to the statue, mock Theagenes, and even scourge the statue as though it were alive. The Thasians put the statue on trial for murder, condemned it, and threw it into the sea, as Plato and Athenian law provide. Then a plague fell upon Thasos, Delphi advised restoring the statue, and the Thasians worshiped the outraged Theagenes as a hero. The familiarly ironic tale of the origin of a hero cult aside, Pausanias shows that the guilty object is a substitute for a human assailant, in this case the spirit of the infuriated Theagenes, just as a guilty animal might be a substitute for a human (*Descr.* 6.11.6–9).

In a story of another murder trial, in Elis, Pausanias combines the categories of animal and object. After a boy playing underneath a bronze bull struck his head against the sculpture and died, the Elians tried and condemned the bull. They worried whether they had dealt with the threat of pollution, and consulted Delphi. If we take the text as it is, the oracle of Apollo

> … told the Elians to make as many purifications concerning the sculpture as Greeks customarily do in cases of involuntary homicide. (*Descr.* 5.27.10)[6]

Apollo means that the Elians should follow Greek homicide law by disposing of the felonious object while making expiatory sacrifices. That would rid the community of the source of pollution.

If we follow Bekker's supplement, however, Apollo

> … told them to make as many purifications as Greeks customarily do and let the sculpture be.[7]

---

6. *Spiritus lenis* is not indicated: *ho de sphas [ho] theos ho en Delphois kata <chōran ean> to anathēma katharsia echra ep' autō poiēsamenous hopósa Hellēnes epi akousiō phonō nomizousin.*

7. *ho de sphas [ho] theos ho en Delphois kata <chōran ean> to anathēma katharsia echra ep' autō poiēsamenous hopósa Hellēnes epi akousiō phonō nomizousin* (August Immanuel Bekker, *Pausanias, De Situ Greciae* [Berlin: G. Reimer, 1826–27]).

This supplement means that Apollo gave the Elians surprising, unconventional advice. Although they had tried and condemned the brazen animal, they should treat it as though they had acquitted it, in other words, "let the sculpture be" rather than dispose of it. I do not know of another case in which Apollo tells a Greek court to reverse itself. Accordingly, we should reject Bekker's supplement.

Roman law recognized two kinds of *homicidium*. The more severe was *parricidium* (murder of a relative); the less severe, all other *homicidium*. Both crimes required a manifest intent to kill, as would be shown by striking a man with a sword, say, rather than with a metal bar. Given that an animal could not commit parricide, the remaining question was whether an animal could display a manifest intent to kill and thus commit ordinary *homicidium*. The *Digest* and *Institutes* agreed that an animal could not meet this standard.[8]

Unlike the Greeks, the Romans did not think of animals as murderers. They did think of them as substitutes for humans in another context. This was forfeiting an animal by way of a procedure called *pauperies*. Ulpian explains,

> If an animal does harm, there is an available action provided by the Twelve Tables. This provided that the master transfer the offending animal to the injured party unless he preferred to pay the animal's asking price. This action, called *noxia*, applied to all quadrupeds. (*Digesta* 9.1.1.pr., 9.1.2)

This procedure applied to both homicide and battery. Gaius gives an example for wounding a person:

> If, say, an animal wounds a man who is the head of a household, or his son, there is no doubt that the action of *pauperies* is available. (Gaius 7 ad ed. provinc., *Digesta* 9.1.3)

In a case like this, the wrong done was the responsibility of the animal's master, not the animal. Yet the master thrust the consequences upon the animal and thus escaped punishment.

Although Attic law did not provide for noxal surrender in cases of animal homicide, archaic law at Gortyn provided that a slave who killed a free man be surrendered by his master to the relatives of the victim. The relatives could deal with the slave in whatever way they saw fit. If a slave wounded a free man, a master could do the same thing. (Only one Roman report features such a surrender of a human being, and this report does not concern slaves, as at Gortyn. After the Romans failed to honor a treaty

---

8. *Digesta* 48.7.1.3 (sword versus bar). For the manifest act, see Paulus, *Sententiae* 5.23.

made with the Samnites, they surrendered to them the emissary who had made the treaty. As Livy says, they were atoning for their own wrong by thrusting it upon a substitute.[9])

To generalize, Romans and Greeks granted some agency to animals, yet both also said that animals lacked reasoning powers. As Ulpian says,

> ... an animal is incapable of committing a legal wrong because it is devoid of reasoning powers. (*Digesta* 9.1.1.3)[10]

Similarly, Demosthenes describes animals put on trial as "having no share of reason" (*mē metechontōn tou phronein*). Aristotle or the author writing in his name distinguishes between a human killer who "does the deed," or *poiein*, and some other agent to be held responsible, like an animal, for which the verb is *dran*.

What was the Greek law if an animal committed battery? We know only through a law of Solon. It provides for the noxal surrender of vicious dogs. Plato's *Laws* provides the same remedy for damage done by animals:

> If some animal — a horse, a dog, or any other — does harm to the property of a neighbor (of the animal's owner), the owner will pay damages in the same way.[11]

The last phrase, "in the same way," refers to the preceding sentences, which concern slaves:

> If a slave or slave woman damages property belonging to someone other than his or her master ... the owner of the slave at fault will pay compensation.

Plato now offers noxal surrender as an alternative to compensation:

> Or the owner may choose to transfer to the injured party the slave who has done the injury.

The same would presumably apply to an animal. Where animals doing damage are concerned — but not animals causing human deaths — Athenian and Roman laws were apparently the same.

---

9. *I. Cret.* 1.1.18. A Roman ambassador is made subject to noxal surrender in Livy 9.1–10.

10. See Demosthenes and Aristotle as in n. 4 above. For partial agency for animals according to Christian teaching, see Thomas Aquinas, *Summa* II 2, q. 90, art. 3.

11. The law of Solon regarding noxal surrender (Plutarch, *Sol.* 22.4) also required that dogs be kept on short leases; followed by Plato, *Leg.* 9.936d-e.

Granting animals agency, yet denying them reasoning powers, raises the question of their legal status, and, in particular, whether they should be subject to noxal surrender. Greek writers do not answer this question, but the Roman jurists say that some animal behavior was unnatural or atypical, and should be the occasion for noxal surrender, but other behavior was natural and typical, and should not. Ulpian says,

> This action [of noxal surrender] is available when a four-footed animal becomes excited because of exceptional wildness. A horse prone to bucking may kick someone, and an ox prone to goring may toss its victim. (*Digesta* 9.1.1.6–7)

"Exceptional wildness" is unnatural or atypical. Ulpian continues,

> [Noxal surrender] is unavailable if a horse kicks because pain upsets it.... Yet it is available if a horse kicks someone who has been stroking or patting it.

Reacting to pain is natural and typical. Kicking the hand that strokes you, as in Ulpian's example, is not. The criterion of the animal's behaving naturally or typically is, in practice, an expectation that the animal has been domesticated. It should behave normally as a master understands this word.

This criterion of normality helps explains the procedure of noxal surrender. It lets the master shed himself of something abnormal, and, in the case of homicide at Gortyn, of something accursed. He is safeguarding his own integrity and well-being. He is protecting himself, as the *Institutes* say when explaining the noxal surrender of slaves:

> There is an excellent reason for the practice of noxal surrender [of a slave], for it would be unjust that the misdeed of a slave should involve his master in any detriment beyond the loss of the slave's own body. (4.8.2)

This passage effectively says that noxal surrender protects the master from severe punishment. Severe punishment is for the slave to suffer—for the master's substitute to suffer, not the master himself.

The noxal surrender of slaves was a complicated legal topic, thanks to the greater measure of agency conceded to slaves than to animals. Besides murder and battery, slaves could commit robbery, theft, rapine, and wrongdoing under the rubric of *injuria*. For example, a slave might neglect a fireplace and cause a building to burn; the owner of the slave could surrender him to the owner of the building. Thanks to the *Lex Aquilia*, the owner could also pay monetary damages. The damages for homicide were high, and if the victim was a free person, they were enormous, amounting to 200 *solidi*, that is, about 900 grams of gold, valued today at some $37,000 but worth far more in antiquity. This alternative to noxal surrender did not come cheap.[12]

The following table summarizes Greek and Roman law for homicide, battery, and damages due to animals:

	Greece	Rome
Homicide	Murder trials	Noxal surrender
Battery	Noxal surrender	Noxal surrender or fines
Damages	Noxal surrender or fines	Chiefly fines, but also noxal surrender

If we compare the alternatives of noxal surrender or fines to the homicide alternatives of trials or surrender, the peculiarity of homicide stands out. The animal that kills a human being is especially threatening, and this is the very animal that the human master regards as a substitute. Such an animal is subhuman yet quasi-human, whereas the legal status of human beings, or at least free persons, is unambiguous. The animal, in other words, is a parasocial quiddity, whereas the master is a normative being. We are, to be sure, speaking only of domesticated animals. Among wild animals, such as lions and boars, an ambiguous creature would be something very different, a monster like Echidna or a sphinx—a *Mischwesen* to be slain by a hero, not a defendant to be condemned by a court.

The Roman law of *pauperies* sheds light on the socioeconomic background for the contents of this table. *Pauperies* always refers to *quadrupedes*, practically speaking, to flocks and herds. Gaius specifies that quadrupeds, or *pecora*, may or may not include pigs, but exclude untamed animals such as bears and lions. The reason, it seems, is that animals that commonly run wild do not rank among those that the Roman farmer can regard as substitutes for himself. They differ from the ox who helps the owner with the plow or the cow who supplements a human mother's milk. (Two foreign species, the elephant and the camel, are hard to classify, *quasi mixti sunt*: beasts of burden, yes, but hard to tame.) (Gaius, *Institutes* 2.14a–16).

As the Roman Empire grew, the exclusion of wild animals from the law proved troublesome. First came the wild animals brought into the cities for use in public games. In response, the aediles, the officials in charge of games, issued an edict that forbade any boar, bear, or "other

---

12. For noxal surrender in cases of damages, see *Digesta* 9.1.1.4. For sources concerning the law of damages, see Bernard Jackson, "Liability for Animals in Roman Law: A Historical Sketch," *Cambridge Law Journal* 37 (1978): 122–43. According to *Digesta* 2.21.42, the damages would be 200 *solidi* if animals were "defective." For chaining defective animals, see 2.21.4. Under the *Lex Aquilia*, the treatment of slaves and animals was more similar than it was under the law of *pauperies*. See Jackson, passim.

animal likely to do harm" to be put on a street or public road unless properly restrained. The aediles would prosecute violators of the law and impose fines, including the previously mentioned fine of 200 *solidi* for the death of a free man. In less serious cases, the offending owner would pay double damages. Later came private importation of panthers and probably lions. The aediles banned it. At some point, the law began regulating household dogs.[13]

These laws, with their urban flavor, imply that animals eventually fared better in the big cities than they did on farms, for in cities they were spared noxal surrender. Yet they fared better at the price of being chained, caged, and regulated. This evolution from possible death to imprisonment and bracelets evokes the paradoxical progress, if that is the word, of modern penology. Roman law envisioned increasing control over animals as well decreasing criminalization.

If we put aside the subject of animal or slave perpetrators and consider animal and slave victims, in Greece the owner of such a victim could sue for damages. If the slave was kidnapped, or the animal seized, the owner could prosecute to repossess his property. In these respects, an animal or a slave did not differ from other property. As for Roman law, the owner of the slain or wounded slave or animal prosecuted under the *Lex Aquilia* and asked for damages. In just one instance, when a slave had harmed the animal, the slave's owner could surrender the slave and thus use noxal surrender to avoid paying damages. Save for this complication, animals or slaves did not differ from other property.

Although an animal could do physical harm and be regarded as its master's responsibility, it could not commit other crimes and be regarded as acting on its own responsibility. For example, animals are never said to steal and be liable for it. They are said to do some damage and to share responsibility with a master in just one circumstance—and this was peculiar, if not rare. If a plow animal upset a boundary stone, the animal and the plowman were both put to death to appease Jupiter Terminus, the offended god of boundaries. Man and beast shared responsibility only when the property being damaged belonged to a god.[14]

This review of the status of animals as both criminals and victims makes it no surprise that Greek and Roman law ignored cruelty toward or neglect of animals and also ignored blood sports. The Greeks and Romans reserved laws against cruelty and the like to free persons, especially citi-

---

13. For panthers, see Pliny, *Nat.* 8.17.64. Regarding household dogs in the *edictum de feris*, see Jackson, "Liability for Animals," 128–29.

14. Salvatore Riccobono, Giovanni Baviera, Contardo Ferrini, Giuseppe Furlani, and Vincenzo Arangio-Ruiz, *Fontes iuris romani antejustiniani*, 2nd ed., 3 vols. (Florence: G. Barbèra, 1940–1943), Numa no. 20. For medieval parallels for prosecuting owners and animals, see von Amira, *Thierstrafen und Thierprocesse*, 550 n. 3.

92 *Animals and the Law in Antiquity*

zens, and most especially heads of households. This explains why *hybris* committed against a slave, a crime mentioned in both Demosthenes and the Old Oligarch, was legally *hybris* against the slave's master.[15] If *hybris* against an animal were possible—for no source says it was—it would also be *hybris* against the master. *Injuria*, or harm done to reputation, was not a crime committable against slaves or animals.

Similarly, Greek and Roman legal texts do not mention injured animals. Classical literature thus differs markedly from the ancient Babylonian legal texts described by Seth Richardson elsewhere in this volume. This omission is all the more remarkable because one Greek writer, Aesop, features talking animals, and such animals appear in Homer, Apuleius, and authors in between. On the whole, classical literature takes some interest in animal suffering. As noticed below, philosophers did. The law did not.

What about other ancient societies besides Babylonia? Early China, for one, used slaves and large populations of domesticated animals as beasts of burden; so did parts of sub-Saharan Africa as well as much of the Near East. Yet trials of animals for homicide occurred in only two societies, ancient Greece and medieval Europe, whereas noxal surrender for homicide occurred mainly in Rome and in medieval England through deodands.[16]

***

How did this odd state of legal affairs arise? Evolutionary answers are dubious. One such answer concerns borrowing. Even if the Romans somehow borrowed noxal surrender from the Greeks, medieval Europe did not

---

15. For *hybris* towards slaves, see MacDowell, *Law in Classical Athens*, 129–32; Alberto Maffi, "Family and Property Law," in *The Cambridge Companion to Ancient Greek Law*, ed. Michael Gagarin and David Cohen (Cambridge: Cambridge University Press, 2007), 254–67, here 258. The parallel between slaves and domesticated animals resembles the parallel drawn by two phrases in French Law, *femme covert* and *beste covert*, as in Bracton, *On the Laws and Customs*, 1:3, c. 5. Bracton also likens animals to serfs (3:36). Uniquely Christian is the idea of animals killing people and then expecting to be punished, as in Johann Thoma, *Tractatus de noxia animalium continens pauperiei, pastus etc.* (Jena: G. Sengenuvaldi, 1553), 191.

16. On noxal surrender, as opposed to a trial, of homicidal animals in medieval France, see *Customs of Touraine and Anjou*, #125, in *The Établissements de Saint Louis: Thirteenth-Century Law Texts from Tours, Orleans, and Paris*, trans. F. R. P. Akehurst (Philadelphia: University of Pennsylvania Press, 1996). Trials, however, were typical, as in Evans, *Criminal Prosecution*, passim. How widespread these trials were is impossible to say, but Evans found evidence as far north as Scotland (265–86). Jacob Finkelstein found one as far east as Russia (*The Ox That Gored*, TAPS 71.2 [Philadelphia: American Philosophical Society, 1981], 85 n. 28). None of this is to say that animals were not punished or slain without process of law; Finkelstein's theme, the goring ox of Hebrew and Near Eastern law, offers an ancient illustration. When the last trial occurred is also uncertain; authors tend to find contemporary or at least recent examples, as Evans did (286) in citing one from the year his book was published. No doubt the author of the *Athenian Constitution* attributed to Aristotle could have done likewise.

borrow animal trials from the Greeks. The Greeks themselves have no one to borrow from—not the Babylonians, Hittites, or Hebrews, whose law collections exclude animal trials, even if they provide for the destruction of nuisances such a goring ox. Another unsatisfactory evolutionary answer is that notions of pollution passed from antiquity to the Middle Ages before expiring in the light of scientific progress. Yet pollution due to homicide differs from the medieval belief that an unavenged murder left a community prey to devils. Deducing the one from the other is problematic.

Another explanation for animal trials or, in medieval England, for coroners' inquests, is a society's wish to account for every wrongful death. As MacDowell says, Antiphon illustrates this wish in his *Second Tetralogy*, concerning a boy who killed someone while practicing with javelins in a gymnasium. Either the javelin thrower was to blame, the orator says, or the victim was, or the javelin: Some party must be held responsible. To use the language of Aristotle, there must be retribution for any act of wrongdoing.[17] One trouble with this explanation is that medieval English coroners did not know Classical Greek. Another is that a wish like this should be universal. It should not appeal to the coroner in the shire, and to certain schoolboy authors, yet fail to reach other peoples, like the early Germans or Chinese.[18]

Evolutionary explanations are etic, and thus culturally external to the evidence. An emic, or culturally internal, explanation is to derive animal trials and noxal surrender from commonplaces of ancient and medieval religious thought. As I have noted elsewhere, Greek and Roman law dictated animal sacrifices; it also dictated the occasional use of animals as scapegoats. The law even dictated sacrifices to commemorate *mirabilia* performed by animals.[19] These laws treat an animal as an agent of a god's

---

17. In *Eth. nic.* 1132a, Aristotle regards the perpetrator and the victim as morally equal and describes murder as negating their equal standing. By assuming that both are human beings, he leaves the question of the status of animals unresolved.
18. Aside from "murder will out," as in MacDowell, *Law in Classical Athens*, 117–18, a similar idea, which is fear of lawlessness, appears in both MacDowell and Humphreys, "Introduction," 17. Anticipating these two is Jean Thonissen, *Études sur l'histoire du droit criminel de la France* (Paris, 1869), 2:198–99. So also St. Augustine in *Corpus juris canonici, curas brevi adnotatione critica instructum ad exemplar romanum*, ed. Louis Richter, 2 vols. (Leipzig: Tauchnitz, 1839), 1:640. Another version of the argument about accounting for human deaths is the argument that rituals or ritualistic acts provide significance to human life, in particular, the ritual of animal sacrifice; see Richard Wollheim, *The Sheep and the Ceremony*, Leslie Stephen Lecture 1979 (Cambridge: Cambridge University Press, 1979), 2–4. Wollheim does not mention animal trials.
19. For animal *mirabilia, thaumata*, or the like, see Aelian, *Nat. an.* 11.4; Aeschylus, *Agamemnon* 1297; Aristotle, *Mir. ausc.* 844b no. 137; Apollonius, *Mirabilia* 13; Philostratus, *Heroicus* 294, 329; Pliny, *Nat*.32.17; Plutarch, *Luc.* 24.7, *Pel.* 22. For violence done against animals in acts of sacrifice, see F. S. Naiden, "Violent Sacrifice in Greece and Rome," in *Cambridge World History of Violence*, ed. Garrett G. Fagan, Linda Fibiger, and Mark Hudson, 4 vols. (Cambridge:

94 *Animals and the Law in Antiquity*

will, as in the case of a *mirabilium*, or as the agent of some hostile or wicked force, as in the case of an animal trial or of a scapegoat ritual. An animal could also be an agent, or rather be a victim, of its own unnatural impulses, as in the case of Roman noxal surrender. Divine agency, diabolical agency, and natural agency all affected animals, and so ancient and medieval law provided for all three. Save for the obsolete category of the act of God, modern law provides only for the last.

Greek and Roman sources do not provide any example of a community's being confused about which of these three agencies might be at work, but the medieval French sources surveyed in the standard work of Everett Evans provide many. To cite but one: If swarms of insects caused a famine, either God sent them, and the people must acknowledge as much and repent, or the devil sent them, and the church must exorcise the insects, or the insects were swarming, and the people must take some action and dispose of the creatures. Priests and judges decide which, and sometimes disagree with each other. This example happens to concern insects, not the mammals who are the subject of ancient laws. The Greek and Roman sources pay much less attention to wild animals than the medieval European ones do, and less to flying creatures. An exception illustrating the rule is Heracles's killing the eagle of Zeus in the Caucasus. A demigod is the killer, the victim is a divine familiar, and the location is uninhabited.[20]

Some ancient philosophers and theologians dissented from the *communis opinio* condemning animals. Empedocles and Porphyry, among others, reasoned that animals suffered because of human transgressions, and not the other way around. Plotinus, however, held that animals suffered according to a divine plan, and thus deserved no protection (*Enn.* 3.2.15).[21]

Some Pythagoreans viewed animals as rational, independent agents. According to Porphyry, Pythagoras concluded that animals, like people,

---

Cambridge University Press, 2020), 1: 475–92. For other views of the role of animals in acts of sacrifice, see Daniel Ullucci in this volume.

20. On Heracles and the eagle, see Wilhelm Roscher, *Ausführliches Lexikon der griechischen und römischen Mythologie*, 6 vols. (Leipzig: Teubner, 1884–1937), vol. 1, s.v. Aetos (A. Rapp). On medieval attention to insects due to the conflation of preventative measures against them with punitive measures against individual quadrupeds, see Esther Cohen, *The Crossroads of Justice: Law and Culture in Late Medieval France*, Brill's Studies in Intellectual History 36 (Leiden: Brill, 1992), 121.

21. For a Christian version of a divine plan, see John Hildrop, *A Commentary upon the Second Psalm* (London: R. Minors, 1742), arguing that animals were immortal in Eden, and thus were punished by divine decree. On Germanic as well as Greek metempsychosis, but only for storks, see Jacob Grimm, *Deutsche Mythologie*, 4th ed., 3 vols. (Gütersloh: Bertelsmann, 1876–1877), 2:638. For Pythagorean views, see Plutarch, *De esu* 99e; *Quaest. conv.* 729e; *Soll. an.* 965b; Aristotle, *Eth. nic.* 1111a-b; 1161b; *Pol.* 1256b; Empedocles, 131 B 127-30, as in Hermann Diels and Walter Kranz, *Die Fragmente der Vorsokratiker, griechisch und deutsch*, 9th ed. (Berlin: Weidmann, 1959–1960), hereafter abbreviated as D-K.

should not commit murder and should not even commit murder by killing other animals. Animals and people both should become vegetarians. Bears, for example, should give up meat and should learn to eat fruits and vegetables. Pythagoras exempted beans from this diet, since he thought this legume was akin to human flesh.

All Pythagoreans thought animals could have human souls thanks to metempsychosis. That gave animals powers of reason, they concluded, and so animals could commit wrongs and could and should be punished, even put to death. Pythagoras and his followers never mention trials of animals, but they must have thought these trials were permissible, provided they were fair. Fairness would mean that animals should not be arbitrarily accused or punished. (Comparisons between animals and slaves occur in one work showing Pythagorean influence, Plutarch's essay on *The Cleverness of Animals*. Both are rational, says the author, and both should be treated justly; put on trial if need be, but treated kindly.)

Other schools of philosophy denied animals reasoning powers. Aristotle said humans had nothing in common with horses or oxen, and drew the conclusion that there was no such thing as justice in regard to animals. Animal trials would be nonsensical in this view, but Aristotle does not mention them, even in a passage saying that human beings govern domesticated animals. Yet Aristotle also admits that animals can act voluntarily, and thus could voluntarily kill a human being. Like Athenian law, Aristotle put animals in the position of being sub-human in some ways, but quasi-human in others. Animals remained a kind of quiddity, just as slaves did.[22]

Only one philosopher surely escaped this confusion. According to the *Florilegium* of Stobaeus, Democritus says,

> As for killing or not killing animals, a man who kills animals that do wrong and do it willingly should not be prosecuted....People must kill animals that unjustly cause harm, and one must kill all of them, no matter the cost. In every community, the man who does so will have a bigger share of contentment, justice, courage, and wealth. (Stobaeus, *Flor.* 2.1.13; D-K 257–59)

So far, Democritus agrees with Aristotle and others. He goes on to say,

> As for killing human beings, it seems to me that people should do the same thing as is right for foxes and snakes: in other words, kill them if they are hostile, and do so in accordance with ancestral laws.

---

22. A survey: Richard Sorabji, *Animal Minds and Human Morals: Origins of the Western Debate* (Ithaca, NY: Cornell University Press, 1993), esp. chapters 9 and 11, on these and other texts.

This implies putting animals on a par with people. The passage in Stobaeus does not explore the consequences of this view. Would Democritus approve of Athenian trials of animals, which put animals on a par with mere objects? (Diogenes Laertius reports that he visited Athens [*Vitae* 9.36].) Would he regard noxal surrender as an evasion of responsibility by culpable humans? The extant fragments of Democritus say nothing about slavery, and thus overlook the common ancient comparisons between animals and slaves. Many fragments mention polis laws, showing that issues like the criminal liability of animals should have interested Democritus.

Common to the philosophers is the lack of any notion of animal rights. As Richard Sorabji observed, the closest they come is the doctrine of metempsychosis. Having human souls gives animals some human attributes, and so, Pythagoreans argue, animals deserve to be protected. Even this position falls short of giving animals rights of their own. Instead it extends human rights. The conceptual core of this position is not the animal owner or slave owner, as in Greek and Roman law, but the human being as opposed to other, lesser beings.

In giving a religious explanation for animal trials and noxal surrender, we should confine ourselves to Greek and Roman paganism and medieval Christianity, in other words, to monotheistic or polytheistic religions in which anthropomorphic gods favored human beings who more or less resembled them, in which animals were at most divine familiars or mere symbols, like the lamb of god, and also in which slavery and animal husbandry complemented one another. This set of characteristics rules out many early religions, for example, the religion of the Aztecs. It even rules out ancient Egyptian religion, in which some animals were gods.

In paganism and medieval Christianity, animals were fellow creatures, as they are in the verses of Coleridge in the epigraph to this essay. Without being on a par with human beings, they were akin to them. Only the learned would state reservations to this culturally conditioned common sense.[23] The same kind of "common sense" applied to ancient slaves, another kind of fellow creature. Both animals and slaves were thus eligible to be substitutes. The governing duality in daily intercourse between free men and other beings was not rationality versus irrationality, the pair of concepts found in some philosophers, but substitution versus subordi-

---

23. The learned against "common sense": e.g., the French Jesuit Guillaume-Hyacinthe Bougeant, *Amusement philosophique sur le langage des bestes* (1739; repr., Paris: Hachette, 2018). According to Evans, "Beasts in that case would be a species of man, or men a species of beast, both of which propositions are incompatible with the teaching of religion" (*Criminal Prosecution*, 67). A modern theologian who sympathizes with this same sort of common sense, and thus claims that Bougeant is writing satirically, is Alvin Plantinga, *God and Other Minds: A Study of the Rational Justification of Belief in God*, Contemporary Philosophy (Ithaca, NY: Cornell University Press, 1967), 149–50.

nation, a mutually complementary pair appearing in ritual, folklore, and polis laws.[24]

This explanation, however, cannot say why animal trials occur in Greece, not Rome, and on the Continent, not in England. I can only observe that a murder trial imputes more humanity to the accused than does the alternative of noxal surrender. In particular, it imputes the trait of malice prepense. The Greeks and the Continentals of the Middle Ages found these traits in animals more than the Romans and the medieval English did.

Coke's definition of the English procedure of deodands illustrates the malign common sense that I am trying to describe:

> Deodands: when any moveable thing inanimate, or beast animate, does move to or cause the untimely death of any reasonable creature by mischance and without the will, offence, or fault of itself or of any person. They being so found by lawful inquisition of twelve men count as the *pretium sanguinis*, the price of blood, and are forfeited to God, that is, to the king, God's lieutenant on earth, to be distributed in works of charity for the appeasing of God's wrath.[25]

Here as in some ancient law, murder is the crime, forfeit is the response, appeasement is the purpose, and an animal is the means to this end. The difference between Coke and the ancients is that Coke evidently expects the animal to be slaughtered by the king's butchers rather than executed. The use of the felon animal to provide charity introduces a Christian element, yet one with a pagan counterpart: just as Christians used deodand money to purchase masses, pagans could use surrendered animals for sacrifices. Also linking Coke to the ancients is the notion that a murderous animal evokes God's wrath. Humanity remains God's favorite, and animals should know it.

A last link between Coke and the ancients is the ambiguity of the words "move to or cause." Is the animal doing the moving, or is it causing the victim to move? Coke (who is following Bracton) does not decide how responsible the animal is. In describing guilty fellow creatures, he does not say how much they are fellows, and how much they are only creatures.[26]

---

24. The contrast of the miraculous versus the routine, as opposed to the rational versus the irrational is suggested by Felix Hemmerlin, *Opuscula et tractatus* (Strasbourg: Georg Husner, 1497), describing premodern animal husbandry in unusual detail. For a much tighter link between men and animals, see Albert Post, *Die Grundlagen des Rechts und die Grundzüge seiner Entwickelungsgeschichte: Leitgedanken für den Aufbau einer allgemeinen Rechtswissenschaft auf sociologischer Basis* (Oldenburg: A. Schwartz, 1884), 354, speaking of *Personifikation*.

25. Coke, *Institutes*, 1:38–40. *Pretium sanguinis*: so also *Fleta seu commentarius juris Anglicani*, ed. H. G. Richardson and G. O. Sayles (London: Selden Society, 1955–84), 1:19.

26. Coke and Bracton: the latter's words, *mouent ad mortem,* with *OLD* s.v. *moueo* 1, 2.

* * *

Religious factors aside, trials and noxal surrender may have appealed to the ancients for a reason still felt today. These two procedures take justice out of the hands of both the victim and the human being who might be at fault and achieve some resolution by way of a third party. They transfer responsibility. We expect every criminal trial to accomplish this — to take the offender out of the community's hands and deliver him to his lawful fate. This kind of transfer keeps the peace and assuages the family of the victim.

In contemporary American law, this kind of transfer sometimes occurs by way of forfeiture. The term *deodand* may even be used. For example, in a recent New Jersey case a vicious dog was to be euthanized according to law, but the owner asked to have the beast spared, and the public sympathized with him. New Jersey did not provide for sparing an animal, so the governor declared it to be forfeit and transferred it to a third party acceptable to all concerned. The animal would then either be confined or taken out of state.[27] These cases of forfeiture occur instead of a civil proceeding under a law such as New Jersey's against vicious dogs. The animal received some modicum of justice.

Otherwise the offending Akita would have received only the summary justice administered by the dogcatcher and the veterinarian performing the act of euthanasia.

Euthanasia without appeal makes the ancient practice of animal trials seem benign. Whatever its anomalies, the practice of animal trials provided substantive, not summary, justice. The mammalian defendant had some measure of legal personality and some rights, and the government had a case to prove, not merely a law to enforce. A jury, albeit a jury of priests or magistrates, served to involve the community in the proceedings, as did the use of witnesses. The notion that the quadruped was a fellow creature was legal, not sentimental; it could save lives as well as take them.[28]

Granting some measure of legal personality to entities that are not persons is sure to involve anomalies, but this is not always a reason to avoid it. Under American law, corporations have some measure of legal personality, and thus may take shelter under the Fourteenth Amendment to the Constitution, one that guarantees due process and "equal protec-

---

27. *New York Times*, 29 January 1994, an act misunderstood as a "pardon" by the *Times*. Since the dog had never been tried, it could not be pardoned. Instead it was forfeit.

28. I owe the phrase "summary justice" to Joan Girgen, "The Historical and Contemporary Prosecution and Punishment of Animals," *Animal Law Review* 9 (2003): 97–133, here 127–29; she argues against euthanasia for vicious animals (131–33), and she summarizes the case against the New Jersey Akita (124–26).

tion" to all "persons." This view of corporations dates back to 1886 and has persisted in spite of modification and debate. In the last important case, Chief Justice Rehnquist termed corporations "artificial" and not "natural" persons, and Justice Stevens said they were not "part of 'We, the people.'"[29] Similar qualifications might apply to animals, once the Fourteenth Amendment protected them. So far, it does not. In this respect, American law is unwittingly following Roman precedent. The Romans developed noxal surrender in a way that protected slaves more than it did animals. The slave was less likely to be destroyed, and more likely to be retained by the owner's paying a fine. In the same way, the Fourteenth Amendment protected ex-slaves, not animals, and now protects artificial persons, not animals.

As the interpretation of the Fourteenth Amendment would suggest, American law features a broader notion of property than did Greek and Roman law. A merely proprietary entity, a corporation, is more like a human being than animals are, whereas in ancient law, corporations did not exist, and the status of animals was complicated by the presence of slaves, a kind of property that reminded property owners of their own precarious position: they might become pieces of property, too. Since we are all enslavable, the Greek or Roman might reason, mere animals may become our stable-mates, our partners in turning the mill and plowing the furrow. Philosophical speculation about some persons or groups being "natural slaves," and others being naturally free, never led Greek writers to deny that even well-favored peoples like Thebans and Tyrians could be enslaved.[30]

The lack of animal rights in ancient law does not dull this contrast but instead sharpens it. Animals lacked rights for the same reason ancient human beings supposedly did—divine malfeasance. Zeus approves of slavery and never mind human rights; Apollo sends famines, and Poseidon earthquakes, and never mind individual guilt or innocence; the Olympians' predecessors were worse and they shall have no successors. Zeus is a god of polis procedure, and Demeter is, too, but they are not gods of universal justice. True, the *interpretatio graeca* means that foreign gods are taken to be Greek gods, but it does not mean justice is the same everywhere. *Nomoi*, or laws, differ by nationality, even though the gods supposedly do not.

---

29. First National Bank of Boston v. Bellotti, 435 U.S. 765 (1978); Citizens United v. Federal Election Commission 558 U.S. 310 (2010). For a polemical but detailed history of this doctrine, see R. Sprague and M. E. Wells, "The Supreme Court as Prometheus: Breathing Life into the Corporate Supercitizen," *American Business Law Journal* 49 (2012): 507–56.

30. Peter Garnsey, *Ideas of Slavery from Aristotle to Augustine*, W. B. Stanford Memorial Lectures (Cambridge: Cambridge University Press, 1996), 23–35, surveying general acceptance of slavery, and 87–97, on the "easing of slavery," a topic that excludes mass enslavement by conquerors.

In *The Law Is a White Dog*, Colin Dayan writes that what she calls "rituals" influence whether the law grants a low or high status to individuals, and even whether individuals count as legal persons. She might have added that every religious ritual has some god or gods to go with it, and so the Greek and Roman ritual of bringing the defendant to what we call the bar of justice meant bringing him (or it) before the gods as well as the people. The ultimate judge was divine, and he (or she) passed judgment on the court as well as on any kind of defendant. The advantage that the court enjoyed, as compared to a defendant with four legs, was that it worshiped the gods in charge. The court knew how to please the gods; it watched closely, as lawyers watch juries; and it knew the gods were partial to certain animals. Besides being divine familiars and sacrificial offerings, animals provided victims useful in ancient prophecy. Most tellingly, gods metamorphosed into animals. In a religion like this, the categories of the superhuman, the human, and the bestial overlapped. For animals, this overlap was both a plus and a minus.[31]

For lack of case law, this chapter has avoided the question of how animals responded to standing trial. Aesop, the obvious source, does not provide any examples, and neither do other ancient writers. So, like some guilty ancient master, I offer a substitute from eighteenth-century England. The title is *The Trial of Farmer Carter's Dog Porter, for Murder*.[32] The persons in this skit are the judge, two associate justices, Matthews and Ponser, a constable, and a counsel for the prosecution; see the next page.

The story of Porter continues for a few pages more, but he never testifies. The court nevertheless convicts of him of killing a hare and hangs him. After the trial comes Porter's epitaph, which gives the moral of this satire, one having nothing to do with animals. This moral is that the trial of Porter illustrates a despotic tendency in British courts, not British

---

31. Colin Dayan, *The Law Is a White Dog: How Legal Rituals Make and Unmake Persons* (Princeton: Princeton University Press, 2011). The interplay of ritual and belief is one of the oldest subjects of controversy in the field of Greek religion. For recent views, see F. S. Naiden, *Smoke Signals for the Gods: Greek Sacrifice from the Archaic through Roman Periods* (Oxford: Oxford University Press, 2015), beginning with the epigraph, "Only God has the right to be an atheist," and the essays in Esther Eidinow, Julia Kindt, and Robin Osborne, eds., *Theologies of Ancient Greek Religion*, Cambridge Classical Studies (Cambridge: Cambridge University Press, 2016).

32. *The Trial of Farmer Carter's Dog Porter, for Murder. Taken down Verbatim et Literatim in Short-Hand, and now Published by Authority, from the Corrected Manuscript of Counsellor Clear-Point, Barrister at Law* (London: T. Lowndes, 1771), unattributed to any author in William Hone, *The Every-Day Book and Table Book: or, Everlasting Calendar of Popular Amusements, Sports, Pastimes, Ceremonies, Manners, Customs, and Events*, 3 vols. (London: Thomas Tegg, 1826–1827), 2:198-210. For possible authors, see Piers Bierne, Ian O'Donnell, and Janine Janssen, *Murdering Animals: Writings on Theriocide, Homicide, and Nonspeciesist Criminology*, Palgrave Studies in Green Criminology (New York: Palgrave Macmillan, 2018), 101–6.

6   THE TRIAL

COURT.
Set the Prisoner to the Bar.

[This was done, and the Indictment read; which we omit, for Sake of Brevity.]

COURT.
Prisoner, hold up your Paw at the Bar.

FIRST COUNCIL.
He is sullen, and refuses.

COURT.
Is he so? Why then let the Constable hold it up, *nolens volens*.

[Which was done, according to Orders.]

COURT.
What is the Prisoner's Name?

CONSTABLE.
P-P-Po-rt-er, an't please your Worship.

COURT.
What does the Fellow say?—We can't hear him.— Speak louder!— What?—The Fellow snuffles like a Parish-Clerk.

CONSTABLE.

OF PORTER.   7

CONSTABLE, hallowing.
Porter! an't please you; *Porter!*

MAT.
He says *Porter*. It's the Name of a Liquor the London *Kennel** much delight in.

PONSER.
Aye, 'tis so; and I remember another Name-sake of his, that was our Ambassador at *Constantinople*.—You have heard of Mr. *Porter?* I was Hand in Glove with him. I'll tell you a droll Story about him.—You must know, one Day as He and I were standing in the Grand Seignior's *Seraglio*, we saw—

COURT.
Hush, Brother!—*Culprit*, how will you be tried?

FIRST COUNCIL.
Please your Worship, he won't say a Word.—*Stat mutus*— as mute as a Fish.

COURT.
How?—what?— won't the Dog speak?— Won't he do what the Court bids him?

* His Worship meant *Canaille*.

COURT.

cruelty toward dogs or others. Britain's despotic tendency explains the reference to the seraglio of the Ottoman sultan.

Is the story of Porter true? The oldest source for it, a nineteenth-century British journal, reports that the satire draws upon an unconfirmed trial of a dog in Chichester, England, in 1771. Surely, this trial could not have taken place. Yet an illustration of Porter at the dock may tempt us to doubt this conclusion. Please see immediately below, and ask how much separates a canine defendant from a human one in canine guise.

Source: W. Hone. (1827). *Everyday book and table-book or everlasting calendar of popular amusements*, p.100.

The Greek language itself may strengthen our doubts. Greek has a word for *dog*, of course, but no word for *animal*. Two common words translated as *animal* mean something broader. *Zōon*, common in Aristotle, means "living thing," and *empsychon* means "living and breathing." A third word, *thēr*, means something narrower, "beast of prey." Ancient Greek distinguishes humans, *anthrōpoi*, from other beings but does not contrast them with a general class of animals. Whether this feature of Greek is due to the character of Greek religion is imponderable, but Coleridge's *Ancient Mariner* evokes this same feature, and so does the anonymous and mediocre satire imagining Porter at the dock.[33]

Seeing the animal in ourselves cannot rightly be said to be a way of humanizing us, but we need not regard it as a way of animalizing us, as though we were brutes. The category of brute is one the *Ancient Mariner* does away with. Animal trials do away with this category, too, and they suggest that if we give animals rights, our legal work has only just begun. We must also give them procedures, and where shall we get them? The Greek sources require us to imagine juries, whereas the Roman sources do not. How could we provide Porter a jury of his peers, as in American and British courts? What other sort of jury could be acceptable? I do not know what to say to Porter, except *non liquet*, the Latin for "verdict not proved."

---

33. In contrast, Latin *animal* sometimes does mean "animal" but may also refer to plants and by extension to the earth as a whole, as in *OLD*, s.v. *animal* 2, 5. *Animans* also may refer to plants as well as animals (*OLD*, s.v, *animans*, 3).

Animal Acts

Diet and Law in the Acts of the Apostles and Early Christian Practice

ANDREW MCGOWAN
Yale University

The most obvious interest in animals evident in earliest Christianity has to do with whether, when, and how to eat them. While the beliefs and practices of Christians in the period before about 200 CE were not uniform in relation to these questions, the issue itself was of general concern. The organic relationship between the new movement and Judaism led to questions concerning dietary law, and the ubiquitous cultic slaughter of the wider Greco-Roman world also raised issues of proper eating. These issues of diet were often linked intimately with those of commensality. Eating or not eating animals, or certain animals, functioned to establish identity not only relative to foodstuffs but also to companions, and to wider issues of identity.

This essay considers two passages in the Acts of the Apostles, the sequel to what is known as the Gospel of Luke, where a portrait of the very earliest Christian communities is painted from a later but still very ancient perspective, perhaps at the end of the first century or early in the second.[1] While animals may not seem especially prominent in Acts as a whole, these two sections do address animal bodies, and are among the most important in the work. The story of Peter and Cornelius (Acts 10) is

---

I am grateful to Saul Olyan and Jordan Rosenblum for the opportunity to take part in the symposium on Animals and the Law in Antiquity at Brown University, and to the discussants there, especially Beth Berkowitz, for their comments and suggestions. My thanks also to Dakota Hampton, Felicity Harley, Yii-Jan Lin, Zachary Smith, and Larry Wills for their expertise and assistance.

1. See Carl R. Holladay, *Acts: A Commentary*, NTL (Louisville: Westminster John Knox, 2016), 4–5; Richard I. Pervo, *Acts: A Commentary*, Hermeneia (Minneapolis: Fortress, 2009), 5–6.

the longest in Acts and is typically seen as a watershed in the overall narrative of Christian expansion and identity formation that is the central theme of the book.[2] The story of the "Jerusalem Council" (Acts 15) is often regarded as the center of the work and is in some respects a counterpoint to the Cornelius narrative.[3] In both stories the author draws on traditional material, which, through literary artifice, helps construct a picture of the expanding Christian movement negotiating socialization and commensality, especially relative to Judaism. In each case, key questions are raised with specific reference to animal food, and the answers are presented to later readers not just as issues of diet but as questions of community or identity, and of law.

I will suggest that the treatment of animal food in Acts does not tell us all that much about animals, or even quite as much about diet as may often be assumed; it tells somewhat more about commensality and related questions of identity. This is not a new suggestion in itself; commentators have often claimed that these stories, which of course support Christian understandings and practices, present a clear renunciation of Jewish law—and dietary law in particular. I will suggest, however, that these narratives are not opposed to the Torah, as is often assumed. More generally, I will consider how both stories make use of law, both in the sense of interpreting authoritative precepts from Jewish Scripture and in the wider sense of using legal ideas and terminology to establish a basis for their preferred practices, and by implication for the identity of the Christian movement and the forms of authority that attend it. While legal restrictions on, or at least rules for, meat eating do appear more clearly as the narrative progresses, these rules focus less on eating the flesh of particular animals than on how the uses of animal food constitute necessary aspects of commensality.

Peter's Vision

In Acts 10, the apostle Peter and a centurion named Cornelius are presented on intersecting narrative trajectories. Each has a visionary experience about the other; Cornelius is told by an angel about the man Peter who is in Joppa, while Peter receives a threefold vision, not about his counterpart but about animals, which is less informative than imperative:

> Peter went up on the roof to pray around the sixth hour. He became very hungry and wanted to eat. While they were preparing, he fell into a trance

---

2. Holladay, *Acts*, 226.
3. Hans Conzelmann, *Acts of the Apostles: A Commentary on the Acts of the Apostles*, Hermeneia (Philadelphia: Augsburg Fortress, 1988), 121.

and saw the heaven opened and a sort of container like a large sheet descending, held at four corners, let down to the earth, in which were all kinds of quadrupeds and reptiles of the earth and birds of the air. Then a voice came to him, "Get up, Peter; slaughter [*thyson*] and eat." But Peter said, "By no means, Lord, for I have never eaten anything common and unclean." The voice came to him again, a second time, "What God has cleansed, you must not consider common." This happened three times, and straightaway the container was taken up to heaven. (10:9b–16)[4]

The divine authority of this vision, especially compared to Cornelius's explicitly angelic annunciation, is underscored by its unnamed agent, whom Peter addresses as "Lord" and whose allusion to the divinity in verse 15 seems to be a self-reference. This mysterious source or medium, emphasized further by the threefold proclamation, gives the vision the force of divine executive order.

The animals in the vision—"all kinds of quadrupeds and reptiles of the earth and birds of the air" (v. 12)—are living beings, the categories in themselves suggesting a compendious array, invoking the order of creation itself (cf. Gen 1:24; 6:20). The description seems designed for comprehensiveness rather than for any analysis that might implicitly emphasize issues related to Jewish dietary prohibitions, to which Peter is clearly understood as subject.

The divine voice instructs him to kill and eat, and Peter objects, "I have never eaten anything common [*koinon*] and unclean [*akatharton*]" (v. 14b).[5] There is an echo of the prophet Ezekiel's response to another divine set of dietary commands here; in that older story God tells the prophet to adopt a diet of mixed-grain bread baked on dung, and he responds, "Ah Lord God! I have never been unclean; from my youth up to now I have never eaten what died by itself or was ravaged by animals, nor has carrion flesh entered my mouth" (Ezek 4:14). There is a closer connection between Ezekiel's response and Peter's than between the actual dietary challenges; here the echo of familiar biblical drama adds something affective to the story about divine command in the realm of food.

Peter's objection may include irregular means of obtaining the food, as well as the variety of animals; although the verb *thyō* can refer to sacrifice, and at least one commentator suggests the command to "slaughter and eat" implies kosher practice, such ideas are at best unclear in this case.[6] The emphasis here is on the animals and their kinds, rather than on the means of processing their meat.

---

4. All translations of biblical and other ancient texts are my own.
5. The NRSV has "or" for "and," but this could be misleading; see Mikeal C. Parsons, "'Nothing Defiled AND Unclean': The Conjunction's Function in Acts 10:14," *Perspectives in Religious Studies* 27 (2000): 263–74.
6. Ibid., 265, referencing Deut 12.

Although there were "all kinds" of animals, Peter objects to some implication of indiscriminate action, which is difficult to find in the divine command itself. Peter's response indicates not just that unclean or impure foods were among the options offered but that somehow it was all unclean (or "common"; see further below) even though different kinds of animals have explicitly been presented, and some choice seems possible. The voice then supports this tendency in the conversation with the retort, "What God has cleansed, you must not consider common" (v. 15).

The meaning of the vision—at least for the present author and text—is revealed and applied in the course of the narrative, through the interaction that follows with Cornelius and his envoys. Peter welcomes the messengers who have come to fetch him and gives them lodging, then accompanies them to Caesarea but expresses caution: "he said to them, 'You know that it is unlawful [*athemiton*] for a Jewish male to associate with or to visit a foreigner; but God has shown me that I should not call any *person* common or unclean'" (v. 28). A punchline of sorts for the vision story has been given here; it was all about how one treats people, not animals. Such a concern about association may reflect a position held by some (other) Jews, but it was not necessarily universal; both Peter's initial objections and his different subsequent actions could have been conceivable to various Jews as well.[7]

After this, a crucial event for the whole Acts narrative takes place: Peter preaches the message about Jesus to this mixed Jewish and gentile audience at Cornelius's house, and "the Holy Spirit fell on all who heard the word" (v. 44), by implication with some accompanying phenomena such as the glossolalia of the earlier Pentecost story (see Acts 2). In the course of a short speech, Peter gives a further human moral to the animal story: "In truth I know that God shows he is not partial, but in every nation the person who fears him and does what is right is acceptable to him" (vv. 34–35).

The connections with law in this narrative are various. Most obviously there is the question of eating animals of different kinds, including those not sanctioned by Levitical dietary rules. Peter's vision may seem to work by challenging the distinctions between animals provided in Lev 11,[8] but this is not as clear as is often assumed. Peter initially articulates the problem during the vision, applying to the hypothetical animal food the phrase "common and unclean." This might initially be read as a form of hendiadys, but it deserves more careful scrutiny.

Mikael Parsons points out that the language shifts subtly from "common and unclean" to "common *or* unclean" in the reported-speech version (v. 28). Each of these terms may refer to specific forms of impurity (cf.

---

7. Holladay, *Acts*, 235.
8. See, e.g., ibid., 232.

1 Macc 1), and context certainly suggests that *koinos* should be understood negatively here (cf. Mark 7:2, Rom 14:14, Heb 10:29; see also Letter of Aristeas 315),[9] although elsewhere it can have a more neutral or even positive meaning. In any event, there may be two categories of marginal or excluded persons (or foods) requiring some negotiation here, and not just one. The allegory, rather than merely suggesting an end to the distinction between Jews and gentiles, in fact refers both to the "common" (or as some translate, profane)—perhaps meaning Jews who had associated with gentiles—and to the "impure" or unclean, who are the gentiles themselves. Thus, while Peter linked the two concepts in the original vision with "and" as a single whole to be avoided, in his subsequent account "or" may be a way of distinguishing the two, which would be to set out more precisely the distinctions between him and all these whom God has purified.

Being Animals: Zoomorphism

As already noted, the implications that Peter draws from the vision of animals-as-people are obviously intended by the narrative as a whole but are not particularly clear in the text of the vision itself. There is a subtlety about the vision and its significance that sits alongside, and is not erased by, Peter's straightforward, if sluggish, interpretation of the animals as a sort of happy and ethnically diverse human community.

In a recent major study on early Christian thinking with and about animals, Patricia Cox Miller considers the sort of interpretive procedure manifested in Peter's explanation as "zoomorphism," the presentation or figuring of human agents or communities as animals.[10] This story in Acts is a rudimentary form of such a process, but slightly later Christian authors were to read this same passage more robustly and intertextually to support such interpretations. Origen of Alexandria, for instance, justifies a wider allegorical approach to biblical animals as a whole by using Peter's vision and its interpretation, claiming it as an apostolic mandate for his own zoomorphic hermeneutics:

> … we need the witness of the divine scriptures, lest anyone … think that I do violence to divine scriptures, and apply what is related in the Law about animals, quadrupeds, or even birds, or fish—pure or impure—to human beings, and take these things to have been said of humans….

---

9. Richard Bauckham, "James, Peter, and the Gentiles," in *The Missions of James, Peter, and Paul: Tensions in Early Christianity*, ed. Bruce D. Chilton and Craig A. Evans, NovTSup 115 (Leiden: Brill, 2004), 102–4.

10. Patricia Cox Miller, *In the Eye of the Animal: Zoological Imagination in Ancient Christianity*, Divinations (Philadelphia: University of Pennsylvania Press, 2018), 42–78.

> Does it not appear to you that Peter the apostle clearly translated all those quadrupeds and reptiles and birds in human terms, and understood as human beings the things shown to him in the sheet lowered from heaven? (*Hom. in Lev.* 7.4.1, 7; PG 12:483–86)

From this perspective, Peter's vision concerns something other than its immediate and apparent subject. Animals are good to think with, but the story does not concern them.

This zoomorphic approach to the problem that arose for Christ-followers negotiating either the practice or the theory of Jewish dietary prohibitions was only to expand from here, but it may have begun even earlier. Probably a bit later in the second century than Acts, the Letter of Barnabas attempts an interpretation of the dietary laws in moralizing terms:

> When Moses said, "you shall not eat the pig, nor the eagle, nor the hawk, nor the raven, nor any fish that does not have scales on it," he held three doctrines in mind.... Regarding the pig he means, you shall not associate with the sort of people who are like pigs. For when they live in plenty, they forget their Lord; but when they are in need, they acknowledge the Lord.... "Do not eat," he says, "the eagle, nor the hawk, nor the kite, nor the raven" (Lev 11:14). "Do not associate," he means, "or assimilate with the sort of people who do not know how to procure food for themselves by labor and sweat, but seize that of others in their lawlessness."... "And do not eat," he says, "the eel or the octopus or the squid."[11] He means, "You shall not associate with people who are impious to the end, and are already condemned to death," as those sea-creatures are uniquely accursed that float in the deep, not swimming [on the surface] like the rest, but living in the mud at the bottom. (10.1–5)[12]

Although uncompromisingly supersessionist, the Letter of Barnabas places the highest value on the Jewish Scriptures, invoking Moses, David, and the prophets as authorities of immediate relevance to the Christian audience. As Robert Kraft suggested some time ago, Barnabas is probably making use of arguments already developed by Jewish interpreters.[13] The material in this section has nothing specifically Christian about it but could have come from a hellenized Jewish source.[14]

---

11. Apparently an expansion (by the source of the Letter of Barnabas?) of Lev 11:10.

12. Text in LCL 25:46-48, ed. Bart D. Ehrman; Origen seems to know the same interpretation of the fin- and scale-less sea creatures as bottom-feeders, literally and otherwise; see *Hom. in Lev.* 7.7.1.

13. Robert A. Kraft, "The Epistle of Barnabas: Its Quotations and Their Sources" (PhD diss., Harvard University, 1961).

14. James Carleton Paget, *The Epistle of Barnabas: Outlook and Background*, WUNT 2/64 (Tübingen: Mohr Siebeck, 1994), 151–54.

In all these cases of early Christian (and perhaps Jewish) zoomorphism, some effort is being made to negotiate sociability, as much as or more than diet, but with reference to the dietary laws.[15] This does not, however, mean that law itself is being flouted or invalidated. The Letter of Barnabas clearly seeks to defend a sort of authority for the Torah, at least as an authoritative text; Origen, too, assumes the value and authority of the Pentateuch, although he is clear (in texts we have not examined here) that its present meaning is not always literal. Acts itself, to which Origen responds, offers a new divine revelation from the unseen divinity, but its precise import regarding the previously given law needs to be considered further.

Eating Animals? Commensality

A zoomorphic approach as just described, where visionary animals turn out to be prosaic people, is at work in the literary frame of the Acts narrative, but this does not justify ignoring a different sense of the text. The story of Peter and Cornelius also works literally, by synecdoche, as well as allegorically and thus zoomorphically. That is, the story can also be read as really about animals, or their bodies, and when and whether to eat them, and in particular perhaps with whom to eat them. In this case the text is (also) about actual animals in relation to people, rather than just about animals as representations of people.

The significant emphasis in the Acts narrative on hospitality and commensality supports the idea that a concern for real practice, and for the treatment of animal bodies as food, accompanies and exemplifies the more typically emphasized Petrine zoomorphic allegory just discussed. Cornelius the Roman centurion we have seen presented as a pious and righteous householder—the archetype of that contested category of "God-fearers"[16]—and therefore perhaps a relatively safe dinner host for Peter anyway, as these things go. Numerous elements of the text mark a more specific hermeneutical territory concerning eating and commensality, however.

Cornelius has his vision concerning hospitality to Peter at the ninth hour, the time for the *cena*, or main meal.[17] The next day, when Peter has his vision, it is only the sixth hour but he is explicitly hungry, and food is being prepared as the trance takes place. Of its meal-related content, we

---

15. Jordan D. Rosenblum, *The Jewish Dietary Laws in the Ancient World* (New York: Cambridge University Press, 2016), 60–70.

16. For discussion and bibliography, see Pervo, *Acts*, 332–34.

17. Dennis E. Smith, *From Symposium to Eucharist: The Banquet in the Early Christian World* (Minneapolis: Fortress, 2003), 21.

are well enough aware. When the messengers from Cornelius come, the meal theme continues: Peter offers them not merely "lodging" (NRSV) but *xenia*, or "hospitality," despite the later claim about having avoided association with gentiles. The implication is that Peter and the envoys dined together. It may be notable that the event takes place in Peter's (current) household; ancient Jewish sources suggest that the source of food and of cooking may be at least as important as more general issues of the presence of non-Jews, when commensality was being negotiated.[18] Yet, when the company arrives in Caesarea, Cornelius has "called together" (or invited—*synkalesamenos*) relatives and friends, which is also hospitality language.[19] Peter's subsequent speech to this party makes a unique (to that point in Acts) reference to the fact that the resurrected Christ appeared "not to all the people, but to those who were chosen by God as witnesses, us, *who ate and drank with him* after his resurrection from the dead" (v. 41).

All this is to say that the question posed by the animals in Peter's vision may not be just about who is acceptable to God as persons but about something more like who is an acceptable guest or host; and even then, the mechanism by which the question is answered is not purely allegorical or zoomorphic. Differentiation in diet or lack thereof—of which animal flesh was a key marker—was not just a symbol of rules of sociability, but the most concrete aspect of them. You are what you eat, as well as with whom you eat it. Even in its zoomorphic aspect of course, the vision was not merely about the nature of persons, but about the propriety of association with persons, itself an issue that raises the very questions of food and eating presented as the literal meaning of the vision.

So the story of Peter and Cornelius does seem to emphasize more than a general principle of indifference to persons, such as that of allowing gentiles into the Christian community, which would be the obvious allegorical or zoomorphic reading of the vision in particular. Despite its frequent interpretation as a watershed for the proclamation of the gospel to the nations, the passage actually comes after a number of others in Luke-Acts where this question of gentile inclusion has been presented as settled (Luke 24:47; Acts 2:39; 3:25–26; 8:27–39). The issue remaining is the more practical one of the extension of this concrete human association of the believers past the potential boundaries of commensality.

This establishment of associational and commensal openness also implies some particular—but so far undefined—approach to the dietary laws of Judaism. The vision of animals could have provided an answer, but it remains frustratingly vague. While divine command had proclaimed

---

18. See Jordan D. Rosenblum, *Food and Identity in Early Rabbinic Judaism* (New York: Cambridge University Press, 2010), 36–45; and Rosenblum, *Jewish Dietary Laws in the Ancient World*, 70–71.

19. LSJ, s.v. "συγκᾰλέω."

a lack of distinction between animals, the explicit zoomorphic interpretation of the vision leaves the conclusions to be drawn about actual diet unclear. Peter might have dined with Cornelius, but are we to imagine him eating his new friend's *ficatum* (liver)?[20] I suspect not.

In fact this uncertainty belongs to the literary art of Acts; for in the following chapter (11:1–2) Peter is immediately challenged, not for breaking the dietary laws but for his liberal approach to commensality.[21] This is all the conclusion the author draws or wants to focus on at this point; the more specific question of what to eat becomes more prominent in the next passage we will consider, and its resolution is being left for that episode.

If the story of Peter and Cornelius is about commensality rather than about diet, we should certainly balk at the common but tendentious scholarly conclusion that the story of Peter and Cornelius is a "clear and blunt reversal of Jewish food laws."[22] This is to confuse (under all-too-typical supersessionist interpretive assumptions) the metaphorical frame of the vision with its ethical application. The explicit interpretation of the vision has nothing to do with food laws. While the two interpretive strands presented here, of allegory and zoomorphy, on the one hand, and synecdoche, on the other, do involve renegotiation of commensality and perhaps hence ultimately of diet itself, the question of diet is raised only implicitly, and not answered. The vision of animals may play with the idea of some reversal of Jewish dietary law, but this is part of the metaphor rather than the moral.

The Jerusalem Council

After Peter's encounter with Cornelius, the narrative of Acts pursues its theme of gentile inclusion and geographical expansion largely though the activity of the other great apostolic actor, Paul. Questions of identity also emerge in this narrative, not by divine revelation but through controversy, and in Acts 15 comes an account of a gathering in Jerusalem involving Paul and Barnabas along with Peter, James, and a group of "the apostles and elders" (15:6), resulting from a dispute about whether gentile converts to the Christian movement were required to be circumcised.[23]

---

20. Apicius's recipes for fig-fed pork are found in book 7 of *De re coquinaria*.
21. David M. Freidenreich, *Foreigners and Their Food: Constructing Otherness in Jewish, Christian, and Islamic Law* (Berkeley: University of California Press, 2011), 98.
22. Eldon Jay Epp, "Early Christian Attitudes toward 'Things Jewish' as Narrated by Textual Variants in Acts: A Case Study of the D-Textual Cluster," in *Bridging between Sister Religions: Studies of Jewish and Christian Scriptures Offered in Honor of Prof. John T. Townsend*, ed. Isaac Kalimi, Brill Reference Library of Judaism 51 (Leiden: Brill, 2016), 141–71, here 153.
23. I make no effort here to harmonize these accounts with the more contemporary

While this question of ceremonial observance is not dietary, Torah observance is still at issue.

Peter refers back to the story of Acts 10 in his speech to this meeting, saying "God who knows the heart testified to [the gentiles], giving the Holy Spirit, just as to us; he has made no distinction between them and us, cleansing [*katharisas*] their hearts by faith" (15:8–9). Again this indicates that the story was about association or inclusion, and only implicitly about diet and law. James, the leader of the Jerusalem community of followers of Jesus and apparently of the wider Christian network, responds with an initial decision framed personally: "I rule [*egō krinō*] that we should not trouble those from the nations who are turning to God, but we should write to them to abstain from the pollutions of idols and from immorality and from strangled things and from blood" (vv. 19–20). The legal framework or idiom of this judgment is clear enough, even if its content has some curiosities.[24]

In the aftermath of James's ruling, something like a more legislative element is added to the juridical. "Then it seemed good to the apostles and elders, with the whole church [*edoxen tois apostolois kai tois presbyterois syn holē tē ecclēsia*], to send chosen men from among them to Antioch with Paul and Barnabas" (v. 22). This is the first of three times that a formula related to Greek statutes is used in this passage. The form "it seemed good to x and y (and z)," where the entities are either different bodies with legislative power such as a senate and an assembly, or an executive leader and council, is typical of legal prescriptions; Josephus preserves one instance in a letter including a decree of Augustus confirming the rights of the Judeans (*edoxe moi kai tō emō symboliō*; A.J. 16.163).[25]

A few verses later, in the body of a formal letter or decree (which opens with, "The apostles and elders who are brothers, to those from among the nations in Antioch and Syria and Cilicia who are brothers, greetings" [v. 23]), the group refers back to the decision to send representatives, using the same legislative formula: "it seemed good to us with one accord [*edoxen hēmin genonemois homothymadon*] to send chosen men to you" (v. 25a). The crucial resolution for present purposes echoes James in presenting the question of animal diet as the primary answer to a problem that had ostensibly been about male circumcision:

> For it seemed good to the Holy Spirit and to us [*edoxen gar tō pneumati tō hagiō kai hēmin*] to impose on you no burden beyond these necessities: that

---

evidence from Paul in the Letter to the Galatians, which touches on some similar issues; see, e.g., Freidenreich, *Foreigners and Their Food*, 96–98; Pervo, *Acts*, 369 n.10.

24. Pervo, *Acts*, 376 n. 84; Conzelmann suggests that it is the proposal for what follows as the decree; see *Acts of the Apostles*, 117–18.

25. See also *IG* II/III³ 1, 1292 and elsewhere.

you abstain from idol offerings, from blood, from strangled things, and from immorality; if you observe these exclusions, you will do well. Farewell. (15:28–29)

This is obviously the most audacious of the set of *edoxe(n)* resolutions, for which the Holy Spirit's authority has now been added to the roster of the apostolic caucus, the divinity taking the equivalent place of Caesar or other executive, relative to the elders as a sort of council. Thus, while Conzelmann can suggest that the result here is "not to retain the law as valid," embodying again the curious enthusiasm of Christian interpreters to seek abrogation of the Mosaic law in these passages, it is obvious that the apostles are making law rather than flouting it. In fact, there is no hint here that the law is anything other than valid, at least for those already understood as subject to it, namely, Jews. In any case, the more obvious result may be to present the Christian elders as a sort of shadow Sanhedrin,[26] or else as an emergent polity, capable of making law independently.

In the most widely accepted and disseminated text of Acts, cited above—generally described as the Byzantine, or B text—the same four items are listed, in different order, both in James's initial proposal and in the legislative confirmation by the elders: idol offerings, blood, strangled things, and immorality (*porneia*). The complex textual tradition of Acts witnesses, however, to a measure of consternation or confusion about the dietary proscriptions. Although an original something like that quoted above seems likely, the manuscript tradition supplies an array of different versions of the prohibitions that ought, as Yi-Jan Lin puts it, to be seen as "neither authentic nor corrupt but useful for interpretation in many fields."[27] One more or less representative example of the alternative "Western" or D trajectory of 15:28–29—although in fact there are many variants—goes like this:

> For it seemed good to the Holy Spirit and to us to impose on you no burden beyond these necessities: that you abstain from idol offerings, from blood, from immorality, and whatever you do not want to happen to you, do not do to another; if you observe these exclusions, you will do well, continuing in the Holy Spirit. Farewell.[28]

It does seem likely that these differences involve an interpretive trajectory, from the relatively terse categories characteristic of the B text to more

---

26. Pervo, *Acts*, 369.
27. Epp, "Early Christian Attitudes toward 'Things Jewish,'" 141–71; Zachary G. Smith, "Reading the Past: Acts of the Apostles among Early Christians" (PhD diss., Yale University, 2019), 253–60; Yii-Jan Lin, "The Multivalence of the Ethiopian Eunuch and Acts 8:37," *TC: A Journal of Textual Criticism* 26 (2021): forthcoming.
28. See the apparatus to NA[28] for these readings.

expansive and general ethical ones in the D version, as represented in the appearance of the "golden rule" as well as the absence of strangulation.[29] The number of variants witnesses to scribal consternation as well as to theological and ethical preferences. The fourth-century commentator known as Ambrosiaster offers both a text-critical and an interpretive intervention on behalf of the (D) version they know, suggesting,

> Besides, these three commands given by the apostles and elders are not known in Roman law.... But some intellectual Greeks, who did not understand but knew about the prohibition on blood, amended what was written by adding a fourth commandment, about refraining from what was strangled. (*Ad Galatas* 2.2.4; CSEL 81.3:19)

Despite Ambrosiaster's rationalization of their preferred text as providing for lacunae in Roman law, the differences in the D tradition are far easier to understand as adaptations where the specific ritual prescriptions related to Levitical tradition were not well understood, than as original ideas reversed. The curiosity of strangling in particular is not convincingly accounted for as a later addition rather than as an early element sometimes removed.[30] The interpretive trajectory in any case blends textual transmission and reception; the references to idol offerings and to "blood" seem to have been applied by early readers to idolatry in general, and to shedding blood rather than eating it, respectively.[31] While the history of these two textual traditions is thus very amenable to a sort of ritual *versus* moral opposition, this dichotomy is simplistic.

The B-text requirements seem related to the stipulations made in Lev 17–18, regarding blood, carrion, and animal prey, which are applied to aliens. If this parallel is accepted, then the references to "strangulation" fit fairly well into an order that proscribes illicit slaughter (Lev 17:1–9), consuming blood and animals that die naturally or by the actions of other animals (17:10–17), and incest and forms of sexual deviance (18:6–23). The B form has largely to do with commensality and, more broadly, common life between Jews and others.[32] This tradition thus offers, or retains, a greater emphasis on animal bodies as such: idol offerings will typically have meant the meat of sacrifices; "blood" means the blood of animals (not of humans); and the prohibition of strangled animals is perhaps the most obvious—granted still rather oblique—way that an animal body is

---

29. Conzelmann, *Acts of the Apostles*, 118–19; Epp, "Early Christian Attitudes toward 'Things Jewish,'" 160.

30. There have been contrary voices; see Smith, "Reading the Past," 258; Conzelmann, *Acts of the Apostles*, 118 n.19.

31. Epp, "Early Christian Attitudes toward 'Things Jewish,'" 161.

32. Conzelmann, *Acts of the Apostles*, 118–19.

invoked in the text, since it refers not merely to a ritual process (sacrifice), or to blood as a by-product of slaughter, but to the act of killing itself.

The quest for some pure original account in the Acts text can be driven by misconceptions. The existence of different versions from a very early point is clear, and it is not possible to place the interpretive trajectory of the "Western," or D, tradition so far outside the thought world of Acts that it has to be seen as a sort of foreign contaminant to an early pure source. Likewise, the B text maintained relevance not (just) because it was older but because questions of proper eating as well as of relationships with Jewish traditions and communities hardly disappeared quickly or simply. Granted the benign retrospect with which the author of Acts attempts to convey a neat legal resolution of the questions of gentile Christian identity, relative to Jewish dietary and other law and practice, the issue was still relevant for centuries.

One more issue favors privileging the B tradition, broadly speaking, relative to the narrative art of Acts. We have seen scholarly claims that Acts 10 resolves questions of diet and law, when in reality it hardly does so at all. The encounter between Cornelius and Peter concerns association and commensality and merely elevates and defers questions of diet and ritual, rather than resolving them. It is in Acts 15 that the denouement of the legal and dietary tensions invoked in Acts 10 takes place, and the B text represents the more effective expression of that resolution. The issue of commensality had raised the question of how diet would be negotiated in the new Christian social formations; the author, from a later vantage point of course, seeks to resolve this drama with reference to the apostolic decree. While a version of the text-critical argument of *lectio difficilior* could be invoked against this suggestion—that is, an editor might conceivably have smoothed the Acts 15 text to reinforce the literary art—this is less plausible at the narrative level than at the more minute level of scribal conundrums. It is precisely by moving animal bodies from the realm of the metaphorical and implicit to the center of apostolic law making that the author resolves in the Jerusalem Council the tension left hanging in the story of Peter and Cornelius.

Conclusions

While the animals in the vision story of Acts 10 seem initially to be actors or agents in a story, they turn out to be virtual animals, mere signs of different things, of people in fact. Real animals make only an implied appearance there, under the guise of commensality, which may have meant consumption of animal flesh. For this reason among others, the scholarly overreading of that story as representing some sort of abrogation of the

Mosaic law is fanciful at best. In Acts 15, however, there are real if hypothetical animals on center stage, but they are always already dead, instrumentalized as foods just as clearly as the visionary animals in Acts 10 are made use of as ideas. People, however, are always the real point in these texts, and the animal body is either a sign of (as in Acts 10) or a mechanism for (as in Acts 15) the Christian movement's negotiation of its identity, relationships, and practices.

The peculiarly concrete focus on diet in Acts 15 (especially in the B text) helps explain the fuzziness of its treatment in Acts 10. The author has been narrating a grand design of Christian expansion and of the progress of the gentile mission; while in Acts 10 they perhaps use, as fodder for a narrative project about commensality, traditional material—the vision of animals—that was as well or better suited for presenting a sea change on food itself, this was not in keeping with the narrative design. Association, not consumption, was the key issue there. In Acts 15, however, the use of animal bodies, while still oblique, is actually the issue because it is more narratively or dramatically appropriate; it is here, not in chapter 10, that the questions of diet are addressed.

This is one of the reasons to read the B text as reflecting the concerns of an earlier narrator and community, despite the important hesitations that can be expressed toward text-critical assumptions about original purity. The narrative development, even if it lurches somewhat relative to its own sources, has some greater logic and clarity in this form. In both stories animals are used to negotiate aspects of law, yet, despite the invocation of a Sinai-like authority in Acts 10, and an almost imperial rescript in Acts 15, nothing about change to the Torah itself is mooted, let alone its abrogation. Peter's vision, as we saw, remained ambiguous regarding diet itself, while delivering a stentorian message about commensality. The Jerusalem Council event determines not the practices of Jewish believers but those of gentile converts.

Subsequent Christian interest in diet shows little influence from the specific considerations raised in Acts 15, at least in that early (B) form. In the next century or two, idol offerings were indeed significant for Christians, leading even to a widespread concern about the use of meat regardless of slaughter, and also about wine.[33] Discourse about these anxieties, however, shows little sign of drawing on this decree or any similar source. The other specific dietary exclusions of blood, and of meat from (otherwise) dead or strangled animals, slip largely into obscurity. This is a further indication that, whatever the real history of any Jerusalem Council may have been, in Acts 15 as well as Acts 10 we are dealing with the theo-

---

33. See Andrew B. McGowan, *Ascetic Eucharists: Food and Drink in Early Christian Ritual Meals*, Oxford Early Christian Studies (Oxford: Clarendon, 1999).

logically driven vision of the author, rather than with direct evidence for how most Christian communities actually negotiated these problems.

This encourages the conclusion already hinted at, namely, that the presentations of both real and imagined animal bodies in Acts are not so much about the consumption of animals as about the ways sociability was to be constructed, hospitality shared, and identity formed. This was important for the author and early readers of Acts because commensality was a defining characteristic of the earliest Christian communities, whose identity was created and expressed in the context of meals.[34] Acts presents these stories perhaps as a kind of "pseudarchaeography" of Christian commensality, as David P. Wright has put it,[35] wherein animals serve not only as a means of thinking about meals but also as the centerpiece of Christian negotiation of Jewish dietary law, which is often evoked in these passages, but in fact only obliquely addressed.

If animals are thus ciphers or signs in Acts, so too is the law. It may be that the communities who first read Acts were still negotiating issues of commensality and diet relative to Jewish norms in active ways. Yet the Acts narrative is not so much a direct answer to pressing questions of Torah observance as it is a picture of how issues of law and ethics are understood to have moved from one locus of authority to another. The text addresses dietary anxieties, not via casuistry or by any abrogation of the Mosaic law, but by presenting the emergent Christian community as a political and legal authority that, with the Holy Spirit as its imperial overseer, decrees for its people a new law, via a story inscribed on the bodies of animals.

---

34. Smith, *From Symposium to Eucharist*; Matthias Klinghardt, *Gemeinschaftsmahl und Mahlgemeinschaft: Soziologie und Liturgie frühchristlicher Mahlfeiern*, Texte und Arbeiten zum neutestamentlichen Zeitalter 13 (Tübingen: Francke, 1996).

35. David P. Wright, "Ritual Theory, Ritual Texts, and the Priestly-Holiness Writings of the Pentateuch," in *Social Theory and the Study of Israelite Religion: Essays in Retrospect and Prospect*, ed. Saul M. Olyan, RBS 71 (Atlanta: Society of Biblical Literature, 2012), 195–216, here 200.

The Role of Laws in Porphyry's Arguments against Animal Sacrifice

MIIRA TUOMINEN
University of Stockholm

In his treatise *On Abstinence from Killing Animals*, as Gillian Clark translates it,[1] more literally *On Abstinence from Animate Beings* (*Peri apochēs tōn empsychōn*; *De abstinentia ab esu animalium*), Porphyry (234/5–305 CE) argues that philosophers aiming at the highest goal in life, assimilation to god[2] to the extent that it is possible in bodily life, should refrain from inflicting injury on animate[3] beings that do not cause harm. On the one hand, this means that such philosophers will not eat meat or otherwise harm animals. Yet no absolute ban on killing animals is implied, since justice as restraint from inflicting injury is limited to harmless creatures (*Abst.* 3.26.9). Therefore, even the highest forms of justice allow self-defense and

---

1. Porphyry, *On Abstinence from Killing Animals*, trans. Gillian Clark, Ancient Commentators on Aristotle (London: Duckworth, 2000). Nauck's Greek text is available online in the *Thesaurus Linguae Graecae* (*TLG*), unfortunately with a different line numberins. See Augustus Nauck, *Porphyrii philosophi Platonici opuscula selecta* (Leipzig: Teubner, 1886; repr., Hildesheim: Olms, 1963). For the *TLG*, see http://stephanus.tlg.uci.edu/abridged.php. In this essay, I refer mainly to the sections found in translations and to Nauck's edition only for individual terms or expressions.

2. This formulation of the goal of human life became standard in late ancient Platonism. The theology of the Platonists was philosophical and pagan, so the god should not be identified with the Christian God. Late ancient Platonists also assumed a hierarchy of gods and discussed which god is the object of assimilation. For the present, the most important aspect of the assimilation is a hierarchy of virtue in which philosophers should aim at the greatest possible good that is, in essence, divine, not human.

3. I use *animate* to refer to creatures having life or soul (Greek *psychē*). Therefore, in addition to human beings and other animals, animate beings include plants. Although Porphyry at times uses the Greek *empsychon* ("animate") to refer to animals excluding plants, this does not necessarily mean that he would deny that plants have souls. The argument of the treatise concerns plants as well, as is seen in *On Abstinence* 2.12–13 and 3.26.12 (Clark); see also n. 8 below. Even Aristotle, who clearly attributes souls to plants, occasionally uses *empsychon* to refer to animals as opposed to plants; see, e.g., *Phys.* 7.2.244b8–245a1.

controlling harmful populations such as vermin.[4] On the other hand, philosophers striving to assimilate themselves to god also need to extend justice to plants, which means harming them as little as possible.

Porphyry's argument is addressed to a fellow Plotinian Firmus Castricius, and, although for a longer treatise by Porphyry it is exceptionally well preserved, it does not survive in its entirety. The manuscripts break off mid-sentence ("brutally" as Michel Patillon and Alain Segonds put it)[5] in book 4, chapter 22. It is reasonable to assume that not very much is missing from the treatise, but this of course cannot be determined with certainty.[6] While Porphyry's objections to arguments against vegetarianism are central in the treatise, I argue that the whole is not only about vegetarianism.[7] One reason for this is that, ideally, justice as restraint from causing harm is extended to plants, not only to human beings and nonhuman animals.[8] As indicated, Porphyry allows using plants for nourishment, provided that the harm caused to them is minimized: eating fruit that trees drop, taking only a part of the organism so that it can continue living, using agricultural products to whose existence and well-being human beings have contributed, and using animal products (milk and honey) in exchange for the care given to the animals that produce them (2.12–13; 3.26). Starving oneself to death is not an option for Porphyry. It

---

4. These qualifications are important for Porphyry, since some objections to abstinence he quotes in book 1 (see, e.g., 1.16) refer to the need of humans to defend themselves against threatening or otherwise dangerous animals as well as the need to restrict populations that (allegedly) increase uncontrollably. Porphyry also views those who live in areas where only animal nourishment is available as justified in eating meat.

5. Porphyre, *De l'abstinence*, vol. 3, ed. and trans. Michel Patillon and Alain Segonds, 2nd ed., Collection des universités de France (Paris: Belles lettres, 2003), 102 n. 358.

6. For an estimate as to how much is missing, see Patillon and Segonds (*De l'abstinence*, 3:LV–LVI).

7. Miira Tuominen, *Injuring No-One, Living with Justice: On Porphyry's Ethics of On Abstinence* (forthcoming). I disagree with those scholars who take the treatise to be merely about vegetarianism, e.g., G. Fay Edwards, "Reincarnation, Rationality and Temperance: Platonists on Not Eating Animals," in *Animals: A History*, ed. Peter Adamson and G. Fay Edwards, Oxford Philosophical Concepts (Oxford: Oxford University Press, 2018), 27–55; Daniel A. Dombrowski, "Porphyry on Vegetarianism: A Contemporary Philosophical Approach" *ANRW* 2.36.2 (1987): 774–91; Catherine Osborne, "Ancient Vegetarianism," in *Food in Antiquity*, ed. John Wilkins, David Harvey, and Mike Dobson (Exeter: University of Exeter Press, 1995), 214–24; Giuseppe Girgenti, "Porfirio nel vegetarianesimo antico," *Bollettino Filosofico: Dipartimento di Filosofia dell'Università della Calabria* 17 (2001): 75–84.

8. Clark claims that Porphyry, by the term *animate creatures* (*ta empsycha*) in the title of his work, refers only to animals; see Gillian Clark, "Fattening the Soul: Christian Asceticism and Porphyry on Abstinence," *Ascetica, Gnostica, Liturgica, Orientalia: Papers Presented at the Thirteenth International Conference on Patristic Studies Held in Oxford 1999*, ed. Maurice Wiles, Edward Yarnold, and Paul M. Parvis, StPatr 35 (Leuven: Peeters, 2001), 41–51. Sections 2.13 (quoted from Theophrastus) and 3.26.12 (describing Porphyry's own position), however, make it clear that Porphyry includes plants in the scope of justice.

would perhaps be unjust to oneself[9] and could not produce the soul's liberation from the body (1.38.2; 2.47.1 [Clark]).

We do not know very much about Porphyry's life. He was a native of Tyre in Phoenicia—his name was Malchus ("king") in the language of his family—and he studied in Athens before moving to Rome.[10] In his own words, he arrived in Rome when he was thirty years old and met Plotinus (204/5–270 CE), his teacher there (*Life of Plotinus* 4.8–13). Porphyry joined Plotinus's philosophical circle and remained a member until an incident in 267/268 related in *Life of Plotinus* (ch. 11). When living in Rome, Porphyry developed a serious melancholy and even contemplated taking his own life. Plotinus intervened and instructed Porphyry to leave Rome. Porphyry did and went to Lilybaeum in Sicily (today's Marsala). This seems to have cured the melancholy, since Porphyry lived more than thirty years after the episode. As a result of being in Sicily, however, he was prevented from being with Plotinus during his last years. Scholars often date *On Abstinence* to the Sicilian period, but the dating, although probable, cannot be confirmed with certainty.[11] Neither do we know where Porphyry went after his sojourn in Sicily.

It is perhaps from Lilybaeum (Marsala) that Porphyry writes to his friend Firmus, who, according to Porphyry's informants, had resumed the habit of eating meat (1.1.1). Instead of emotional reproach, Porphyry decides that he must persuade his friend by reason, refuting the objections to abstinence that have been presented (1.1.3) and that he quotes in book 1. The longest discussion is against the Stoics in book 3 on the point about animal rationality. Porphyry argues that the Stoics do not have sufficient grounds for excluding animals from the scope of justice because they do not succeed in showing that animals are not rational. Traditionally, scholars have taken Porphyry to subscribe to the claim that animals belong to the scope of justice (i.e., human beings have to act with justice toward animals) because, contrary to what the Stoics claim, animals are rational. This traditional view, however, has been challenged on the grounds that Porphyry's argument in book 3 is dialectical; that is, the aim is to show that, *on the basis of their notion of rationality*, the Stoics should extend it to nonhuman animals.[12] I agree that Porphyry's objective in book 3 is mainly

---

9. This perhaps follows from the claim that abstinence is not unjust toward oneself (3.26.13). This seems to imply that starving oneself to death is.

10. For Porphyry's life, see, e.g., Andrew Smith, "Porphyrian Studies since 1913," *ANRW* 2.36.2 (1987): 717–73, here 719–22; see also Porphyre, *De l'abstinence*, vol. 1, 2nd ed., ed. and trans. Jean Bouffartigue and Michel Patillon (Paris: Belles lettres, 2003), xi–xii; Aron P. Johnson, *Religion and Identity in Porphyry of Tyre: The Limits of Hellenism in Late Antiquity*, Greek Culture in the Roman World (Cambridge: Cambridge University Press, 2013), 15–21.

11. See, e.g., Smith, "Porphyrian Studies," 721 n. 18.

12. See G. Fay Edwards, "Irrational Animals in Porphyry's Logical Works: A Problem for the Consensus Interpretation of *On Abstinence*," *Phronesis* 59 (2014): 22–43; Edwards, "The

to refute the Stoics and, more important, that his grounds for arguing for animal justice are not dependent on the question of animal rationality.

Some scholars have also argued that it is not rationality but sentience that is the relevant criterion for justice for Porphyry.[13] However, I do not think this can be right either, since it would leave the inclusion of plants in the scope of justice inexplicable. Rather, in the overall argument of *On Abstinence*, the argument about animal sentience and the capacity of animals to feel pain (3.19.2, quoted or adapted from Plutarch)[14] is directed at an objection (mentioned in 1.18), that since we need to eat plants anyway, we are justified in using animals for nourishment as well. In Porphyry's overall argument, animal sentience blocks this objection by pointing out that animals differ from plants exactly because of their capacity to feel pain. Therefore, the justification of considerate use of plants does not carry over to killing, eating, or otherwise harming animals. Yet the capacity to feel pain, or sentience more generally, is not the criterion for justice because, as mentioned, plants must be included as well, and they are not sentient.

Instead of animal sentience or rationality, Porphyry builds on an argument quoted from Aristotle's junior colleague Theophrastus (ca. 371–287 BCE)[15] in book 2, according to which it is intrinsically unjust to harm other creatures and depriving a living creature of its life causes great harm to it (2.12.3–4). It is analogous to stealing but an even greater wrong because life is a greater good than external possessions that one might

---

Purpose of Porphyry's Rational Animals: A Dialectical Attack on the Stoics," in *Aristotle Re-Interpreted: New Findings on Seven Hundred Years of Ancient Commentators*, ed. Richard Sorabji, Ancient Commentators on Aristotle (New York: Bloomsbury Academic, 2016), 263–90. In a forthcoming article, "Porphyry on Justice towards Animals: Are Animals Rational and Does It Matter for Justice?" Riin Sirkel challenges Edwards's view about the nature of Porphyry's argument.

13. Dombrowski, "Porphyry on Vegetarianism" and Girgenti, "Porfirio nel vegetarianismo," although he also points to "a sober life-style" and animal rationality. Richard Sorabji counts animals' capacity to feel pain as among the similarities between human beings and animals on the basis of which he takes Porphyry as arguing for animal justice (*Animal Minds and Human Morals: The Origins of the Western Debate*, Cornell Studies in Classical Philology 54 (Ithaca, NY: Cornell University Press, 1993), 184. However, he does not articulate which criterion, if any, he thinks is decisive.

14. In this passage, it is argued that plants cannot be harmed. This, however, reflects Plutarch's view and not that of Porphyry, who follows Theophrastus (2.12–13) in claiming that plants are harmed by stealing their parts or taking their lives and that, ideally, a just person should minimize harming plants by using fruit dropping from trees or dead plants (3.26.12). See also 3.27.2 for the inclusion of plants in justice.

15. I talk about Theophrastus when referring to the passages that Porphyry says he has quoted from Theophrastus's *On piety*; see Porphyre, *De l'abstinence*, vol. 2, 2nd ed., ed. and trans. Jean Bouffartigue and Michel Patillon (Paris: Belles lettres, 2003). See their table (on p. 29) showing how different scholars have identified the quotations. I will not address the question of whether the quotations are genuine.

steal from another person (2.12.4). In fact, it follows from this that, contrary to much of the modern discussion of the moral status of animals, Porphyry is not committed to any version of the argument of desert, that is, the claim that animals only "deserve" moral consideration if they can be shown to have a certain relevant feature (such as rationality, sentience, linguistic capacities, personhood, ritual practices, or tool use) that they share with human beings. In fact, it seems that, although such a great harm that is constituted by taking lives is possible only for living creatures, it does not seem that an ideally just person would, according to Porphyry, cause harm to inanimate creatures either; he once notes that such people restrain themselves from harming anything whatsoever (3.26.10). Although it is possible that this refers only to all animate things in the context (3.26.9), the extension of justice to plants shows that the criterion is none of the features typically used in arguments based on the assumption of desert.

The Goals and Structure of This Essay

An important part of *On Abstinence* consists in arguments to the effect that piety and reverence for gods (*eusebeia, hosiotēs*) do not require animal sacrifice but rather preclude it. References to laws and conventions (Greek *nomos*) occur in several different contexts within the argument, and, in this essay, I consider how the notions function in those arguments. One important claim quoted from Theophrastus is that it is not lawful to sacrifice animals (cf. *nomimos* in 2.12.2). The claim is also connected to other statements in book 2 according to which animal sacrifice is not permissible[16] or that one ought not[17] sacrifice animals. However, Porphyry also makes the much weaker claim that the laws of his city or state do not require animal sacrifice and notes that this makes it possible for philosophers to follow justice in accordance with the laws of the city, respecting the gods with offerings that are appropriate for the gods (2.33.1). Moreover, later on he also claims that, even if a city engages in animal sacrifice, "this has nothing to do with us" (2.43.2), that is, us as philosophers aiming at the assimilation to god.

Therefore, there seems to be some tension or inconsistency in Porphyry's claims about the laws. If they preclude animal sacrifice, why does he also make the weaker claim that they do not require it? Moreover, is he saying that philosophers should aim at changing laws or not? If he is, why

---

16. The Greek expression is *prosēkein* and its negation, *ou prosēkein*; see, e.g., 2.2.2 (= 133.11 Nauck); 2.12.4 (= 143.3 Nauck).

17. Indicated by the Greek *dein* ("ought") and *mē dein* ("ought not"); see, e.g., 2.4.1–2 (= 134.4–10 Nauck); 2.44.1 (= 173.12 Nauck).

does he say at the opening of 2.33 that he is not doing so himself? I argue below that Porphyry's view is consistent, although his rhetorical moves do not seem so. For the purposes of the argument, I have divided Porphyry's references to laws and conventions into the following seven groups:

1. Porphyry's own arguments for the claim that ancestral laws or customs forbid eating meat and/or sacrificing and harming animals (e.g., 1.2.3).

2. Objections to abstinence that maintain, to the contrary, that laws protect human communities against animals (1.5.3). Therefore, according to the objection, we are entitled to harm animals because they are not able to obey laws.

3. Porphyry's arguments for abstinence that distinguish between (actual written) laws and laws of nature, divine laws or what virtue ordains (e.g., 1.28.4). The claim is that, even if existing laws do not forbid harming animals, this does not entail that natural/divine law or (supreme) virtue would not do so.

4. Porphyry's arguments for abstinence on the basis of the claim that although laws allow punishing wrongdoers, this does not justify killing, eating, or otherwise injuring harmless animals (2.2.1).

5. An argument for abstinence on the basis of the claim that, while human language functions on the basis of human conventions, animal language is based on animal conventions (*nomoi*) (3.3.3). Therefore, from the fact that animal communication does not follow human linguistic conventions one cannot deduce that animals have no language.

6. Porphyry's claim that existing laws do not require animal sacrifice, that is, that it is possible for philosophers to refrain from the practice without being sanctioned (2.33.1).

7. The puzzling combination of Porphyry's declaration that he does not aim at abolishing any laws (2.33.1) with the note that philosophers should not conform to any bad customs or laws but aim at changing them (2.61.6).

In the following, I consider Porphyry's statements about laws and conventions falling into these groups. The main claim I want to make is that we can best understand Porphyry's different references to laws in the light of the distinction between actual written laws and divine laws or laws of nature (3). A corollary of this is that, when Porphyry is claiming that laws prohibit animal sacrifice, he is making a normative rather than descriptive claim: he is mainly concerned not with whether some existing laws ordain animal sacrifice but, rather, with outlining what he takes to be morally correct ritual practice.

I will not discuss group (5) in this context, although it is rather striking. The claim that animal languages are governed by animal conventions (*nomoi*) rather than human ones occurs in Porphyry's arguments against the Stoics on animal rationality. The point is that, although animal communication is not governed by linguistic conventions similar to those of human communication,[18] it does not mean that animals do not have "a language," that is, a significant system of communication, of their own. From Porphyry's point of view, the fact that animals have expressive speech even though it is not a human language, shows that they have a share in reason, contrary to what the Stoics claim.

Before considering the groups of claims about laws and conventions, we need to recognize that assessing whether Porphyry's claim that laws of his city or state do not require animal sacrifice is empirically true is complicated by the fact that we do not know to which city or state he is referring. Since his time in Rome with Plotinus was so important and since *On Abstinence* was perhaps written in Sicily right after that time, it is likely that he is speaking about Rome. As mentioned, however, we do not know where Porphyry went from Sicily, and therefore it is not impossible that he means some other city's laws. On the island of Cos, for instance, laws had imposed an obligation on citizens to sacrifice animals,[19] and it has also been argued that animal sacrifice was still central in Rome during Porphyry's time, although wine was important as well, an offering "equivalent to blood."[20] Therefore, assuming that Porphyry is talking about the laws of Rome, he might be right that one could have been able to avoid animal sacrifice without sanctions. However, this has been the subject of

---

18. This claim might not hit the mark with the Stoics because their conception of human language is not a conventionalist one. For an analysis of name giving and nature in Stoicism, see James Allen, "The Stoics on the Origin of Language and the Foundations of Etymology," in *Language and Learning: Philosophy of Language in the Hellenistic Era; Proceedings of the Ninth Symposium Hellenisticum*, ed. Dorothea Frede and Brad Inwood (Cambridge: Cambridge University Press, 2005), 14–35.

19. Robert Parker and Dirk Obbink, "Aus der Arbeit der *Inscriptiones Graecae* IV: Sales of Priesthoods on Cos I," *Chiron* 30 (2000): 415–49, here 427–29; see also Daniel C. Ullucci, *The Christian Rejection of Animal Sacrifice* (New York: Oxford University Press, 2011). Marco Zambon simply claims that the cult of Porphyry's day was sanguineous and he knew it; see Alberto Camplani and Marco Zambon, "Il sacrifice come problema in alcune correnti filosofiche di età imperiale," *Annali di storia dell'esegesi* 19 (2002): 59–99, here 72.

20. John Scheid, "Roman Animal Sacrifice and the System of Being," in *Greek and Roman Animal Sacrifice: Ancient Victims, Modern Observers*, ed. Christopher Faraone and F. S. Naiden (Cambridge: Cambridge University Press, 2012), 84–95, here 94; Francesca Prescendi, *Décrire et comprendre le sacrifice: Les réflexions des Romains sur leur propre religion à partir de la littérature antiquaire*, Potsdamer altertumswissenschaftliche Beiträge 19 (Stuttgart: F. Steiner, 2007), 88–90. For wine's function of generating social hierarchies, see Georges Dumézil, "Vin et souveraineté: Vinalia," in *Fêtes romaines d'été et d'automne suive de Dix questions romaines*, Bibliothèque des sciences humaines (Paris: Gallimard, 1975), 87–97; he calls it "the drink of sovereignty"; see also Prescendi, *Décrire et comprendre*, 90–93.

controversy as well, since some scholars have argued that a decree by Decius in 249 CE ordered the practice of animal sacrifice.[21] In short, because Porphyry's argument is normative—one should not sacrifice animals and the laws should not require it—rather than empirical—these are the existent laws with respect to animal sacrifice—and since we do not quite know which city to consider, I will not focus on the question of the truth of the empirical claim.

Ancestral Customs and Laws

With respect to the arguments of group (1), Porphyry notes that he does not believe that his friend Firmus would have abandoned "the ancestral laws of the philosophy" to which the two had been committed (1.2.3). The implication is that those ancestral laws ordain abstinence from harming animals and that Firmus had rejected them. Porphyry adds that he does not think this has happened because of excessive and erroneous love of pleasure but rather through some error of reason that he is eager to correct. It is not specified in the context what those ancestral laws of philosophy are. Much later in the treatise, in book 4, Porphyry mentions some examples of Attican lawgivers, for example, Triptolemus, who had forbidden harming animals:

> Xenokrates the philosopher says three ... [of Triptolemus' laws] are still in force at Eleusis: respect parents, honour the gods with crops, do not harm animals. (4.22.2 [Clark])

Another case is found where the manuscripts break off and the surviving text of *On Abstinence* ends. A law of Drakon is said to ordain people to honor the gods and heroes with

> ... good words, first-fruits of crops, and annual offerings of cakes. The law required the divine to be honoured with first-fruits of those crops that people use, and with cakes.... (4.22.7 [Clark])

---

21. For the discussion, see J. B. Rives, "The Decree of Decius and the Religion of Empire," *JRS* 89 (1999): 135–54. In the fourth century, the Christian emperors issued decrees against public animal sacrifice, but there were ways to keep private animal sacrifices alive, about which see Ullucci, *Christian Rejection of Animal Sacrifice*, 51 n. 96. For recent accounts, see Michele Renee Salzman, "The End of Public Sacrifice," in *Ancient Mediterranean Sacrifice*, ed. Jennifer Wright Knust and Zsuzsanna Varhelyi (Oxford: Oxford University Press, 2011), 167–87; Benedikt Eckhardt, "'Bloodless Sacrifice': A Note on Greek Cultic Language in the Imperial Era," *GRBS* 54 (2014): 255–73. Therefore, even though Decius's decree from 249 CE ordered animal sacrifice, there might have been ways around it.

Since the text ends exactly here, we do not know how Porphyry comments on the claim or how the list continues. It must be noted, however, that Porphyry's framing of the law is rather tendentious. In the quoted passage, the instructions apply to private rituals, while the public offerings must be made "following ancestral custom" (4.22.7). It is not unlikely that the original formulation referred, by ancestral customs, to animal sacrifice, while it is Porphyry (following Theophrastus's history of humanity quoted in 2.5–6) who claims that according to such ancestral customs animal sacrifice is forbidden.[22]

The objection to abstinence is precisely that ancestral laws justify human practices of killing, eating, sacrificing, and otherwise harming nonhuman animals. In Hesiod's words, while justice does not exist among nonhuman animals, Zeus gave it to human beings.

> To fish, to beasts, to winged birds granted
> to eat each other, for there is no justice among them;
> To human beings [Zeus] gave justice. (1.5.3 [Clark])

The point of the objection is that there is no justice or injustice in human action with animals, and the same claim is made also in Epicurean objections that Porphyry quotes in book 1 (chs. 7–12). Those objections state, first, that ancient lawgivers wanted to protect the human community against other animals and that such protection requires limiting excessive populations and defense against attacks (1.7–9, 11). Second, the reason why justice does not apply to nonhuman animals is, according to the Epicurean Hermarchus (1.12),[23] that animals cannot make agreements with us because they "are not receptive of reason" (1.12.6); that is, they do not come to have rational capacities that are required for making agreements.

Even though Porphyry's claim that ancestral laws and customs forbid animal sacrifice is empirically wrong—Greek ritual traditions required animal sacrifice—his responses to the objection make sense. He points out that the need to protect human communities against the attacks of harmful animals does not entail that tame and harmless animals could justifiably be killed (Porphyry's claim in group 4 distinguished on p. 126 above). Moreover, Porphyry himself also restricts the requirement of restraint from harming animate creatures to the harmless ones. This means that he allows self-defense and protection of human communities, and this makes his position resistant to the objection. Therefore, as mentioned, his view

---

22. See also 2.18.3: "Hesiod was right to say in praise of the rule of ancient sacrifices: For sacrifice from the city, the ancient law is the best."

23. For Hermarchus, see Diogenes Laertius, *Lives of Eminent Philosophers* (10.16–21); Paul Vander Waerdt, "Hermarchus and the Epicurean Genealogy of Morals," *TAPA* 118 (1988): 87–106.

differs from those of today's arguments that attribute intrinsic value to life and thus cannot allow restriction of harmful populations.[24]

Human and Divine Laws

As I indicated earlier, a crucial move that Porphyry makes in his arguments concerning laws and customs with respect to animal sacrifice is the positing of a distinction between actual written laws in cities and states and divine laws or laws of nature that he identifies with his own view about what is morally correct (3). He makes it very clear that the divine or natural laws are superior to the written ones. In book 1, for example, Porphyry compares different lives and describes one of them as being governed by laws that ordinary people would choose. By "ordinary people" he means those whose conception of what is good is related to external things and bodily concerns. He asks, rhetorically:

> [W]hy would anyone cite their law to subvert a way of life which is superior to every written law designed for the many, because it aims at the unwritten, divine law? (1.28.4 [Clark])

The claim is that the unwritten divine law is superior to written laws of cities. The latter are viewed as expressing the conceptions of good and bad characteristic of most people, who take as good external things like health and wealth, fame and status, or things that satisfy desires for food, drink, and sexual pleasure. To this Porphyry contrasts a life dictated by unwritten, divine laws, that is, what is truly good.[25] A curious point that he makes in this context is that even written laws "aim at" the divine ones. It does not seem that such "aiming" could mean that written laws are made with an eye to divine laws, the life of the intellect, and what is truly good, since Porphyry later notes that such a life is not what written laws ordain. Rather, the claim probably is that written laws "aim at" a good because they aim at restricting people's actions and preventing them from harming each other. In this sense they have a likeness to the real good or approximate it. For instance, the justice of restraining oneself from harming other human beings can be seen as similar to or perhaps even approxi-

---

24. For the criticism of those modern views along these lines, see Elizabeth Anderson, "Animal Rights and the Values of Non-Human Life," in *Animal Rights: Current Debates and New Directions*, ed. Cass R. Sunstein and Martha C. Nussbaum (New York: Oxford University Press, 2004), 277–98.

25. See also the contrast Porphyry makes between the laws of the body and the laws of the intellect in 1.56.4.

mating what Porphyry takes the divine law to prescribe, that is, to restrain oneself from harming harmless living creatures across the board.

In a similar manner, he also exclaims, if only the legislators were acting in accordance with the intellect, that is, with true principles concerning the good. Acting like this, they would make people in general obey such principles also with respect to food (1.28.3). Therefore, although, strictly speaking, Porphyry's arguments are directed only at philosophers aiming at the greatest possible assimilation to god (2.3.1)—and he seems to assume that his friend Firmus wants to be one—he would be quite happy if there were laws for everyone that would make them follow the requirements of real justice, that is, minimizing the harm caused to living creatures. He does not argue for abstinence for all in the treatise—his argument would probably not convince people who are not already committed to a life of philosophy. However, the passage shows that he would be content if people were made to abstain through actual legislation.

On the whole, his argument is not based on such a scenario but, rather, on a distinction between what philosophers aiming at the greatest possible virtue are required to do as opposed to what ordinary laws prescribe. He likens the philosophers' moral maxims (of which the most important one in the treatise is not to inflict injury on harmless living creatures) to the kinds of laws that regulate the actions of priests in existing societies as opposed to laws that are for everyone (2.3.1). Consequently, there are many things that the law allows to "the many,"[26] that is, people in general, but not to philosophers (4.18.7). The point of course is not to say that there actually are different written laws for philosophers. Rather, philosophers must follow the dictates of the divine law (what is morally right). For instance:

> The law has not forbidden people to spend their time in wine-bars, but nevertheless that is reprehensible in a decent person. (4.18.8 [Clark's translation slightly modified])

Similarly, Porphyry points out in book 4 that, although written laws of cities prohibit some wrongful actions, they do not ordain virtue for everyone. Importantly, there is not even a law requiring the sages and priests to abstain from eating meat; rather, the law left them autonomous (Greek *autonomos*), considering them to be superior to itself (4.18.5). As sitting in bars is allowed but not in accordance with virtue, visiting a courtesan is not prohibited for the many (4.18.8),[27] but it would be shameful for a virtuous person. In general, there are many things that the laws allow for the

---

26. In addition to the classical *hoi polloi* for "the many," a Hellenistic word *chydaios* is also used here; see references in Patillon and Segonds, *De l'abstinence*, 3:31 n. 276.

27. He even mentions a tax collected from courtesans, apparently implying that, if

many, while a moderate person (4.18.8),[28] a philosopher or a citizen of a well-organized city (4.18.7 = 260.2–3 Nauck) sees those things as shameful and contrary to virtue.

Although at first sight the last-mentioned remark seems just like the earlier ones—virtue requires different actions from those who follow what is truly good and those whose action is regulated by written laws—it makes a different, rather remarkable claim. One might think that to be a good citizen it is quite enough to follow the laws of one's city. Here, however, Porphyry requires more: the citizen of a well-organized city needs to follow virtue, preventing him or her from actions that would be permissible by the written laws but that contradict virtue, for example, visiting courtesans and sitting in cabarets. Yet there is no indication that abstinence from harming animals and plants (to the extent it is possible) would be required from the moderate person and the good citizen. That seems to be a requirement that holds only for philosophers aiming at the greatest possible virtue.

All in all, the seeming inconsistency between what Porphyry says about the law—namely, that, on the one hand, it precludes animal sacrifice and, on the other hand, it does not require it (the weaker claim)—can be solved by reference to the distinction between the two senses in which he talks about the laws. In one sense, he means the written laws of existing cities, and the weaker sense applies to such laws. The second meaning, divine laws, the laws of nature,[29] divine announcements,[30] or the laws of intellect, refers to what Porphyry takes to be correct morality, what is truly good. Morality in this sense is, in his scheme of things, superior to written laws, and it is the divine law—what is truly good and just—that is violated by sacrificing living creatures.[31] Therefore, his crucial point is that morality is superior to legislation, and, notwithstanding what the written law says about it, animal sacrifice is against what is truly good, the law of nature or divine law. This is also consistent with the claim he makes in

---

something is taxed, it must be legal. On the tax, see Clark, *On Abstinence*, 190 n. 655; Patillon and Segonds, *De l'abstinence*, 3:90–91 n. 278.

28. Clark translates the Greek *metriois andrasi* (260.11 Nauck) ("moderate men") as "decent men."

29. Porphyry calls them literally "laws of nature" (*physeōs nomoi*, 2.61.7 = 186.7 Nauck), and the reference to natural law recurs later in book 4 (*ho nomos physikos* in 4.15.2 = 252.12 Nauck). For natural laws in Porphyry, see also *Letter to Marcella* (25.12–26.1), in Porphyrios, Πρὸς Μαρκέλλαν, ed. Walter Pötscher, Philosophia antiqua 15 (Leiden: Brill, 1969).

30. The Greek for this is *theia parangelia* (2.61.7 = 186.7–8 Nauck).

31. Porphyry refers in passing to the Plotinian notion of cosmic justice (2.45.3), which maintains everything at its place and allots proper punishment for those who violate it. For cosmic justice in Plotinus, see *Enn.* 2.3.8.2–5; Paul Kalligas, *The Enneads of Plotinus: A Commentary*, trans. by Elizabeth Key Fowden and Nicolas Pilavachi (Princeton: Princeton University Press, 2014), 1:293 as a note on *Enn.* 2.3.8.1–9; Bouffartigue and Patillon, *De l'abstinence*, 2:47.

passing that he would hope that legislators would ordain laws in accordance with the intellect and also make laws about food in this manner. The point is of course that he would like laws to forbid using animals for nourishment, in which case people who are not willing to abstain from eating meat because of virtue would do so in order to follow the laws of their city.

Finally, although Porphyry would prefer laws against using animals for nourishment, he does not seem to think that such a scenario is likely to be realized. More important, the way in which he wants the divine laws (what really is just and good) to be followed in action is not by people being "forced" by the law but rather by making autonomous choices, as philosophers, whom he compares to priests of the god above all, do. It is as if they set the divine law as the moral code for themselves—a thought that is surprisingly modern. In the modern context, a similar claim is familiar from Kantian deontology, that is, a moral theory operating on the notion of duties or obligations. It is important to note, however, that this notion—the notion of duty—is not found in Porphyry's analysis of how the philosophers autonomously choose to act in accordance with the divine law and the nature of justice. The notion of duty is not easily reconciled with Porphyry's framework, in which there are higher and higher levels of virtue, not required by ordinary morality (for citizens of a well-organized city) but required only of those philosophers who strive for assimilation to god to the maximal degree. Consequently, another important difference between Porphyry's analysis and Kantian deontology is that, for Porphyry, what he takes the divine law to instruct one to do is not necessarily generalizable. While the highest requirements of justice apply to philosophers aiming at assimilation to god to the greatest possible degree, for others—and even for other philosophers—those requirements do not apply.

Abolishing or Changing Laws?

Let me now move to the final puzzle related to Porphyry's view of existing laws and philosophers' relation to them. After his extended quotations from Theophrastus in book 2, he makes an emphatic entrance to the discussion in chapter 33 with the first-person pronoun *I* (*egō*), saying that he is not abolishing any laws because it is not his task to talk about political matters or the constitution (*politeia*, 2.33.1 = 162.22 Nauck). Combined with the claim that the laws of his city do not require animal sacrifice and that one is thus allowed to follow the truly good and the just without breaking these laws, Porphyry gives one the impression that he is willing to accept the laws of his city and is not interested in reforming them. He also says later, however, that if there are bad customs or laws, philosophers should not let themselves be changed by them but rather should change those laws or customs (2.61.6). What, then, is he saying about existing laws? Should one accept them or aim at changing them?

The scholarly debate related to this question has focused on whether Porphyry accepts traditional rituals or not. Gillian Clark, for instance, has argued that Porphyry rejects the traditional cult in *On Abstinence* and therefore holds a different view from the one he puts forward in his *Letter to Marcella* 18.[32] Others, by contrast, have argued that Porphyry does not need to question the civic cult.[33] In my view, the question of whether he rejects the traditional cult is too straightforward as such and needs to be nuanced. In a nutshell, a crucial point is whether the laws of one's city sanction restraint from animal sacrifice. If they do not, then one can make sacrifices in accordance with the laws of the city (with some further specifications that I will clarify below). If they do, one should aim at changing those laws and not accept them. Therefore, to the extent that Porphyry claims that the laws of his own city do not require animal sacrifice, he himself does not need to aim at abolishing the laws of his city. This can be reconciled with his claim that philosophers should not concede to bad customs by noting that he also makes the following conditional claim: *if* the laws of a particular city require animal sacrifice (and sanction refraining from it), philosophers must not take part in such rituals but rather aim at changing those laws. Therefore, my claim is that, when we make these distinctions, there is no contradiction or ambiguity in Porphyry's position about how one should act with respect to existing laws.

In order to make this claim more concrete, let us briefly consider the ritual practices that Porphyry recommends for philosophers aiming at maximal assimilation to god. In order to discuss the guidelines for philosophical ritual practices, we need to consider a distinction Porphyry makes between different kinds of divinities.[34] In fact, he gives three ver-

---

32. Gillian Clark, "Philosophic Lives and the Philosophic Life: Porphyry and Iamblichus," in *Greek Biography and Panegyric in Late Antiquity*, ed. Tomas Hägg and Philip Rousseau, Transformation of the Classical Heritage 31 (Berkeley: University of California Press, 2000), 29–51, here 41.

33. Andrei Timotin, *La démonologie platonicienne: Histoire de la notion de daimōn de Platon aux derniers néoplatoniciens*, Philosophia antiqua 128 (Leiden: Brill, 2019), 210 n. 147, with reference to Camplani and Zambon, "Il sacrifice come problema," 70–74. According to Timotin, there is no tension or contradiction when we recognize Porphyry's distinction between beneficent and maleficent *daimones*, that is, demigods. In brief, animal sacrifice will strengthen maleficent *daimones*, while modest offerings of barley, flowers, oil, and wine can be made to the beneficent *daimones*. I will return to the distinction in the body of the text, and, while it is certainly important, I will argue that it is not sufficient to explain Porphyry's guidelines for philosophical ritual practices.

34. Some scholars have even called Porphyry's exposition of divinities "a system"; see Luc Brisson, "What Is a *daimon* for Porphyry?," in *Neoplatonic Demons and Angels*, ed. Luc

sions of the guidelines that are not quite the same, but the differences of detail need not concern us for the moment. One important distinction is the one made between divinities proper and demigods, *daimones* (2.38-43). Of divinities, we need to distinguish between the god above all (*theos epi pasin*) and its offspring (2.34) among which there are further distinctions. The most important point is that, according to Porphyry, to divinities proper only immaterial offerings are appropriate. This means that not even the modest offerings that Theophrastus recommends instead of the "blooded ones," that is, barley, flowers, and libations, should be made to divinities proper. They have their role as offerings to the beneficent demigods (*daimones*) but are not appropriate to full gods. As to divinities properly speaking, the god above all is appropriately respected only through "offerings" of pure silence[35] and pure thoughts that are not mixed with the affections of the soul (2.34.2), that is, emotions and perceptions. I am using "offering" in quotation marks because such offerings differ from the traditional ones. While animal sacrifice and even flowers require the destruction of the "victim,"[36] immaterial offerings of pure thoughts and silence do not do so. By contrast, it could be argued that pure thoughts and silence are increased when "offered" to god. The question of course is what such offering can mean.

It seems to me that the pure thoughts Porphyry is talking about can be clarified with reference to Plotinus's distinction between two kinds of thoughts in the intellect (*Enn.* 6.9.[9].3.33–39). All of the intellect's thoughts (or acts of knowing or understanding) are directly about intelligible objects (roughly Platonic Forms) and not about their perceptible images or copies and, thus, are pure in the sense of not being mixed with perceptions and emotions.[37] However, some of the intellect's thoughts are purer than others. The purest ones are those that are about what is before it. Since only the One (i.e., unity as the supreme principle) is before the intellect,

---

Brisson, Seamus O'Neill, and Andrei Timotin, Studies in Platonism, Neoplatonism, and the Platonic Tradition 20 (Leiden: Brill, 2018), 86–101, here 88. However, I would also like to stress the somewhat undeveloped character of Porphyry's hierarchy of divinities. As mentioned in the body text below, he gives three different versions of the account (in 2.34, 2.36, and 2.37), and each one is slightly different from the others. I will not discuss this question in detail here, however.

35. The idea that the supreme god is revered by pure silence is attributed to "a wise man" (2.34.2) who, since Eusebius of Caesarea (*Preparatio evangelica* 4.10.7), has been identified with Apollonius of Tyana; see Bouffartigue and Patillon, *De l'abstinence*, 2:30 n. 1. However, there are differences in the texts of Eusebius and Porphyry.

36. For the traditional conception, see Jean-Pierre Vernant, "A General Theory of Sacrifice and the Slaying of the Victim in the Greek Thusia," in Vernant, *Mortals and Immortals: Collected Essays*, ed. I. Zeitlin (Princeton: Princeton University Press, 1991), 290–302.

37. For the Plotinian distinction between intellectual understanding and ordinary forms of thought that are mixed with the affections of the soul, see Eyjólfur K. Emilsson, *Plotinus on Intellect* (New York: Oxford University Press, 2007), 176–213.

such purest thoughts must be about the One. In Porphyry's case, he also talks about theoretical contemplation or understanding of god (*theou theōria*, 2.34.3 = 164.4 Nauck), and thus he can be taken to identify the One with the god above all. The philosophical ritual of offering to the god above all thus consists in theoretically contemplating and understanding god.

Pure silence, in its turn, is perhaps best explained by reference to Plotinus's distinction between two kinds of prayer.[38] While the lower prayers are directed at the cosmos and can be seen as attempts to influence what is happening in the world (*Enn.* 4.4.[28]), the higher ones focus on uniting the One in ourselves with the One in itself.[39] Plotinus describes the preparation for such a union in terms of silence (*Enn.* 5.1.[10].6.11–16). According to Plotinus, we should not seek the vision of the One but should remain in quietness so that it can appear to us. This, it seems to me, requires an inner silence in which even the processes of thinking and understanding come to a halt and we prepare for the One dawning on us in a way that is beyond intellectual understanding. I take this as a likely account of the pure silence Porphyry is talking about. The silence we dedicate or devote ("sacrifice") to god above all (the One in Plotinus) is not destructive of anything but something that makes it possible for us to be with the god.

In sum, the god above all is, according to Porphyry, best respected through intellectual contemplation of it and inner silence in preparation for a nonintellectual appearance of god corresponding to the Plotinian One. The "offerings" philosophers can make to the offspring of the god above all are also immaterial, and they consist in the contemplation of the heavens, mathematical objects, and—probably in general—intelligible objects that make up the structure of the perceptible world as well. Insofar

---

38. For a discussion, see John M. Rist, *Plotinus: The Road to Reality* (Cambridge: Cambridge University Press 1967), 199–212. Iamblichus introduced a threefold hierarchy of prayer (*Myst.* 5.26, 237.16–238.6) for which, see John Dillon, "Introduction," in *Iamblichi Chalcidensis In Platonis Dialogos Commentarium Fragmenta*, ed. and trans. John Dillon, Philosophia antiqua 23 (Leiden: Brill, 1973; repr., Westbury: Prometheus Trust, 2009), 3–66; Richard Sorabji, *The Philosophy of the Commentators 200–600 AD: A Sourcebook*, vol.1, *Psychology* (London: Duckworth, 2004), 392. For a recent account of Porphyry's relation to Iamblichus, see Crystal Addey, *Divination and Theurgy in Neoplatonism: Oracles of the Gods* (Farnham: Ashgate, 2014), who argues that the traditional strict opposition between the two is overstated. On Porphyry within the tradition of Platonic philosophical theology, see Andrew Smith, "Porphyry and Pagan Religious Practices," in *Plotinus, Porphyry and Iamblichus: Philosophy and Religion in Neoplatonism* (Farnham: Ashgate, 2011), 29–35.

39. This is how Rist describes it in *Plotinus*, 212. For such a prayer, see *Enn.* 5.1.[10].6 and 5.8.[31].9. For Porphyry on prayer from a slightly different perspective, see Andrei Timotin, "Porphyry on Prayer: Platonic Tradition and Religious Trends in the Third Century," in *Platonic Theories of Prayer*, ed. John M. Dillon and Andrei Timotin, Studies in Platonism, Neoplatonism, and the Platonic Tradition 19 (Leiden: Brill, 2015), 88–107.

as heavenly bodies are also gods, fires can be lit to them (2.36.3), and this includes a material aspect of the offering and the destruction of the fuel. Perhaps the point is that, since the gods as heavenly bodies are more connected to bodily nature than purely immaterial gods are because heavenly bodies are luminous, lighting fires for them as an offering accords with their nature.[40]

While divinities properly speaking are thus best respected through immaterial offerings, material offerings (provided that they are not "blooded") can be made to demigods, in Porphyry's rather lengthy analysis *daimones* (singular *daimōn*) (2.38–43). According to Porphyry, the *daimones* are of two kinds, beneficent and maleficent. The beneficent *daimones* have an important function in cosmic providence, providing sufficient but not excessive rain, the change of seasons, and so on (2.38), while the maleficent ones cause all kinds of disasters such as droughts, floods, and the like (2.40). The central claim with respect to sacrifice is that the modest material offerings that Theophrastus recommends (i.e., flowers, grain, oil, honey, and wine) can be made to the beneficent *daimones* (2.36.4). However, animal sacrifice, in addition to being unjust, only ends up going to the maleficent ones, strengthening them and their power to cause disaster (2.36.5). The maleficent *daimones* also lead people astray, disguising themselves as gods and making them believe that real divinities want blooded offerings (2.40.3).

Porphyry's claim is that philosophers aiming at maximal assimilation to god can also take part in the rituals of a city provided that animal sacrifice is avoided and only flowers, grain, and libations are offered. They need to be clear, however, that the offerings are in reality directed to beneficent *daimones* and not to real gods (2.58.2).[41] By contrast, animal sacrifice is not only unjust but also harmful, not only to the person making the offering, but in the universe more generally through the natural disasters that the maleficent *daimones* bring about.

Therefore, if one asks to what extent Porphyry accepts traditional rituals, one needs to distinguish whether the rituals can be performed without animal (or human) sacrifice. If they can, even philosophers aiming at maximal assimilation to god can take part in them provided that they

---

40. Here Porphyry refers to "a theologian" (2.36.3 = 165.15 Nauck) who in this context is taken to be Pythagoras; see Bouffartigue and Patillon, *De l'abstinence*, 2:11, and Clark, *On Abstinence*, 154 n. 297.

41. I agree with Timotin (*La démonologie*, 211) that the distinction between beneficent and maleficent *daimones* is important for Porphyry's argument. However, since the "offerings" made to real divinities are immaterial and deviate from traditional offerings, Porphyry's revision of ritual practices for philosophers is more radical than the one proposed by Theophrastus (as quoted by Porphyry). This means that the distinction between two kinds of *daimones* is not sufficient for Porphyry's reform of ritual practices for philosophers aiming at maximal assimilation to god.

keep in mind that material offerings of flowers and grain as well as libations are made to beneficent *daimones*. If laws require animal sacrifice, philosophers must aim at changing them. Moreover, to the divinities proper philosophers aiming at assimilation to god make only immaterial "offerings" such as theoretical contemplation and pure silence. As to citizens who are not philosophers, Porphyry perhaps assumes that material offerings to beneficent *daimones* are sufficient (given that they are not blooded). However, since he addresses his friend Firmus Castricius and seems to assume that Firmus wants maximal assimilation, he is not explicitly considering the practices suitable for nonphilosophers.[42]

Conclusion

In this essay, I have discussed the notion of law (Greek *nomos*) in Porphyry's arguments against animal sacrifice in book 2 of his treatise *On Abstinence from Animate Beings* (translated as *On Abstinence from Killing Animals* by Gillian Clark). I have argued that his discussion is consistent if we recognize, on the one hand, a distinction between laws as morality — the divine law or natural law, law according to the intellect — and existing laws of cities or states. On the other hand, we need to distinguish between Porphyry's instructions to philosophers aiming at maximal assimilation to god and his account of different kinds of divinities and demigods (Greek *daimones*). Moreover, his instructions to nonphilosophers and philosophers not aiming at maximal assimilation to god probably differ from the ones he gives in *On Abstinence*, which is addressed to his fellow Plotinian Firmus. However, the discussion of maleficent *daimones* shows that he would not recommend animal sacrifice for anyone. Let me now summarize the main claims of this essay.

First, Porphyry's argument is of a normative rather than a descriptive nature, which means that he is concerned with what laws *should* prescribe and how one *should* sacrifice. This is especially relevant with respect to his claims about ancestral customs (group 1 discussed above). He claims that they forbid animal sacrifice, while we know that the practice was central in Greek rituals. Porphyry's argument, however, cannot be refuted simply by pointing this out, since his aim is to argue that one *should* understand ancestral customs as precluding animal sacrifice. He also has some evidence of traditional regulations or laws against harming animals. While I do not think that the arguments are refuted by the empirical dubiousness

---

42. He also grants that not even all philosophers aim at maximal assimilation to god, but his argument is directed at those who do (see 2.3.1). There, assimilation is referred to as "imitation" or "emulation" (Greek *mimēsis*).

of his claims, it would perhaps have been a better rhetorical strategy for Porphyry not to refer to ancestral customs.

Second, Porphyry's claim that laws forbid animal sacrifice concerns what he calls "divine laws," "laws of nature," or "laws of the intellect." In a remarkable passage using the expression "autonomous," he also states that philosophers aiming at maximal assimilation to god should prescribe this law to themselves (4.18.9). Therefore, distinguishing between actual laws of cities and true morality (incorporated in the divine law), he maintains that the latter is superior and the one that philosophers should follow. Although this passage uses language that sounds Kantian, Porphyry's approach differs from Kantianism, since his argument does not operate on the notion of moral obligation or duty. This also means that he does not use the notion of rights, and, although he argues that maximal justice requires restraint from inflicting harm on living beings, this does not entail that, for Porphyry, animate creatures (human beings, animals, or plants) would have rights. From Porphyry's perspective, the crucial point about divine laws is that, while the laws of the city might allow certain kinds of actions (such as visiting courtesans), they conflict with virtue (i.e., what is good and divine law) and a virtuous person refrains from them. Similarly, even if the laws of a city allow animal sacrifice, philosophers aiming at maximal assimilation to god and the highest degree of virtue should abstain from it.

Third, and with respect to existing laws, Porphyry's rhetoric is slightly confusing. I have argued, however, that he has a consistent view when we recognize the following distinctions. First, he makes a rhetorical declaration that he is not aiming at abolishing the laws of his city, which may or may not be true. However, his considered view later in book 2 is more refined. The crucial claim is that, insofar as the laws of one's city do not require animal sacrifice, even philosophers can offer libations, grain, and flowers to beneficent *daimones*. If animal sacrifice is ordained and restraint from it sanctioned, philosophers must work toward changing the laws.

Finally, Porphyry also outlines a reform of ritual practices for philosophers aiming at assimilation to god. Moving forward from the Theophrastean guidelines for offerings that do not conflict with justice as Porphyry understands it in the treatise, he gives instructions for offerings that transform the traditional notion of sacrifice involving the destruction of a victim (a human being, an animal, or a plant). The immaterial "offerings" directed at divinities properly speaking involve activities such as theoretical contemplation or a practice of silence in which even intellectual understanding ceases. Such "offerings" can be devoted to real gods, Porphyry seems to assume, because they correspond to the nature of the real good that is immaterial. When the reformed offerings are devoted or "sacrificed" to gods, they do not destroy anything. Rather, contemplating and understanding god as well as silence increase when we devote them to god. The more we contemplate and understand god, the more we are able to do so, and the more silence we practice in preparation for the appearance of the god (or the One), the more silence we are able to create in our minds.

From a more general point of view, it is noteworthy how different Porphyry's view is from other arguments against inflicting injury on animals, ancient and modern. As opposed to most arguments for including animals in the scope of justice in the history of Western philosophy, Porphyry's argument is not based on any version of what can be called "the assumption of desert." The argument of desert maintains that we must extend moral concern to animals if and only if animals satisfy some general condition, typically if they can be shown to possess some feature shared with human beings such as rationality, capacity to feel pain, personhood, self-awareness, or concern for others. While Porphyry attributes the capacity to feel pain to nonhuman animals, his argument for why philosophers aiming at assimilation to god to the greatest possible degree should refrain from harming animals is not dependent on that claim. As I have argued, he also extends the ideal form of justice to plants, and there is no indication that he would attribute the capacity to feel pain to plants—in fact the passage pointing to animal sentience distinguishes animals from plants precisely on these grounds.

However, although Porphyry extends justice in its highest form to nonhuman animals and plants, his argument is not based on the claim that life has intrinsic value. Even the highest form of justice extends only to harmless animate creatures, thus allowing self-defense and the restriction of harmful populations. Therefore, his position is not open to the kind of criticism, also presented against modern versions of the claim of intrinsic value of life, that appeals to the problems that ensue if harmful animals cannot be killed. Porphyry responds to similar criticism adding that, although harmful animals can be killed, this entails no justification for killing or otherwise harming harmless creatures.

Partly for similar reasons, Porphyry's view also differs from the arguments for animal rights. It is controversial whether the notion of moral right can be found in ancient philosophical discussions, and I think one should not insert the notion of right unless there is clear evidence for its presence. As mentioned in the discussion above, Porphyry builds on Theophrastus's argument quoted in book 2 that it is intrinsically wrong to deprive living creatures of their lives. This is explained by saying that taking lives is analogous to stealing, rather than with reference to the right to life. Assuming that people typically recognize that stealing is wrong, it would be odd to maintain that taking an even greater good from its owner, an animal or a plant, would not be wrong.

Although Porphyry's ideal for the life of philosophers aiming at the assimilation to god to the maximal possible degree is certainly austere or ascetic, he also has something quite different and rather original to offer for discussion. This is because he does not attempt to reduce the guidelines for action to a single principle, such as utility or value of life, and to assume that that single principle solves all moral dilemmas one might face concerning saving lives or inflicting injury. Most important, he does not assume that one should be able to solve all such dilemmas in order to start cutting down on the killing and reducing injury caused to living beings. Neither does he require that one strive perfectly for the highest justice for one's striving to be valuable. While he certainly prefers a wide-ranging application of restraint from causing harm to living creatures, he also assumes that it is better to practice abstinence from harming animate creatures to a certain extent than not to practice it at all because one is unable to attain perfection in it.

Banning Animal Sacrifice ad Infinitum: Cui Bono?

DANIEL ULLUCCI
Stonehill College

The Codex Theodosianus, or Theodosian Code, a monumental though quirky collection of Roman law compiled under Theodosius II between 429 and 437 CE, preserves a series of laws banning the performance of animal sacrifice in the late Roman Empire. These laws coincide with a precipitous decline in traditional civic sacrifices and a simultaneous rise in the power of Christian ecclesiastical elites and the churches they ran. The "end of animal sacrifice" and the laws mandating this end would, seemingly, represent the high point in the history of ancient animal rights. But of course, the laws were not about animal welfare at all, and it is not apparent that they had any impact on either animal husbandry or meat consumption. They definitely did impact economic systems significantly, but not by saving a single animal from death. The laws against sacrifice did not ban the killing of animals. Rather, they shifted (1) the ideological and symbolic context for conceptualizing the killing and butchering of animals, and (2) the physical location and "social site" in which these activities took place.[1] This was a significant change, not simply in religious ideology but also in social and economic systems. None of this was spurred by an interest in animals or an awakening of human obligations toward animals. The laws banning sacrifice are an example of a recurring theme of this volume and the conference that spawned it: the manipulation of ideology and practices involving animals in the service of human social formation and competition.

I am enormously grateful to Saul Olyan and Jordan Rosenblum for the invitation to contribute to this volume and the very well planned and fruitful conference at Brown University that preceded it, also to Jessica Pesce, who edited the manuscript and prepared the translations of Codex Theodosianus below.

1. For the theorization of social "site," see Theodore Schatzki, *The Site of the Social: A Philosophical Account of the Constitution of Social Life and Change* (University Park: Pennsylvania State University Press, 2002), 123–88.

The laws banning sacrifice renegotiated whether the ritualized killing, butchering, offering, and consuming of animal parts did or did not index large identity constructs such as piety and *Romanitas* in the late empire. That is, they reordered the associations between major Roman identity constructs and the ritual of animal sacrifice. This reframing of animal sacrifice (as pious or impious, Roman or not Roman, rational or irrational) actually had little to do with the specific activities of sacrifice (gathering, butchering, burning, cooking, distributing, eating). Rather, sacrifice was a floating signifier—a practice that could be freely reinterpreted and rebranded as part of the complex religious discourse of the late empire.[2] That discourse is the focus of this essay.

My interest in the laws against sacrifice comes from a larger interest in how and why Christianity spread the way it did. The laws on sacrifice are obviously a key part of this question since they would seem to suggest that people became Christians *de jure*—the alternative, "paganism," being explicitly outlawed. I argue (1) that the traditional scholarly framing of the laws as *in support of* Christianity and *against* paganism needs to be reconsidered, and (2) that while these laws did benefit some Christians, they did not, in fact, benefit *all* Christians, and that this is a critical point for understanding the spread of Christianity in the fourth century.

Legal Vacillations and Traditional Framing of the Issue

The period from the middle of the third century CE into the early fifth century saw a flood of contradictory laws on animal sacrifice. In 249 CE the emperor Decius decreed that all inhabitants of the empire had to perform animal sacrifice and, in some cases, actually obtain proof that they had done so.[3] Sacrifice was also a component of the imperial policies of Diocletian and a key factor in the so-called Great Persecution of the early 300s.[4]

---

2. While the term *floating signifier* originated with Claude Lévi-Strauss, it now has a broad history of reapplication. In calling sacrifice a floating signifier I mean both that the actions of sacrifice were open to multiple interpretations and also that what constituted "real" sacrifice, or the "essence" of sacrifice, was equally open to interpretation in the ancient Mediterranean. See Claude Lévi-Strauss, *Introduction to the Work of Marcel Mauss* (London: Routledge & Kegan Paul, 1987), 63–64; Jeffrey Mehlman, "The 'Floating Signifier': From Lévi-Strauss to Lacan," *Yale French Studies* 48 (1972): 10–37.

3. We have evidence from Egypt in the form of sacrifice receipts, *libelli*, that show that even people in rural areas really did go to the effort of proving that they had sacrificed. On the *libelli*, see James Rives, "The Decree of Decius and the Religion of Empire," *JRS* 89 (1999): 135–54, here 137 n. 13. See also Kate Cooper, "Christianity, Private Power, and the Law from Decius to Constantine: The Minimalist View," *JECS* 19 (2011): 340–41.

4. For analysis of these events and the role of sacrifice in them, see Elizabeth DePalma

Just a few years later, however, Constantine seized power and the situation changed. Far from demanding sacrifice, Constantine castigated it, and his sons passed laws actually banning it in some cases. Constantine's sons were critical to the success and stability of all of his policies. As David Potter stresses, Constantine was one of only a handful of emperors in all of Roman history to successfully pass his reign to his sons.[5] But the confusion was not over with the rise of Constantine's dynasty. In 361 Julian, a nephew of Constantine, came to power and attempted to reverse the decline in traditional Roman practices with a vast program of sacrifices. Even Julian's sympathetic supporters thought his sacrificing was excessive, and one quipped that, if Julian's policies continued, there would be no more white birds left in the Eastern Empire.[6] Fortunately for the birds, Julian did not get his way. He was killed in battle in 363, and his successors returned to the antisacrificial policies of Constantine. Throughout the late fourth century and into the fifth, various emperors issued laws banning animal sacrifice, preserved in the Codex Theodosianus.

Vacillations on the value and legality of a social practice as historic and culturally significant as animal sacrifice must have been bewildering. Anyone, particularly any elite, living in a major city of the empire during the period from roughly 300 to 365 could not have failed to notice that animal sacrifice was very much in play in the cultural competition and discourse of their day.

These oscillations are connected to the rise of Christianity and the support it received, or did not receive, from Roman emperors. Past scholarship has generally framed these events in terms of a battle between Christianity and paganism. Decius was a persecutor, Constantine the great champion, and Julian ("the Apostate") the last gasp of paganism. This framing, however, has been questioned.

In the case of Decius, James Rives has shown convincingly that laws mandating sacrifice were not targeted at Christians specifically. Rather, they were part of a broader attempt to promote a particular model of Roman imperial identity that stressed traditional religious practices like sacrifice as the epitome of Roman piety and imperial culture. While Decius had no love for Christianity, he was focused on larger problems, not

---

Digeser, *A Threat to Public Piety: Christians, Platonists, and the Great Persecution* (Ithaca, NY: Cornell University Press, 2012).

5. David S. Potter, "The Transformation of the Empire: 235–337 CE," in *A Companion to the Roman Empire*, ed. David S. Potter (Malden, MA: Blackwell, 2006), 153–73, here 154.

6. For criticism of Julian, see Ammianus Marcellinus, 25.4.17; 22.12.5. On Julian's attempt to revive sacrifice, see Glen Bowersock, *Julian the Apostate* (Cambridge: Harvard University Press, 1978); Scott Bradbury, "Julian's Pagan Revival and the Decline of Blood Sacrifice," *Phoenix* 49 (1995): 331–56. For Julian's program of sacrifice in relation to Christianity, see Daniel Ullucci, *The Christian Rejection of Animal Sacrifice* (Oxford: Oxford University Press, 2012), 137–49.

specific legislation against the relatively insignificant movement that was Christianity in the third century.[7] While some Christian writers certainly saw Decius's policies as targeted attacks on Christianity, Rives shows that this is not the way Decius saw it, and probably not the way the majority of the empire saw it either.

Breaking out of the traditional Christian-versus-pagan framework has proven more challenging in the case of Constantine and his successors. Here the basic framework still comes largely from the Christian apologist Eusebius. It imagines Constantine as a classic Christian convert who rejected traditional Roman religion, which led him to ban its most iconic ritual—animal sacrifice. The model has been soundly falsified but has proven incredibly hard to kill. Many popular and scholarly works still repeat the patently false claim that Constantine made Christianity "the official religion of the Roman Empire" (as if a "®" should follow this phrase).

The laws on sacrifice are part of the problem, and a better understanding of them can be part of the solution. They are part of the problem because they seem to make sense only as part of explicitly Christian, anti-pagan legislation. At the same time, the wording of the laws, their placement in the Codex Theodosianus, and their proliferation over decades force us to consider other models. I hope to show how two different threads of recent scholarship can be put together to force us to see these laws in a new light—as renegotiation of imperial identity, not the legal ratification of a monolithic "Christianity."

There is significant scholarly disagreement about the laws, but I start with two undisputed points and a question that arises from them. First, laws forbidding sacrifice were definitely in place in some parts of the empire by the 340s at the latest—possibly as early as the 320s. Second, these laws were not broadly enforced, and the Code itself is the best evidence for this.[8] Individual statutes in the Code can usually be dated quite accurately to specific years and even months. In the Code, new laws against sacrifice were continually added, decade after decade, for nearly a

---

7. Rives, "Decree of Decius," 140–54.

8. Scott Bradbury, "Constantine and the Problem of Anti-Pagan Legislation in the Fourth Century," *CP* 89 (1994): 120–39, here 133. Bradbury assumes that the laws went unenforced because they were resisted by local magistrates. A critical piece of evidence for the lack of enforcement is the fact that, when Christian bishops in the late fourth century attempted to close or destroy Roman temples, they rarely did so on their own initiative, nor did they cite previously established laws banning sacrifice and ordering temples closed. Rather, they obtained imperial rescripts specifying their authority in a particular situation. See, e.g., Marcus Diaconus, *Vita Porph.* 26; Garth Fowden, "Bishops and Temples in the Eastern Roman Empire A.D. 320–435," *JTS* 29 (1978): 53–78.

century.⁹ There are a total of twenty laws banning sacrifice in the Code; that might not quite be *ad infinitum*, but it is a lot more than we might expect. More tellingly, there is no direct evidence that anyone in the fourth century was actually prosecuted for defying these laws.¹⁰

What, then, were the laws doing? More specifically, *who benefited* from serially recurring laws against sacrifice that were clearly not being enforced? This might seem like a silly question. Christians are the obvious beneficiaries, and the laws are normally interpreted as a critical tipping point when Christianity finally had the political power to assert itself by banning the practices of its enemies. Recent scholarship on the laws, the category "pagan," and the development of the modern category "religion," however, challenges this view.

Reframing "Christian versus Pagan"

The very framing of the issue as Christian versus pagan is a problem since, as many have shown, the concept "religion," as it is commonly used today to mean a set of theological beliefs, did not exist in the fourth century. Equally important, the concept of "a religion" as a discrete social formation or social identity did not operate in the ancient Mediterranean in the way religious studies scholarship has often assumed.¹¹ We are at exactly the point in history when what will become the modern usage of "religion" is developing.¹² It was certainly not established in the early fourth century when laws against sacrifice begin to appear. Isabella Sandwell points out that there existed neither a legal precedent nor even

---

9. The last law is from 435, just two years before the completion of the collection in 437.
10. Bradbury, "Constantine," 134.
11. Brent Nongbri, *Before Religion: A History of a Modern Concept* (New Haven: Yale University Press, 2013); William E. Arnal and Russell T. McCutcheon, *The Sacred Is the Profane: The Political Nature of "Religion"* (New York: Oxford University Press, 2013). For a critical corrective to the claim that "religion" is merely a modern or scholarly creation and therefore does not exist, as well as a discussion of the common confusion between scholarly analysis of "religion" versus "*a* religion," see Stanley K. Stowers, "Religion as a Social Kind" (unpublished paper presented at the symposium "Religion before Religion," at Bowdoin College, 14–15 October 2016) and other venues.
12. The pivotal role that discourse on sacrifice played in developing concepts of religion has been shown by James Rives, "Between Orthopraxy and Orthodoxy: Constantine and Animal Sacrifice," in *Costantino prima e dopo Costantino / Constantine before and after Constantine*, ed. Giorgio Bonamente, Noel Lenski, and Rita Lizzi Testa (Bari: Edipuglia, 2012), 153–63. An alternative view is expressed by Guy G. Stroumsa, *The End of Sacrifice: Religious Transformations in Late Antiquity*, trans. Susan Emanuel (Chicago: University of Chicago Press, 2009). For a critique of Stroumsa, see Daniel Ullucci, "Sacrifice in the Ancient Mediterranean: Recent and Current Research," *CurBR* 13 (2015): 388–439.

an established verbiage for defining paganism as a discrete religion that could be legislated against.[13] It is thus highly implausible that either the emperors creating these laws, or the officials enforcing them, or the populace being affected by them would have understood them as laws against a religion called paganism. "Christian" was a loosely established (and contested) identity construct by the fourth century, but pagan surely was not, at least not outside a few Christian apologists actively engaged in creating the category.

If not antipagan, then what? Again, I think Decius provides the relevant historical precedent. Decius's laws were attempts to negotiate identity, not to promote discrete religions. I will show, following the work of Sandwell, Rives, and Michele Salzman, that many of the laws against sacrifice in the Codex Theodosianus associate sacrifice with practices long seen as dangerous, impious, and irrational in Roman culture. The change here is that sacrifice, once associated with Roman identity, civic pride, and piety, is now associated, in these laws, with impiety, irrationality, and treason.

A renegotiation of law through the lens of "piety" is not unusual. Kate Cooper points out that the principle of piety was a key element of the Roman legal system. Claims about what was or was not pious were often the rationale for changing laws or not enforcing laws in particular situations. The Roman legal system was not so much a system of explicit case law as a system of principles for which the casuistic specifics needed to be worked out. Local officials were granted significant discretionary powers, and piety was often a justifying principle for legislative leeway.[14] The laws on sacrifice are part of a discourse on Roman identity being enacted through statements on proper piety, not a discourse that pits one religion against another. The winner in this discourse is not Christianity *eo ipso*, but a particular idea of what practices constitute correct behavior in relationship to the gods.

This might all seem like a pointless nuance. Since clearly the needle is being moved closer to Christian practice and further from traditional Roman practice, one might argue that the net result is that Christianity wins and traditional Roman religion loses. I argue, however, that seeing this distinction matters for understanding the goals of the laws and how they affected the populace to which they were directed. More importantly, it matters because the winners are not Christians but rather only a specific kind of Christian.

---

13. Isabella Sandwell, "Outlawing 'Magic' or Outlawing 'Religion'? Libanius and the Theodosian Code as Evidence for Legislation against 'Pagan' Practices," in *The Spread of Christianity in the First Four Centuries: Essays in Explanation*, ed. W. V. Harris, Columbia Studies in the Classical Tradition 27 (Leiden: Brill, 2005), 87–123, here 89–90.

14. Cooper, "Christianity, Private Power," 330–31.

Reframing "Christianity" and Christian Sacrifices

The second thread of recent scholarship that must be integrated into this debate is evidence for other Christian offering practices. Put simply, not all early Christians rejected sacrifice. We have strong textual and archaeological evidence that many people who self-identified as Christians were making agricultural offerings, including animals, well into the fifth century and beyond.[15] These offerings often took place in funerary contexts and in veneration of saints and martyrs. The form of Christianity that ultimately rose to dominance vociferously rejected such practices as utterly un-Christian, but they did not speak for everyone. Paulinus of Nola, for example, gives ample evidence that Christians were offering animals in the context of a Christian martyr cult in the early fourth century. Frank Trombley has assembled evidence for animal offerings by Christians in Greece and Anatolia.[16] Ramsay MacMullen characterizes these extraecclesiastical practices as the "second Church."[17]

---

15. Most of our evidence for Christian offering practices consists of agrarian offerings, such as grains, oil, and wine. This is to be expected since many of the offerings are being made by non-elites for whom animal sacrifice was economically inaccessible. However, sufficient evidence for animal offerings does exist. See, in particular, Dennis Trout, "Christianizing the Nolan Countryside: Animal Sacrifice at the Tomb of St. Felix," *JECS* 3 (1995): 281–98. For a condensation of the major evidence for all types of Christian offerings, see Ramsay MacMullen, *The Second Church: Popular Christianity A.D. 200–400*, WGRW 1 (Atlanta: Society of Biblical Literature, 2009); Robin Jensen, "Dining with the Dead: From the Mensa to the Altar in Christian Late Antiquity," in *Commemorating the Dead: Texts and Artifacts in Context; Studies of Roman, Jewish, and Christian Burials*, ed. Laurie Brink and Deborah A. Green (Berlin: de Gruyter, 2008), 107–44; Christophe J. Goddard, "The Evolution of Pagan Sanctuaries in Late Antique Italy (Fourth–Sixth Centuries A.D.): A New Administrative and Legal Framework; A Paradox," in *Les cités de l'Italie tardo-antique, IV–VI siècle: Institutions, économie, société, culture et Religion*, ed. Massimiliano Ghilardi, Christophe J. Goddard, and Pierfrancesco Porena (Rome: École française de Rome, 2006), 281–308; Nichole Belayche, "Realia versus Leges: Les sacrifices de la religion d'état au IVe siècle," in *La cuisine et l'autel: Les sacrifices en questions dans les sociétés de la méditerranée ancienne*, ed. Stella Georgoudi, Renée Koch Piettre, and Francis Schmidt, Bibliothèque de l'École des hautes études: Sciences religieuses 124 (Turnhout: Brepols, 2005), 343–70; Kathleen Corley, *Maranatha: Women's Funerary Rituals and Christian Origins* (Minneapolis: Fortress, 2010); Ekaterina Kovaltchuk, "The Encaenia of St. Sophia: Animal Sacrifice in Christian Context," *Scrinium* 4 (2008): 161–203; Graydon F. Snyder, *Ante Pacem: Archaeological Evidence of Church Life before Constantine* (Macon, GA.: Mercer University Press, 1985); and Frank Trombley, *Hellenic Religion and Christianization c. 370–529*, 2 vols., Religions in the Greco-Roman World 115 (1993–1994; repr., Leiden: Brill, 2001)

16. Frank Trombley, "Paganism in the Greek World at the End of Antiquity: The Case of Rural Anatolia and Greece," *HTR* 78.3–4 (1985): 327–52. See particularly his analysis of the sacrifice in the life of Saint Nicholas (339–40). See also discussion of the tradition that Justinian sacrificed huge numbers of animals at the dedication of the church of Saint Sophia in Constantinople in Kovaltchuk, "Encaenia of St Sophia," 161–203.

17. MacMullen, *Second Church*.

This evidence has been largely neglected by scholars and, thus far, has not been incorporated into macro-level models of the spread and development of early Christianity. Particularly, it has not been incorporated into an analysis of the laws against sacrifice. A rejection of sacrifice is often assumed to be the sine qua non of Christianity; therefore, any law against sacrifice is naturally seen as a pro-Christian, antipagan law. Scott Bradbury for example, in analyzing Constantinian law, asserts that all Christians had a "universal loathing for blood sacrifices."[18] More recently, Maria-Zoe Petropoulou also asserts that a rejection of animal sacrifice was at the core of all Christian identity.[19] Realizing that there were plenty of sacrificing Christians in the fourth century forces us to reframe the laws on sacrifice and how they impacted the spread of Christianity.

The real beneficiaries of these laws turn out to be, primarily, Constantine's imperial dynastic network and, secondarily, a particular form of Christianity that just happened to meld well with this ideology, a form of Christianity characterized by translocal ecclesiastical organization and a long-standing and well-developed antisacrificial discourse.

Constantine and Sacrifice

I begin with a look at the difficult question of Constantine's position on sacrifice and then move on to the laws in the Codex Theodosianus. There is a long-standing scholarly dispute over whether Constantine banned sacrifice.[20] Eusebius says he did.[21] The Roman rhetorician Libanius says he did not.[22] Some scholars have argued that Libanius is the more

---

18. Bradbury, "Constantine," 129.
19. Maria-Zoe Petropoulou, *Animal Sacrifice in Ancient Greek Religion, Judaism, and Christianity, 100 BC–AD 200*, Oxford Classical Monographs (Oxford: Oxford University Press, 2008).
20. As Bradbury points out, this is perhaps the most controversial thing about Constantine. For a summary of positions, see Sandwell, "Outlawing 'Magic,'" 87–101. Bradbury ("Constantine," 120–29) concludes that a lost law against sacrifice from Constantine, probably from 324, is a strong probability. He also stresses the literary context of Eusebius's *Vita Constantini*. For previous scholarship, much of which rejected the notion of a ban on sacrifice originating with Constantine, see Bradbury, "Constantine," 122 n. 9.
21. Eusebius, *Vita Const.* 2.44–45; 3.1.5; 4.23; 4.25. See Bradbury, "Constantine," 121–22. On the literary context of Eusebius's claim and its impact on his credibility, see John Curran, "Constantine and the Ancient Cults of Rome: The Legal Evidence," *Greece & Rome* 43 (1996): 68–80, here 74.
22. Libanius, *Or.* 30.6, states definitively that Constantine did not ban sacrifice. Bradbury's assertion that Libanius, *Or.* 1.27, is a reference to a Constantinian ban on sacrifice seems to me unfounded. The text may be a reference to any number of laws against various religious practices.

reliable source, others that Eusebius is more reliable.[23] I think Rives is right to cut through the speculation and conclude that, whatever law Constantine issued, it must have been ambiguous enough that Eusebius and Libanius could come to diametrically opposed interpretations, which they each presented publicly.[24]

That Constantine had negative views of sacrifice is very likely, though even that is not definitively provable.[25] The evidence comes from Eusebius, who claims several times to be reproducing official documents from Constantine. This becomes a probability argument. We should certainly be suspicious of Eusebius, but it seems unlikely that he could have gotten away with inventing antisacrificial positions out of whole cloth if Constantine had never said anything of the sort. On the other hand, the reworked reliefs of Constantine performing sacrifice on his triumphal arch in Rome provide limiting evidence. As Rives argues, if rejecting sacrifice was at the core of Constantine's public religious identity, it is inconceivable that the elites of Rome would dare to place an image of him sacrificing on such a public monument.[26] I think the best we can say is that it is impossible that Constantine publicly rejected all sacrifice, but improbable that he said nothing against it.

Making sense of Constantine's position has led to scrutiny of the authenticity of his Christian beliefs. Was he a real Christian who caved to practical political realties? Was he a devoted Christian thwarted by underlings who would not enforce his laws? Was he a Christian dabbler who never fully committed one way or the other? All of these models still rely on the basic Christian-versus-pagan framework. There are alternate possibilities for understanding Constantine's positions without resorting exclusively to the notion that he banned sacrifice because he had become a Christian; in fact, we can give a list.

First, Roman (and earlier Greek) intellectual history contains plenty of negative positions on animal sacrifice. Various philosophical traditions

---

23. See Bradbury, "Constantine," 128. Timothy D. Barnes was an aggressive supporter of the latter position in an influential book *Constantine and Eusebius* (Cambridge: Harvard University Press, 1981). He was challenged by H. Drake, review of *Constantine and Eusebius*, by Timothy D. Barnes, *AJP* 103 (1982): 462–66. On the ensuing debate, see Bradbury, "Constantine," 125 n. 20.

24. Codex Theodosianus 16.10.2 is a law against sacrifice from 341 that appears to refer to an earlier law of Constantine, now lost. But the reference and context are too vague to make a definitive conclusion.

25. The question of Constantine's views on sacrifice hinge largely on assumptions about the accuracy of Eusebius. There is, however, a report from the historian Zosimus that Constantine caused a scandal in Rome by not participating in a festival on the Capitoline (Zosimus, *New History* 2.19.5). The exact reasons, however, are unclear from Zosimus's report. For a summary of the evidence and scholarly positions, see Sandwell, "Outlawing 'Magic,'" 100–101.

26. Rives, "Between Orthopraxy and Orthodoxy," 160.

condemned sacrifice, including those associated with Pythagoras and Orpheus, the writings of Theophrastus and Porphyry, and texts such as Philostratus's account of the life of Apollonius of Tyana.[27] Others such as Iamblichus and some Neoplatonists argued that animals might be acceptable offerings to the lower-level gods of the universe, but they were completely inappropriate offerings for the highest gods. These "highest" gods are exactly the gods with whom a Roman emperor like Constantine would imagine himself to be keeping company.[28] (Constantine's religious preferences are not properly separable from his views of himself and his position.) It was also entirely possible for Constantine to be critical of some aspects of sacrifice without rejecting the act altogether; in fact, that would be the normal position.[29] We should not assume that any negative views of sacrifice Constantine had must have come from his contact with Christianity. Bruno Bleckmann, for one, argues for Neoplatonism as a key source of Constantine's religious views.[30]

Second, Constantine knew about the failed religious policies of his predecessors. Decius's and Diocletian's attempts to forge an empire-wide identity around sacrifice had failed to create unity or solidarity. Worse, appeals to the aegis of traditional Roman gods and traditional sacrifices had not protected Constantine's predecessors from a combination of death in battle and serial assassination. Constantine was clearly willing to try something novel, as his interest in Christianity shows.

Third, Constantine's attempts to construct a dynastic imperial identity need to be considered.[31] In his analysis of Constantine's policies, Rives makes the extremely important observation that Constantine's new vision of imperial government continued the trend away from traditional civic

---

27. For a summary of Greek and Roman sources that reject sacrifice see Harold W. Attridge, "The Philosophical Critique of Religion under the Early Empire," *ANRW* 2.16.1 (1978): 45–78; Ullucci, *Christian Rejection of Animal Sacrifice*, 56–64.

28. See Attridge, "Philosophical Critique," 45–47.

29. It is possible that Constantine was not the first emperor to express dislike of sacrifice. These views were ascribed to Philip the Arab by Christian sources. No corroborating evidence exists, but it is possible that views against sacrifice were the impetus for Christian writers to claim Philip as the first Christian emperor. For Eusebius's claim, see *Vita Const.* 4.10; 3.15. The historian Zosimus, while critical of Philip, makes no claims about his religious identifications. See Zosimus, *New History*, 1.13–16. For discussion of ancient sources that debate the meaning and purpose of sacrifice without rejecting the practice, see Ullucci, *Christian Rejection of Animal Sacrifice*, 31–64.

30. Bruno Bleckmann, "Konstantin und die Kritik des blutigen Opfers," in Bonamente, Lenski, and Testa, *Costantino prima e dopo costantino*, 165–80.

31. Constantine was incredibly successful at forging this identity. It is easy to lose sight of the fact that what makes Constantine really unique among the emperors of the third and fourth centuries is the fact that he does not get killed. This is not random chance but evidence of his ability to create a successful image of imperial power that kept him and his sons alive (along with the good luck or savvy not to get killed in battle).

networks of power in favor of broader empire-wide structures. He argues that Constantine, "favored policies that promoted a centrally organized bureaucracy over the leadership of local elites, and so would have had less need for the work that animal sacrifice did in tying together local and imperial hierarchies."[32] As Salzman shows, one way Constantine did this was by advancing a large number of men to the rank of senator, most of whom were not from traditional Roman power networks. These new elites were tied directly to Constantine and derived their power from him, not from traditional civic networks indexed by sacrifice.[33]

Fourth, as Potter points out, later Roman emperors were almost completely occupied with border policing. Indeed, Constantine's desire to move the capital east was, in part, based on a desire to have the seat of government closer to the eastern front, where he spent most of his time. Many American tourists have spent more time in Rome than Constantine ever did. He visited only three times in his life.[34] Perhaps, then, the conflicts he faced in the East impacted his conceptions of identity and proper religious practice more than has normally been assumed.

In the East, Constantine was facing the Sasanian Empire. Sasanian kings explicitly promoted Zoroastrian identity as part of their imperial ideology. Potter observes that what we might broadly term "religious identity" was a key part of Roman/Sasanian hostility and ideological positioning.[35] Animal sacrifice played a central role in Zoroastrian identity, perhaps even more so than in traditional Roman religion.[36] It seems at least possible to me that Constantine's foreign military enemy impacted his own conceptions of Roman identity and the place of sacrifice in that identity.

In short, there is a list of sources for Constantine's dislike of sacrifice other than, or at least in addition to, Christianity. We might consider that, rather than Christianity pushing Constantine to reject sacrifice, perhaps it was the well-developed rejection of sacrifice among some Christians that attracted Constantine to this rather marginal group in the first place.

Ultimately, some combination of these factors led him to articulate a religious identity that rearranged the traditional links between piety, Roman identity, and animal sacrifice. As Rives argues, Constantine effectively "reversed the assessment of [sacrifice's] value" such that "it was

---

32. Rives, "Between Orthopraxy and Orthodoxy," 162.
33. See Michele Renee Salzman, *The Making of a Christian Aristocracy: Social and Religious Change in the Western Roman Empire* (Cambridge: Harvard University Press, 2002).
34. These were in 312, 315, and 326. See Hugh Elton, "The Transformation of Government under Diocletian and Constantine," in Potter, *Companion to the Roman Empire*, 193–205, here 197.
35. Potter, "Transformation of the Empire," 159–61.
36. For an overview of animal sacrifice in the Zoroastrian tradition, see Richard Foltz, "Zoroastrian Attitudes towards Animals," *Society and Animals* 18 (2010): 367–78.

now the rejection of animal sacrifice that marked the socio-political hierarchies and communal identity that he wished to promote."[37]

Laws against Sacrifice in the Codex Theodosianus

I turn now to the Code, focusing on how the laws functioned as identity constructs by associating sacrifice with traditionally unsavory Roman cultural signifiers. Because Theodosius II ordered the compilers of the Code to be as brief as possible and preserve only the final rulings, not their specific context, it is not possible to tell if individual laws were specific or universal or in what locations at what time any particular law may have applied.[38] Moreover, as discussed previously, the Roman legal tradition tended toward broad apodictic statements of principle, what Bradbury calls "moralizing ideology," with the details left to the discretion of local magistrates.[39] This actually makes the Code quite suitable for our interests in that it preserves the statements of principle with which the emperors were defining their administrations.[40] Of the ten earliest laws banning sacrifice in the Code, seven explicitly associate sacrifice with some cultural referent that had a long-standing negative connotation in Roman history. I focus on these laws, laid out in table 1 on the following page.[41]

---

37. Rives, "Between Orthopraxy and Orthodoxy," 163.
38. See *C.Theo.* 1.1.5. For a discussion of the editing and rearranging of laws in the Code, see Sandwell, "Outlawing 'Magic,'" 91–93. For an overview of Roman law in this period, see John Matthews, "Roman Law and Roman History," in Potter, *Companion to the Roman Empire*, 477–91.
39. Bradbury puts the situation succinctly: "Late Roman legislation is often characterized by an admixture of moralizing ideology and operative clauses indicating what was actually to be done" ("Constantine," 135). As Cooper argues, leaving the details to trusted elites was a critical strength ("Christianity, Private Power," 329–30). This approach often frustrated those tasked with actually enforcing the laws. Symmachus reports that when he was urban prefect he often gave up and referred cases to the emperor (Bradbury, "Constantine," 135 n. 62). Bradbury also points out an example of the inconsistency of imperial rulings. After announcing that he "wholly forbid[s] the existence of gladiators," Constantine granted an Umbrian town the right to include gladiatorial combat in a festival to the imperial cult ("Constantine," 135).
40. A. H. M. Jones summarized the laws of the Code as "aspirations" rather than evidence of real change. A. H. M. Jones, *Studies in Roman Government and Law* (Oxford: Blackwell, 1964), viii.
41. For the sake of space, I significantly abbreviate these laws, summarizing passages as needed. For a full translation, see *The Theodosian Code and Novels, and the Sirmondian Constitutions*, trans. Clyde Pharr, Corpus of Roman Law 1 (Princeton: Princeton University Press, 1952). The full text of the Code is available online, "Theodosiani Libri XVI," https://droitromain.univ-grenoble-alpes.fr/Codex_Theod.htm. Translations are by Jessica Pesce and myself.

TABLE 1. Seven of the Ten Earliest Laws against Sacrifice
in the Codex Theodosianus

	C. Theo.	Date	Translation
1	16.10.1	3/8/321	Emperor Constantine Augustus to Maximus: [If a palace or public building is struck by lightning] retain the ancient customs and make inquiries of the *haruspices*.... Permission is also granted to all others to appropriate this custom to themselves, provided only that they abstain from domestic sacrifices [*sacrificiis domesticis*], which are specifically prohibited.
2	16.10.2	341	Emperor Constantius Augustus to Madalianus, Vice Praetorian Prefect: *Superstitio* will cease; the insanity of sacrifices will be abolished [*sacrficiorum aboleatur insania*]. For if anyone, contra the law of the divine Emperor our father and our reasonable decree, dares to perform sacrifices, he will suffer ... suitable punishment.
3	16.10.5	11/23/353	Constantius Augustus to Cerealis, Prefect of the City: Nocturnal Sacrifices [*sacrificia nocturna*], permitted by the authority of Magnentius, will be abolished, and henceforth this nefarious license will be revoked.
4	16.10.4	12/4/356	Constantius Augustus to Taurus, Praetorian Prefect: It is our pleasure that the temples, in all places and all cities, be immediately closed, so that, with access forbidden, all the depraved [*perditis*] seeking to do wrong are denied the opportunity. It is also our will that all people abstain from sacrifices [*sacrificiis*].
5	9.16.7	9/9/364	Emperors Valentinian and Valens Augusti to Secundus, Praetorian Prefect: Hereafter no one will attempt to perform nefarious prayers [*nefarias preces*] or magic preparations [*magicos apparatus*] or funeral sacrifices [*sacrificia funesta*] at night.

	C. Theo.	Date	Translation
6	16.10.7	12/21/381	Emperors Gratian, Valentinian, and Theodosius Augusti to Florus, Praetorian Prefect:
			If any frenzied or sacrilegious [*vesanus ac sacrilegus*] person should immerse himself in forbidden sacrifices [*vetitis sacrificiis*], by day or by night, as a seer, and if he believes he should undertake, or thinks that he should approach, a shrine or a temple for the execution of such a crime, he should know that he will be subject to proscriptions, since we warned by our lawful arrangement that god must be honored by sacred prayers [*castis precibus*] and not be profaned by horrible incantations [*diris carminibus*].
7	16.10.9	5/25/385	Emperors Gratian, Valentinian, and Theodosius Augusti to Cynegius, Praetorian Prefect:
			No mortal will have the audacity of performing sacrifices [*sacrificii*], so that by the inspection of the liver and the examination of the entrails of the sacrificial victims, he may obtain the hope of a false prophecy, or what is worse, he may [claim to] learn the future from execrable consultations.

These laws reveal a repetitive set of fears and distinct ideology of dangerous and illicit sacrificial practices, which can be briefly summarized:

1. The first law, dating from Constantine's reign in 321, bans private sacrifice in the context of interpreting omens. Concern over such private divinatory practices was nothing new. Emperors, in particular, were always concerned about clandestine attempts to predict the rise and fall of new emperors.[42] Interestingly, *public* divinatory sacrifice (the ancient custom of consulting *haruspices*), over which the emperor had more control, is explicitly approved of in this law.[43]

2. The second law, from Constantius in 341, links sacrifice to one of the most evocative polemical words in Roman religious discourse, *superstitio*. The context of this law has been excised, but this may be the first general ban on sacrifice to be preserved. Libanius indeed claimed that it was Constantius who first banned sacrifice (*Or.*

---

42. Sandwell, "Outlawing 'Magic,'" 95–96, 101. For a broad discussion of divination in the ancient Mediterranean, see Leslie Kelly, *Prophets, Prophecy, and Oracles in the Roman Empire: Jewish, Christian, and Greco-Roman Cultures* (London: Routledge, 2018).

43. Curran, "Constantine and the Ancient Cults," 71.

30.7). The law explicitly links sacrifice to *superstitio* and madness. Salzman has done a full study of the novel use of *superstitio* in the Code, showing how it is increasingly applied to elements of traditional Roman worship.[44]

3. The third law, again from Constantius, bans "nocturnal sacrifice." Nocturnal rituals were, of course, highly suspect going all the way back to the Bacchanalia scandal of 186 BCE.

4. The fourth ties temple sites to "depraved" persons, suggesting that only illicit activities take place there, and repeats a ban on sacrifice.

5. The fifth links wicked prayers, magical preparations, and funeral sacrifices performed at night.

6. The sixth again raises concern over the issues of nocturnal rituals and illicit divination performed by "frenzied or sacrilegious" persons.[45] It also makes a distinction between appropriate prayers and the illicit prayers or hymns (*carminibus*) associated with sacrifice.

7. The seventh associates sacrifice, again, with illicit divinatory practices in which people falsely claim to predict the future.[46]

Much more could be said about these laws and the social concerns they reflect, but what is clear is that these emperors were explicitly linking sacrifice to established notions of impiety and *superstitio*. Suspicion of treason is explicit in several laws. Laws 1, 6, and 7 are focused on divinatory practices where the concern is that sacrifice is part of rituals in which people claim to predict the future. Emperors had always seen these rituals as dangerous, because such supposed prophecies of the rise and fall of leaders were used to sway political support.[47] The central problems raised here are not with sacrifice itself but with the association of sacrifice with *superstitio*, clandestine rituals, and treason.

Notice that none of these laws frames the ban on sacrifice as part of a ban on paganism.[48] The laws only project some vaguely defined conception of "crazy" people. It is also important to point out that the mention of

---
44. For a full discussion of *superstitio* in the Code in particular, see Michele R. Salzman, "'Superstitio' in the 'Codex Theodosianus' and the Persecution of Pagans," *VC* 41 (1987): 172–88. For a broad analysis of the term, see also Dale B. Martin, *Inventing Superstition: From the Hippocratics to the Christians* (Cambridge: Harvard University Press, 2004).
45. Sandwell, "Outlawing 'Magic,'" 107.
46. Ibid., 109.
47. Ibid., 111.
48. Sandwell points out that the term *pagani* is notably absent from most of the antisacrificial laws. The term, in fact, never occurs in the main parts of the Code addressing laws against sacrifice (C. Theo. 16.10 and 9.16) (Sandwell, "Outlawing 'Magic,'" 89 n. 6).

Christianity is notably missing from these laws.[49] The absence of specifically Christian references in the laws against sacrifice is telling, because the Code has a lot to say about Christianity in other places. It contains extensive laws upholding Nicene Christianity as the only legitimate form of Christianity, and it explicitly bans a whole range of so-called Christian heresies, often describing them in detail (C. Theo. 16.1–7). These laws are in a different section of the Code, suggesting that the compilers, at least, did not think that the bans on sacrifice fit with the laws about Christianity specifically.

In making these proclamations about sacrifice, Constantine and his successors were articulating a new vision of imperial order and Roman identity in which sacrifice did not play the key role that it had in previous identity constructs. Why? Rives gets us closest when he remarks that Constantine and his heirs are interested in a different model of imperial power, one that is not tied so closely to local civic elites and is instead tied to a new network of imperial officials appointed by the emperors themselves. Sacrifice was a key element of this ideological shift.

Arjan Zuiderhoek has shown that sacrifice played a key role not simply in maintaining and indexing the power of Roman civic elites but in *legitimating* that power.[50] This is significant in a radically unequal society such as that of the late empire. Public acts of sacrifice and euergetism worked to bolster the ideology that rich men were also *great* and *pious* men who deserved their position, what Max Weber called the "theodicy of good fortune."[51] In devaluing sacrifice, Constantine and his followers were devaluing a key support structure of local subimperial elites.

Returning to the question of who benefited: What would the impact of these laws be on the ground? The average person would likely not be

---

49. Indeed, the only laws in the Code that mention both sacrifice and Christianity together are 16.2.5, a law from Constantine stating that Christian clergy should not be forced to sacrifice, and a law from 383 stating that Christians who turn to temples are banned from making testaments. Neither of these laws bans sacrifice; they just ban forcing Christians to do it, and they punish Christian apostates. Not only does this law from 383 assume that temples are still in operation decades after the law of 356 that supposedly closed all temples: it also specifies Christians, leaving out any explicit punishment for non-Christians who "turn to altars and temples." This law seems to be about prohibiting Christian apostasy, not sacrifice in general.

50. Arjan Zuiderhoek, *The Politics of Munificence in the Roman Empire: Citizens, Elites, and Benefactors in Asia Minor* (Cambridge: Cambridge University Press, 2009), 113–53. Rives also makes this point ("Orthopraxy and Orthodoxy," 162–63).

51. H. H. Gerth and C. Wright Mills, eds. *From Max Weber: Essays in Sociology* (New York: Oxford University Press, 1946), 271. See also Cooper, "Christianity, Private Power," 329. Of course, sacrifice had also worked to legitimate the power of emperors going all the way back to Augustus, but the experience of the third century and particularly the experience of Decius showed that it was not working very well anymore. Constantine and his heirs tried a different strategy.

affected much at all. The offering of extremely expensive animals was always a game for the rich. A person who had been accustomed to getting a portion of sacrificial meat at a civic festival would likely no longer get one, but it is not clear that average people got such meat with any regularity anyway, as F. S. Naiden has shown.[52] There is no evidence of an appreciable increase in vegetarianism in the fourth century. Animal husbandry continued as it always had. The slaughter of animals was now no longer a ritualized act, but it still took place.[53] The everyday religious practices of the majority of the population (prayer and small-scale agricultural offerings in the home) would not be disrupted by an imperial ban on sacrifice.

For elites, however, the change would have been significant. Libanius and Symmachus give some evidence of this impact.[54] Julian also provides evidence that civic sacrifice in Antioch had all but ceased by the mid-fourth century (*Misopogon* 361b). This change meant that the key practice by which civic elites signaled their elite status and, again, as Zuiderhoek stresses, the *legitimacy* of their elite status was gone. This change would have strongly favored elites whose power and legitimacy came from imperial imprimatur, people like the new senators created by Constantine. The main losers would have been local civic elites not connected to the imperial regime. Their cultural capital had been tied to civic sacrifices, but these were now associated with *superstitio*, magic, and nocturnal rites and were increasingly being banned outright. Weakening local elites not only enhanced the power of imperially appointed elites, but it was also a good safety measure. Networks of elites not tied to the imperial regime were exactly the kind of people who, if they gained enough power, assassinated emperors and overthrew imperial dynasties.

These laws would have affected Christians differently. Understanding the spread of Christianity is a matter not simply of exploring why Christianity spread at the expense of other traditions but also of considering why one particular form of Christianity came to dominance—it is not simply people becoming Christians, but people becoming a certain kind of Christian. Recalling that many Christians in the fourth century made

---

52. F. S. Naiden, "Blessèd Are the Parasites," in *Greek and Roman Animal Sacrifice: Ancient Victims, Modern Observers*, ed. Christopher A. Faraone and F. S. Naiden (New York: Cambridge University Press, 2012), 55–83.

53. The deritualizing of sacrifice has broader significance for the success of Christianity that cannot be explored here. See Ullucci, *Funding Spiritual Offerings: Wealth, Social Networks, and the Spread of Christianity* (Oxford University Press, forthcoming).

54. See Libanius, *Or.* 1.201; 14.41; 24.36; 30. Libanius several times argues that rituals were performed to traditional gods, but that sacrifice was specifically not performed. See Sandwell, "Outlawing 'Magic,'" 102–9. On Symmachus, see Michele Renee Salzman, "The End of Public Sacrifice: Changing Definitions of Sacrifices in Post-Constantinian Rome and Italy," in *Ancient Mediterranean Sacrifice*, ed. Jennifer Wright Knust and Zsuzsanna Várhelyi (New York: Oxford University Press, 2011), 167–83.

animal offerings, I point out that the laws in the Code make no exception for animals offered to Christian saints, martyrs, or honored dead. These practices too would be associated with impiety and *superstitio* and would be subject to imperial ban. The Christian beneficiaries were the kinds of Christians whose translocal leadership structures and antisacrificial discourse happened to meld well with this new imperial identity.[55]

This is the form of Christianity that comes to dominance in the fourth century. These Christians benefit ideologically and materially from imperial support and also from the ideological shift on the part of elites who bought into the new image of imperial identity. Bans on sacrifice meant rerouting patterns of euergetism for elites at all levels. One part of this was a rerouting of money that had once gone to civic sacrifices and civic temples but that now went to Christian churches. There was a huge influx of wealth into churches of the fourth and fifth centuries, evidenced by their increasing economic impact and their increasingly daring architectural achievements, as Peter Brown has shown.[56]

To conclude, the key winner here is a particular form of Christianity whose complex antisacrificial discourse harmonized perfectly with a fourth-century emperor looking for ways to articulate a pious Roman identity different from the traditional views that had for centuries been articulated through animal sacrifice.

None of this helped the animals who went on providing a key protein source for those who could afford them. Ideologically, though, the killing of animals had been transformed. It was radically dissociated from piety and Roman identity. It was also dissociated from its ritual context. In the newly evolving conception of religion in late antiquity, the killing and butchering of animals had nothing to do with religion. That legacy is still very much with us and can be seen in modern American reactions to religious traditions that still practice sacrifice, such as the Afro-Caribbean tradition known as Santería.[57]

---

55. Stanley Stowers calls this "the religion of literate experts and political power" and stresses this combination as a central feature of the success of the dominant form of Christianity ("The Religion of Plant and Animal Offerings versus the Religion of Meanings, Essences, and Textual Mysteries," in Knust and Várhelyi, *Ancient Mediterranean Sacrifice*, 35–56, here 49–51.

56. Peter Brown, *Through the Eye of a Needle: Wealth, the Fall of Rome, and the Making of Christianity in the West, 350–550 AD* (Princeton: Princeton University Press, 2014).

57. Church of Lukumi Babalu Aye v. City of Hialeah, 508. US Supreme Court 520 (1993).

Dolphins are Humans of the Sea (b. Bekhorot 8a)

Animals and Legal Categorization in Rabbinic Literature

JORDAN D. ROSENBLUM
University of Wisconsin, Madison

The field of Critical Animal Studies troubles the binaries between human and nonhuman animals, exploring how reconsideration of these strict binaries deprivileges humanness and how such a reorientation affects the ethics and representation of both human and nonhuman animals.[1] Recently, scholars have begun to consider how insights from Critical Animal Studies might inform their reading of rabbinic literature.[2] This essay contributes to this trend by focusing on how the ancient rabbis used human and nonhuman animals to interrogate and delineate the boundaries between

---

I thank my fellow participants at the "Animals and Law in Antiquity" Symposium at Brown University, especially Beth Berkowitz and Saul Olyan; the faculty of the Center for Jewish Studies at the University of Minnesota; and Michael Naparstek and Catherine Bonesho for feedback on earlier drafts of this essay. I am the only human animal to whom any remaining errors should be attributed.

1. For an excellent summary of recent scholarship on Critical Animal Studies, with particular attention to how it informs the study of rabbinic literature, see Beth A. Berkowitz, *Animals and Animality in the Babylonian Talmud* (New York: Cambridge University Press, 2018), 1–26. Conversation with Karl Steel informed my formulation of several points in the introduction to this essay.

2. For example, see Berkowitz, *Animals and Animality*; Rachel Neis, "Reproduction of Species: Humans, Animals, and Hybrids in Early Rabbinic Science," *JSQ* 24 (2017): 1–29; and Mira Beth Wasserman, *Jews, Gentiles, and Other Animals: The Talmud after the Humanities*, Divinations (Philadelphia University of Pennsylvania Press, 2017). Julia Watts Belser is also working on this topic. Though my focus is on the classical rabbinic movement, interest in Critical Animal Studies is also evidenced in the work of scholars focusing on biblical and medieval rabbinic literature; see, e.g., Ken Stone, *Reading the Hebrew Bible with Animal Studies* (Stanford, CA: Stanford University Press, 2018); and David I. Shyovitz, *A Remembrance of His Wonders: Nature and the Supernatural in Medieval Ashkenaz*, Jewish Culture and Contexts (Philadelphia: University of Pennsylvania Press, 2017).

certain legal categories. My aim is not to offer an exhaustive catalog but rather to investigate preliminarily some of the fascinating ways that, for the rabbis, animals are good to think with.

More specifically, I focus on a few (of the many) instances in which inquiry into animals is used discursively to dehumanize certain human animals.³ From a modern perspective, these texts are often difficult to digest, as they depict non-Jews as less than human. Seeking neither to critique nor apologize for these texts, I simply state that this discomfort is intentional, as comparing the human Other to the nonhuman serves — by design — to erase the important cultural distinction between their humanity and their animality.⁴ Discussing this discursive function, Beth Berkowitz notes:

> The rabbinic Other is the more obvious category with which to be considering animals. Others become such by being compared to animals. Others associate with the wrong animals. Others relate to animals in ways that they shouldn't. It is hard to even imagine the Other without the animal, who is the Other par excellence.⁵

While Critical Animal Studies may reevaluate the crisp binary between human and nonhuman animals, the ancient rabbis clearly utilized this binary to remove certain people from the category of "Us" and place them firmly across the border, in the territory of "Them."

"What Are Dolphins?" Human/NonHuman Animals and Rabbinic Categorization

The move to dehumanize certain human animals relies on broader rabbinic presumptions about categorization. Everything — whether object, animal, location, time, or other — belongs in a legal category, to which various, specific rules apply. The rabbis devote significant energy to considering interstitial people, periods, places, property, and so on, in order to decide into which category to place them. Hybrid animals are one such

---

3. On how law can deprive personhood and dehumanize categories of human animals, see Colin Dayan, *The Law Is a White Dog: How Legal Rituals Make and Unmake Persons* (Princeton: Princeton University Press, 2011).

4. My use of the term *animality* here is informed by Berkowitz, *Animals and Animality*, 13–14.

5. Berkowitz, *Animals and Animality*, 184. On the Other in rabbinic literature, see Christine Elizabeth Hayes, "The 'Other' in Rabbinic Literature," in *The Cambridge Companion to the Talmud and Rabbinic Literature*, ed. Charlotte Elisheva Fonrobert and Martin S. Jaffee (New York: Cambridge University Press, 2007), 243–69.

area of concern.⁶ For example, m. Bek. 1:2 inquires, If a pure nonhuman animal gives birth to what appears to be an impure nonhuman animal, is that offspring kosher for ingestion?⁷ Working through the many variables that this scenario presents, t. Bek. 1:10–11 notes that different species have different gestational periods. For example, the text asserts that the pig gives birth after sixty days, whereas the ape gives birth after three years. Rachel Neis argues, "This conspicuous display of knowledge about modes of reproduction and gestation periods of a variety of creatures ... serves as a justifying explanation for why interbreeding is not actually possible."⁸ While most of this passage works for Neis's larger argument, there is one statement that does not quite fit. According to t. Bek. 1:11, "Dolphins give birth and grow [offspring] like humans."

What does it mean that dolphins gestate "like humans"?⁹ The Babylonian Talmud considers this very question:

> Our Rabbis taught: ... "Dolphins are fruitful and multiply like humans."
> What are dolphins?
> Said Rav Yehudah: Humans of the sea. (b. Bek. 7b–8a)

Immediately we notice that the version of this tradition quoted here has an important difference in wording: rather than dolphins giving birth and growing like humans, dolphins are explicitly described as *reproducing* like humans. I render the Hebrew text more literally, to further highlight this fact. The wording "fruitful and multiply" [Hebrew: *pārîn wərābîn*] cues an association with Gen 1:28:

> God blessed them and God said to them: "Be fruitful and multiply [Hebrew: *pərû ûrəbû*], fill the earth and master it; and rule the fish of the sea, and the birds of the sky, and all the living things that creep on the earth."¹⁰

---

6. For references to rabbinic discussions of hybrid animals, see Berkowitz, *Animals and Animality*, 46–47; Jordan D. Rosenblum, *The Jewish Dietary Laws in the Ancient World* (New York: Cambridge University Press, 2016), 116 n. 43; and, for a humorous example, see Ann VanderMeer and Jeff VanderMeer, *The Kosher Guide to Imaginary Animals: The Evil Monkey Dialogues* (San Francisco: Tachyon, 2010).

7. Discussed in Neis, "Reproduction of Species," 17–18.

8. Ibid., 23.

9. Hebrew: *kə'ādām* ("like human"). Neis considers issues of "like" [Hebrew *kə*], but not in regard to this specific text (see, e.g., "Reproduction of Species," 17–21). Unless otherwise noted, all translations are my own.

10. For a history of the interpretation of this verse, see Jeremy Cohen, *"Be Fertile and Increase, Fill the Earth and Master It": The Ancient and Medieval Career of a Biblical Text* (Ithaca, NY: Cornell University Press, 1989).

In Gen 1:28, God commands the primordial man and woman to reproduce and rule over the earth in a manner that reflects a rigid, hierarchical binary between human and nonhuman animals. By invoking this language, not only are dolphins engaging in a human reproductive activity, but the audience is expected to know the second part of the verse, which could be read as implying that dolphins are now ruling over the birds in the sky, the living creatures on the earth, and even over all other fish in the sea.

This realization sparks the anonymous voice of the Talmud to inquire, "What are dolphins?" Before answering this question, it is worth pausing to consider an important variant text. The medieval commentator Rashi has a version of this text that states, "Dolphins are fruitful and multiply from humans."[11] The difference between "*like* humans" and "*from* humans" is a single prefix letter [*kaph* and *mem*, respectively]. Whether this variant was known to the editors of the Talmud, the logic of this grammar supports Rav Yehudah's assertion that dolphins are *bənê yamā'*, which literally means in Aramaic "sons of the sea," but which I render "humans of the sea."[12] Dolphins are thus aquatic mammals that, at the very least, share some special similarities with humans and, at most, according to Rashi's text, engage in procreative sex with humans.

As odd as it might seem, the notion of human–dolphin intercourse is actually a common motif, appearing both in the ancient Mediterranean and well beyond.[13] Rashi himself was aware of this motif, which he incorporates into his own commentary on this passage.[14] Yet the ambiguity still remains. Are dolphins *like* humans or *from* humans? And, in either case, how precisely are they legally categorized? Rather than answer these questions, I use them to point toward a larger issue: in the words of Berkowitz, "… animals serve frequently in rabbinic literature to define the limits of reality. Animals sit at the edge of personhood, like a variety of human characters—women, children, slaves, foreigners."[15] To define what it means to be the dolphin (or any other nonhuman animal) is to define

---

11. The Tosafot support Rashi's reading. The relevant Rashi and the Tosafot both appear at the very top of b. Bekhorot 8a.

12. While rabbinic authors likely presumed the human animals to be male and the dolphins to be female when considering the act of copulation, there is no reason to presume a singular gender for the offspring; therefore, I render the phrase "humans of the sea" rather than "sons of the sea."

13. For example, see Craig A. Williams, "When a Dolphin Loves a Boy: Some Greco-Roman and Native American Love Stories," *Classical Antiquity* 32 (2013): 200–242. On the dolphin in folklore and mythology, with particular attention to human–dolphin sexual encounters, see Alan Rauch, *Dolphin* (London: Reaktion Books, 2014), 70–103 (discussion of this talmudic passage appears on 97–98).

14. "'Humans of the sea': There are fish in the sea that are half the form of man and half the form of fish, and in French [they are called] '*sereine*' [derived from the Latin *siren*]" (Rashi on b. Bek. 8a, s.v. *bənê yamā'*).

15. Berkowitz, *Animals and Animality*, 38.

what it means to be the human. It can also serve to define what it means for human animals to lose their status as humans. It is to this conversation that we now turn.

Defining (the) Human

For the rabbis, a human animal is capable of agency, that is, the ability to act with intention and efficacy.[16] Often, however, this legal concept of agency applies only to *Jewish* human animals. In limiting agency, the non-Jew regularly is equated with a nonhuman animal. In this section, we examine two instances in which this process results in dehumanizing the non-Jew.[17]

Is the Butcher a Human or an Ape?

Valid rabbinic slaughter requires that three things be fit (or proper, the literal definition of "kosher"): (1) the nonhuman animal that is slaughtered; (2) the slaughtering procedure itself; and (3) the human animal who is slaughtering. While the Hebrew Bible spells out some of these concerns (mostly in regard to that which is slaughtered, less so in regard to the procedure and the one slaughtering), the rabbis elaborate various related issues.[18] It is in this context that we encounter our first text:

> All may slaughter, and their slaughter is valid [Hebrew: kəšērâ], except for a person who is deaf, a person with cognitive impairment, or a minor, lest they ruin the meat in their act of slaughtering.
> But all of these who slaughter while others observe them, their slaughter is valid.
> An animal slaughtered by a gentile is carcass, and it imparts impurity by carriage.
> One who slaughters at night, and so too a person who is blind who slaughters, his slaughter is valid.

---

16. See Howard Eilberg-Schwartz, *The Human Will in Judaism: The Mishnah's Philosophy of Intention*, BJS 103 (Atlanta: Scholars Press, 1986).

17. There are myriad examples in rabbinic literature in which non-Jews constitute a categorical Other. See, e.g., Steven D. Fraade, "Navigating the Anomalous: Non-Jews at the Intersection of Early Rabbinic Law and Narrative," in *The Other in Jewish Thought and History: Constructions of Jewish Culture and Identity*, ed. Laurence J. Silberstein and Robert L. Cohn, New Perspectives on Jewish Studies (New York: New York University Press, 1994), 145–65.

18. See Jordan D. Rosenblum, *Food and Identity in Early Rabbinic Judaism* (New York: Cambridge University Press, 2010); and Rosenblum, *Jewish Dietary Laws*.

> One who slaughters on the Sabbath or on Yom Kippur, even though he becomes liable for death, his slaughter is valid. (m. Hul. 1:1)[19]

While "all may slaughter, and their slaughter is valid," the next word defines the remainder of this text: "except." In typical rabbinic fashion, a broad statement is made and then immediately exceptions are introduced. For example, we learn that "all" refers to all adults who are neither hearing impaired nor cognitively impaired; we learn that one who slaughters on the Sabbath or on Yom Kippur—actions punishable by death—still produces valid animal slaughter;[20] and, as we shall discuss in more detail, we learn that "all" refers only to Jews.

Tucked into this passage is a provocative claim: "An animal slaughtered by a gentile is carcass." Carcass [Hebrew: nəbēlâ] refers to an animal that has died a natural death.[21] In addition to its purity implications (as the passage mentions, carcass transmits impurity to anyone who carries it), it is important to note that this category of death is not at the hands of a human/nonhuman animal. Further, as I have argued elsewhere, "the tannaitic innovation that an animal slaughtered by a non-Jew is not fit for Jewish consumption *simply because it is slaughtered by a non-Jew* is introduced without justification and, so it would seem, without controversy."[22] Taken together, then, this passage states that slaughter by a non-Jew has the same legal effect as the nonhuman animal in question dying from natural causes.

Slaughter by non-Jews, therefore, is not deemed equivalent to an action performed by a human animal. But does this fully dehumanize non-Jews? After all, their slaughter is simply deemed a death by natural

---

19. Translation based on Jordan D. Rosenblum, "Hulin," in *The Mishnah: An Annotated Translation*, ed. Shaye J. D. Cohen, Robert Goldenberg, and Hayim Lapin (New York: Oxford University Press, forthcoming).

20. Commenting on this latter ruling, Barry Scott Wimpfheimer states, "The existence of multiple registers gives the rabbis a powerful tool to deal with the relationships of morality and the law. The rabbis can accept the possibility that legal acts can be considered simultaneously odious and effective. An animal properly slaughtered on Yom Kippur is kosher even though the slaughterer is liable for the death penalty" (*The Talmud: A Biography*, Lives of Great Religious Books [Princeton: Princeton University Press, 2018], 61; see also 96).

21. On this term, see Rosenblum, *Food and Identity*, 68–69; and Rosenblum, *Jewish Dietary Laws*, 101. As these references point out, the rabbis reinterpret the term "carcass" to refer to an improperly slaughtered animal. A gentile slaughtering an animal results in improper slaughter; yet, as I argue below, the connection between the original meaning of this term (a natural death) continues to influence rabbinic discussion on this topic.

22. Rosenblum, *Food and Identity*, 78 (emphasis original). My discussion in this entire section draws from *Food and Identity*, 77–80, 154–58. See also David M. Freidenreich, *Foreigners and Their Food: Constructing Otherness in Jewish, Christian, and Islamic Law* (Berkeley: University of California Press, 2011), 48–52, 54–55.

causes. This ambiguity is clarified in a text edited shortly after our previous one:

> All are fit to slaughter, even a Samaritan, even an uncircumcised man, and even a Jewish apostate.
> An animal slaughtered by a heretic is [regarded as an act of] idolatry.
> And an animal slaughtered by a gentile, in that case, it is invalid; and an animal slaughtered by an ape, in that case, it is invalid.
> As it is said: "*You* may slaughter ... and *you* may eat" [Deut 12:21].
> [*You*] may not [eat] that which a gentile has slaughtered; and [*you*] may not [eat] that which an ape has slaughtered; and [*you*] may not [eat] that which is slaughtered by its own action. (t. Ḥul. 1:1)

I begin by clarifying that "all" — meaning "all *Jews*" — are fit to slaughter, including three categories of people who might be classified as Jew-*ish*.[23] We then learn that slaughter by a Jewish heretic [Hebrew: *mîn*] is deemed by the text to be equivalent to an idolatrous sacrifice.[24] This is the first pivot point in my argument. Unlike the previous categories of those who are Jew-*ish*, heretics are deemed outside the boundaries of Judaism. But heretics are still technically Jewish. So their slaughter "must 'count' for something; hence, it is classified as idolatrous."[25]

After establishing that slaughter by the heretic is idolatrous — the polar opposite of proper rabbinic ritual practice — we turn our attention to the second pivot point of this text: slaughter by gentiles and apes are equated, both resulting in invalid slaughter. Elsewhere, I have argued the following:

> Butchery — a cultural practice that separates humans from animals — is now marked by the Tannaim as a distinctly Jewish practice. Gentile slaughter is (pejoratively, it would seem) equated with slaughter by an ape.... Unlike the heretic, whose slaughter is recognized as actually occurring (and hence is pejoratively branded as idolatrous), the Gentile's slaughter is likened to the action of an animal; it is a natural, not human, act.[26]

The exclusion of gentiles from the human cultural practice of butchery is furthered by the inclusion of a biblical reference. The full verse of Deut 12:21 states:

---

23. On these categories in this text, see Rosenblum, *Food and Identity*, 154–61.
24. On apostate versus heretic in this text, see Rosenblum, *Food and Identity*, 155–56.
25. Ibid., 157; see also Freidenreich, *Foreigners and Their Food*, 49.
26. Rosenblum, *Food and Identity*, 79–80.

> If the place where the Lord has chosen to establish His name is too far from you, *you may slaughter* from your cattle and your sheep that the Lord gave you, as I have commanded you; *and you may eat* to your heart's content in your settlements.

Our text assumes that the implicit *you* in this text is a normative rabbinic Jew. *You* may eat only that which *you* slaughtered. Their slaughter is invalid for ingestion by *you*. And not only that, but the three categories of Them are equated in a way that marks each as the product of nonhuman action: gentile slaughter, ape slaughter, and carcass.[27]

In sum, slaughter by a gentile is deemed, at best, a nonhuman action and, at worst, the action of a nonhuman animal. In establishing this legal principle, the gentile is dehumanized, while, concomitantly, the Jew becomes the normative human animal.

Like Cattle-Pens on the Sabbath

Another manner in which the legal agency of non-Jews is limited via their equivalence with nonhuman animals appears in a discussion of the *'êrûb*. Literally meaning "mixture," an *'êrûb* is a legal fiction by which multiple domains can be "mixed"—that is, combined—into a single domain, allowing for the carrying of objects between what would otherwise be separate domains, an action prohibited on the Sabbath.[28] In detailed exposition of this rabbinic principle, conversation turns to a particular type of *'êrûb*, one that merges households that share a courtyard. Without the creation of such an *'êrûb*, residents of each household could not carry objects outside of their home on the Sabbath without violating rabbinic law.

In m. Eruv. 6:1, the shared courtyard of a Jew and a non-Jew is introduced, when we learn:

> [If a Jew] lives with a non-Jew in a courtyard, or with one who does not agree with the *'êrûb*, in that case, that [person] imposes a prohibition [against carrying on the Sabbath] on him [= the Jew], the words of Rabbi Meir.
> Rabbi Eliezer ben Yaakov says: He never prohibits unless there are two Jews, who would prohibit one another.

Without getting bogged down too much in the details of this mishnah, it teaches that, when a Jew shares a courtyard with either a non-Jew or a

---

27. For understanding the phrase "slaughtered by its own action" as referring to carcass, see Freidenreich, *Foreigners and Their Food*, 238 n. 8.

28. See Jer 17:21–22, and the entire tractate of Eruvin, where our texts in this section originate.

(presumably nonrabbinic) Jew who rejects the rabbinic concept of the *'êrûb*, then the Jew is forbidden to carry anything into their shared courtyard on the Sabbath. Another opinion is offered wherein non-Jews do not prohibit; only Jews matters legally.[29]

When we look at how Tosefta treats this topic, a very different narrative emerges:[30]

> A courtyard of a non-Jew, in that case, it is like a cattle-pen [Hebrew: *kədîr šel bəhēmâ*].
> It is permitted to bring in and take out from the courtyard to the houses [surrounding the courtyard]; and from the houses to the courtyard; and utensils that are for the Sabbath that are in the courtyard, it is permissible to carry them in the courtyard.
> [But if even] a single Jew lives in [a courtyard], in that case, it is prohibited [to carry on the Sabbath], because it is like his courtyard. (t. Eruv. 5:19)[31]

The courtyard of a non-Jew is compared to a cattle-pen. Legally and rhetorically, it is worth unpacking this simile. A cattle-pen encloses and contains cattle—that is, explicitly nonhuman animals. A courtyard shared between non-Jews encloses all of its residences (and residents) in a single domain. As a single domain, one can bring objects into and out of homes that share that courtyard without violating rabbinic regulations prohibiting carrying on the Sabbath.[32] The same statement applies to cattle-pens. Beyond the mere legal point of clarifying Sabbath carrying law, the comparison of non-Jewish courtyards to cattle-pens clearly serves to dehumanize non-Jews.

But just in case this rhetorical move is not clear enough, the text continues on to note that, if a single Jew resides in a shared courtyard, then Rabbi Meir's ruling from m. Eruv. 6:1 applies. Now, a Jew cannot carry anything on the Sabbath, since it is no longer a single domain, but separate domains. When only non-Jews lived there, it was an undifferentiated cattle-pen inhabited by non-Jews, that is, by nonhuman animals. But now a human animal—a Jew—has moved in, and hence it is deemed equivalent

---

29. According to b. Eruv. 62b, the latter is the preferred opinion (cf. y. Eruv. 6:1, 23b).

30. This is the second instance I introduce of a toseftan text intensifying the rhetoric of the non-Jew as dehumanized from that found in its mishnaic analogue. While it is well beyond the scope of this essay, it would be interesting to see whether this represents a general trend. What can be said is that there is a general trend, over time, in which this rhetoric of dehumanization intensifies, with the most by far in the Babylonian Talmud.

31. This tradition is discussed in more detail in both Talmuds; see y. Eruv. 6:1, 23a–b; b. Eruv. 61b–62b. Due to space limits, I cannot address these later discussions, though they offer interesting material that further supports my argument above.

32. On this point, see Saul Lieberman, *The Tosefta: According to Codex Vienna, with Variants from Codices Erfurt, London, Genizah Mss. and Editio Princeps (Venice 1521)*, vol. 2, *The Order of Mo'ed*, 2nd printing (New York: Jewish Theological Seminary of America, 2002 [1962]), 115.

to "his courtyard." In short, the shared courtyard is not deemed a human habitation until a rabbinic human moves in; and only Jews are fully human.

Defining Bestiality

Thus far, I have argued that rabbinic literature dehumanizes the non-Jew. This point has been made by scholars previously, so it is certainly not my own insight. However, an important logical extension of this observation has been missed, namely, Can the dehumanized animal *actually* engage in "bestiality"? By definition, bestiality refers to a sexual interaction between human and nonhuman animals. But if neither animal is a human, is "bestiality" the correct nomenclature? In this section, I argue against using "bestiality" for describing such sexual interactions.

"Dearer to Them Than Their Own Wives"

The *locus classicus* for the connection between non-Jews and bestiality is b. Avod. Zar. 22a–23a. Due to limits of space, I will discuss only a piece of this complex and difficult narrative, which nevertheless serves to illustrate my overall argument.[33]

The talmudic passage opens by quoting m. Avod. Zar. 2:1:

> They do not place animals in inns belonging to non-Jews, because They are suspected of mounting.[34]

This mishnah asserts that Jews may not stable their nonhuman animals at inns owned by non-Jews, out of concern for "mounting" (i.e., sexual intercourse). The word that I translate as "mounting" [Hebrew: *rəbîʻâ*], its most literal meaning, is usually rendered "bestiality." Summarizing the standard argument for how the rabbis use the Hebrew root *resh-bet-ayin*, Michael Satlow states, "The word is reserved for animal intercourse, intercourse between a human and an animal, and homoerotic intercourse."[35]

---

33. For recent treatments of this pericope with attention to Critical Animal Studies, see Berkowitz, *Animals and Animality*, 185–87; and Wasserman, *Jews, Gentiles, and Other Animals*, 73–119.

34. Quoted in b. Avod. Zar. 22a. The mishnah continues, but I cite only the part that is relevant for our conversation.

In both this and the following text, I capitalize They/Them when the text is implying this plural third-person pronoun in the manner that modern scholars discuss Us/Them (Self/Other).

35. Michael L. Satlow, *Tasting the Dish: Rabbinic Rhetorics of Sexuality*, BJS 303 (Atlanta:

Though I do not disagree with this general point about its usage, I argue against understanding this term, when applied to non-Jews, as "bestiality," because such a translation obscures important nuances regarding the ways in which the Other is conceived and articulated in rabbinic literature.[36]

To illustrate my point, we turn to the talmudic commentary on this mishnah:

> What is the reason that they do not leave female [animals belonging to Jews] alone with female [non-Jews]?
> Said Mar Uqva bar Hama: Because non-Jews frequent the wives of their friends, and sometimes when he does not find her, he finds the animal and mounts it.
> Or, if you prefer, say that even if he finds her [= his friend's wife], he also mounts her [= the animal belonging to a Jew]; as Master said: Animals belonging to Jews are dearer to Them than Their own wives. (b. Avod. Zar. 22b)[37]

The text opens by presuming that the reader understands why a Jew would not leave his[38] female and male nonhuman animals alone with a male non-Jew, or his male nonhuman animals alone with a female non-Jew; but why would female nonhuman animals and female non-Jews present any concern? The answer is that non-Jews are perceived to lack self-restraint: they frequently visit their male friends' houses in order to have sexual intercourse with their friends' wives. Not only do they not care about the legal and moral concerns of adultery and lack of moderation, but they are depicted as animalistic[39] in their desires. While ideal (that is, male and Jewish) humans engage in self-restraint, non-Jewish men are so driven by their passions that they regularly have sex with their

---

Scholars Press, 1995), 202 (on "bestiality" in general, see 201–3); and, more recently, Wasserman, *Jews, Gentiles, and Other Animals*, 76, 258 n. 3.

36. My argument about dehumanization applies equally to the ways that rabbinic texts deploy this term in regard to male homoerotic intercourse: namely, it rhetorically transforms a sexual activity between two human animals into one that is understood to be between two nonhuman animals. Similarly, see Satlow, *Tasting the Dish*, 202–3.

37. On this text, see also Michael L. Satlow, "'Try to Be a Man': The Rabbinic Construction of Masculinity," *HTR* 89 (1996): 19–40, here 36. Satlow's point about the rabbinic presumption of the civilizing nature of Torah study furthers my argument, though limits of space prevent me from discussing this in detail.

38. My usage of the masculine pronoun here is intentional, as rabbinic texts presume the normative narrator and/or agent. I discuss this issue further below.

39. I use this term fully aware of the problems inherent in the binary it presumes. But that is my very point: the rabbis presume this problematic binary between human and nonhuman animal. See also Wasserman, who refers to this as "bestial desires" (*Jews, Gentiles, and Other Animals*, 88).

friends' wives; and, if their friends' wives are not home, then they have sex with any available female nonhuman animals.

This dehumanizing rhetoric is kicked up a notch when the text continues on to declare that even if non-Jews find their friends' wives at home, they would much rather engage in sexual activity with a nonhuman animal belonging to a Jew.[40] Master's statement makes this presumption crystal clear: "Animals belonging to Jews are dearer to Them than Their own wives." For this reason, Jews may not leave their female nonhuman animals alone even with female non-Jews.

Though scholars describe this sexual activity as "bestiality," I argue that the rhetoric of dehumanizing the non-Jew is not fully considered in their accounts. Jews cannot leave their nonhuman animals alone with non-Jews precisely because, unlike Jews, non-Jews cannot be expected to act as human animals are expected to: not only do they engage in unbridled sexual activity, but their men actually prefer to have sex with Jewish nonhuman animals. In this rhetoric, non-Jewish men are dehumanized; thus, their sexual activity should be interpreted as sexual activity between two nonhuman animals.[41] Hence, it is "mounting" and not "bestiality."

Beautiful Donkey

Thus far, I have attended to how non-Jewish men are dehumanized. Other non-normative human animals are dehumanized, as well: women, enslaved people, minors, people with disabilities, and so on.[42] However, the visual *eros* of rabbinic texts focuses on the male gaze, a distorted lens that we must refocus.[43] In this section, I briefly use two passages about donkeys to show how dehumanized non-Jewish—*and* non-normative—bodies trouble the usage of "bestiality."

---

40. As Wasserman states, "The hyperbole about the superiority of Jewish animals to gentile women is a potent example of rabbinic swagger, as it simultaneously casts aspersions both on the sexual allure of gentile women (less attractive than cattle) and on the moral character of gentile men (they like to sleep with animals)" (*Jews, Gentiles, and Other Animals*, 88).

41. Perhaps this observation is furthered by the fact that, since they are preferred, non-human animals belonging to Jews could be viewed as actually more human than non-Jewish women. One reason for this preference could be their association with Jews—that is, with human animals.

42. To this list, I could also add non-rabbinic Jews. See the famous passage in b. Pesah. 49a–b; and, for brief discussion and scholarly references, Berkowitz, *Animals and Animality*, 185.

43. In general, see Rachel Neis, *The Sense of Sight in Rabbinic Culture: Jewish Ways of Seeing in Late Antiquity*, Greek Culture in the Roman World (New York: Cambridge University Press, 2013), esp. 113–69.

In the first talmudic passage, a famous rabbi gazes at a beautiful non-Jewish woman:

> One who sees beautiful trees or beautiful human beings [Hebrew: bənê-'ādām] says: "Blessed is the One who created such beautiful creatures in His world" [cf. t. Ber. 6:4].
> Once upon a time, Rabban Gamaliel saw a beautiful non-Jewish woman, and he recited the blessing over her.
> Did not Rabbi Zeira say in the name of Rabbi Yosi bar Hanina [and] Rabbi Ba [say that] Rabbi Hiyya [said] in the name of Rabbi Yohanan: "You shall show Them no mercy" [Deut 7:2],[44] [which teaches that] you shall not grant Them favor.
> What did he say? [He did not say]: "Unbewitched!"[45] He said only "... who created such beautiful creatures in His world," because even if one saw a beautiful camel, a beautiful horse, or a beautiful donkey, one says: "Blessed is the One who created beautiful creatures in His world." (y. Ber. 9:2, 13b–c)[46]

This text opens by teaching a general blessing to recite when one encounters a beautiful tree or human animal created by God. It then introduces a story about Rabban Gamaliel gazing at a non-Jewish woman, over whom he recited this blessing due to his perception of her physical appearance. How could he have done this, the text asks, especially given biblical prescriptions against saying anything nice about non-Jews?! Clarifying the concern that Rabban Gamaliel had actually wished that no harm come upon her ("Unbewitched!"), we are told that he merely recited the blessing that one says when one encounters beautiful creatures that God creates, such as beautiful camels, horses, or donkeys.

But notice two subtle discursive moves made in this text. First, the original blessing is recited by "One who sees beautiful trees or beautiful human beings"—it does not refer to nonhuman animals. Second, in addition to including beautiful nonhuman animals in this blessing, the non-Jewish woman is compared implicitly to nonhuman animals. The normative rabbinic male gazing at a non-Jewish woman is therefore compared to a human animal gazing at a nonhuman animal. Were they to

---

44. On the violence against the Other contained in the biblical context of Deut 7:2, see T. M. Lemos, "Dispossessing Nations: Population Growth, Scarcity, and Genocide in Ancient Israel and Twentieth-Century Rwanda," in *Ritual Violence in the Hebrew Bible: New Perspectives*, ed. Saul M. Olyan (New York: Oxford University Press, 2015), 27–65, here 48.

45. I translate this term based on the suggestion of Marcus Jastrow, *Dictionary of the Targumim, the Talmud Babli and Yerushalmi, and the Midrashic Literature*, 2 vols. (1903; repr., Peabody, MA: Hendrickson, 2005), s.v. 'ăbasqanṭâ.

46. For parallels, see y. Avod. Zar. 1:9, 40a–b; b. Ber. 20a–b. For discussion, see Neis, *Sense of Sight*, 114.

engage in sexual activity, "bestiality" would be the proper term to describe their actions.[47]

In the second talmudic passage, we learn about the four things that God hates, the fourth of which is "one who has sexual intercourse in front of any living creature [Hebrew: ḥāy]" (b. Nid. 16b–17a).[48] Commenting on what this means, the following exchange appears:

> Rav Yehudah said to Shmuel: Even in front of mice?
> [Shmuel] said to him: Wise-guy![49] No, rather, for example, this refers to the house of So-and-So, which has sexual intercourse in front of their male and female slaves.
> And as for them, on what biblical basis do they justify [their actions]?
> "You stay here with the donkey" [Gen 22:5], [which teaches that slaves are] people that are similar to the donkey. (b. Nid. 17a)

God hates those who engage in sexual intercourse in the presence of any living creature. Rav Yehudah asks Shmuel if this refers to having sex even when mice are present—that is, small creatures that might hide in the corner and are not easy to detect. Shmuel rejects that view emphatically. Rather, he argues, it refers to the house of So-and-So (i.e., to the rabbinic "John Doe"), where they have sex in front of their male and female slaves. The text inquires on what biblical basis does So-and-So justify this action? On Gen 22:5, which mentions a donkey. And how does that justify this sexual exhibition? Because "[slaves are] people that are similar to the donkey."

The exact mechanism of this exegesis need not detain us. What matters is that slaves are dehumanized.[50] They are donkeys.[51] Human animals

---

47. Support for this claim can be found also in b. Sanh. 67b. In this famous text, a presumably Jewish man detects that a presumably non-Jewish woman tries to utter a magical incantation over a drink that she serves him and casts a counterspell on a beverage that he serves her. The text then reports, "He gave her a drink [and] she turned into a donkey. He rode her down to the marketplace. Her girlfriend came [and] broke the spell. [Thus,] he was seen riding upon a woman in the marketplace." Turning the woman into a donkey clearly dehumanizes her, and riding the donkey in public equates their physical contact with that of a male human sexually mounting a female donkey. For yet another example, see b. Ber. 58a.

48. On this text, see Daniel Boyarin, *Carnal Israel: Reading Sex in Talmudic Culture*, New Historicism 25 (Berkeley: University of California Press, 1993), 125–28; and Satlow, *Tasting the Dish*, 298–302.

49. I adopt this felicitous translation from Boyarin, *Carnal Israel*, 125.

50. As Boyarin argues, "Shmuel regards it simply as an attack on the Roman practice of having intercourse in the presence of slaves, a practice that indeed involved the assumption that slaves are not somehow human" (*Carnal Israel*, 126).

51. I believe another connection to Greek and Roman attitudes to be operative here, namely, the association between slaves and donkeys. Both are seen as a different class of human/nonhuman animals: those who engage in slave labor and those deemed culturally superior to them (i.e., the free man and the horse). See Jill Bough, *Donkey* (London: Reaktion

(i.e., Jews) should not be having sex in front of their slaves, who are deemed biblically equivalent to nonhuman animals.[52] It is this action that God is described as hating. When a similar exegesis of Gen 22:5 appears elsewhere in the Babylonian Talmud, the text clearly refers to Canaanite slaves—that is, to non-Jewish slaves—as "the donkey" (see b. Yev. 62a). I believe that that same understanding underlies our present text, as well, meaning that the slaves are doubly dehumanized as both slave *and* non-Jew. But remove "the donkey" from the bedroom and then normative sex may occur without God hating anything.

Conclusion

When their slaughtering is equated with that of an ape, or their courtyards are equated with cattle-pens, non-Jews are dehumanized. In the binary human/nonhuman animals, non-Jews become legally equivalent to nonhuman animals. As a result, when rabbinic texts depict non-Jews as engaging in sexual activity with nonhuman animals it should not be deemed "bestiality." On the other hand, since Jews can engage in bestiality when they gaze at non-Jews in a sexual manner, then the language of bestiality is appropriate.[53] For this reason, they refer to their non-Jewish slaves who watch them fornicate as "the donkey" and they bless God for creating "beautiful donkeys." In all of these instances, the ancient rabbis interrogate and delineate boundaries between legal categories by means of exploring the boundaries between human and nonhuman animals.

Books, 2011), 59. To this, I would also add that Priapus, the Greek god of fertility, was often depicted as a donkey, which might have led to the connection between the donkey and sexuality that we see throughout this section (see Bough, *Donkey*, 67).

52. Another text that supports my argument is y. Ber. 3:4, 6c, in which a man seeks to have sex with Rabbi's female slave and explicitly compares her to an animal [beast; Hebrew: bəhēmâ], but she invokes Exod 22:18: "Whoever lies with a beast shall surely be put to death."

53. Also, Jews engage in bestiality when they themselves have sex with nonhuman animals. For example, there is a tradition wherein drunk women desire sex with donkeys:

> It is taught: One cup [of wine] is beneficial for a woman; two [cups] is a disgrace; three [cups lead to her] making explicit sexual propositions; four [cups lead to her] making sexual propositions even to a donkey in the marketplace, [since she is so drunk that] she does not care [with whom she has sex]. Rava said: This was taught only when her husband is not with her, but [if] her husband is with her, [then] we have no problem with it. (b. Ketub. 65a)

Rabbinic men, unlike non-normative categories (women, non-Jews, etc.), are deemed capable of self-control. Therefore, drinking with their husbands is understood as a way for women to control their desires; but if they drink too much not in their husbands' presence, wives would be willing to engage in public sex acts with donkeys. Since these women are presumably Jewish, then these sexual acts can be understood as bestiality.

Writing this essay, I often had to grapple with just how deeply troubling many of these texts are to my modern values. I conclude by noting this discomfort not to distance myself from these texts but to remind my audience that this unease is integral to the texts. They are intended to depict the non-Jew as nonhuman. And the rhetoric of dehumanization is, by design, troubling and, dare I say, animalistic.

Response to Bailleul-LeSuer, Olyan, Richardson, and Tuominen

ANDREAS SCHÜLE
Universität Leipzig

Not so long ago, Jacques Derrida pointed out that talking about "animals" is a problematic way to describe nonhuman life. Ultimately, it is not the "animal world" that is depicted when we talk about "animals" but the way in which humans position themselves vis-à-vis nonhuman forms of life.[1] Among all living creatures, only one deserves a special genus designation. Everything else is animal. For Derrida, this marks the beginning of what is ultimately a blurred, biased, and distorted perception that does not correspond to empirical findings. Of course, this partiality is not a modern phenomenon. It is evidenced in European intellectual history at the latest with Aristotle's famous classification of living beings, which he fundamentally depicts in *De Anima* (413a): plants are living beings capable of growth and decay; animals, in addition, are capable of sense perception and movement; and humans, finally, are beings that have the capacity to reason. Seen from the human point of view, animals and plants are living beings that have some but not all characteristics of fully developed vitality as it occurs in humans. In other words, animals (and plants) are determined by a deficit, a lack, a not-having. Thus, our talk of animals always resonates with the sense that they are "not (entirely) human."

Only recently has this view been increasingly called into question, and for two reasons: First, following Derrida and others, one ought to ask whether the binary distinction animal/human is not too superficial and too anthropocentric to do justice to the diversity of life. Second, there is the

---
1. Jacques Derrida, *The Animal That Therefore I Am*, ed. Marie-Louise Mallet, trans. David Wills, Perspectives in Continental Philosophy (New York: Fordham University Press, 2008), 1–51.

question of law. What legal status do humans grant animals? And on what criteria are these legal statuses based? Obviously, there are differences. Looking at factory farming from an ethical and legal standpoint, the question arises as to how animals that are bred solely for the purpose of serving as human food sources ought to be treated. The legal discourse changes when one turns to animals outside the human habitat. What responsibilities do humans have to preserve various species and provide for their need for space and resources? Finally, there are also the rights of animals that are companions of humans in a broader or narrower sense. What standards must be observed, for example, in the keeping of pets? Most people treat pets not unlike human persons. But why do we not actually apply these high standards of responsibility and care to all animals? From a legal point of view, it very quickly becomes clear that animals are not all the same.

Each of the four contributions I discuss here pick out individual aspects of this broad spectrum of questions and topics. They do so with a focus on different cultural regions of the ancient world: Egypt, Mesopotamia, Syria-Palestine, and Greece. All in all, it is clear that thinking about the rights of animals is not a modern phenomenon; rather, it is in fact already documented in the earliest written cultures that have survived. And here, too, it is noticeable that there are no uniform legal systems that apply equally to all "animals," and that it is often the proximity to or remoteness from the human sphere that determines the legal status of different groups of animals. Statements about animals in general and legal statements about animals in particular are always also statements by humans about themselves. Or to put it another way: Law indicates that a preoccupation with the animal world is always also a mirror in which people perceive themselves. As the authors show, legal provisions for animals are often the preliminary stage of, or "experimental field" for, laws pertaining to humans. This generally concerns the perception of animals as legal subjects. In the context of ancient cultures, the relationship between humans and animals often reflects the social disparities among different groups of people. The hierarchy of humans over animals thus also forms the basis to legitimize hierarchies among humans: between free people and slaves, natives and strangers, and also between men and women.

In her contribution, Rozenn Bailleul-LeSuer provides a broad overview of the different roles that animals played in ancient Egyptian society. She distinguishes between high culture and everyday culture. The former is particularly well documented by Egyptian iconography. Here, representations of animals are part of the fixed inventory of religious images, including those found in numerous tombs and temples. But what role did animals play outside this very specific context? How were animals integrated in the different areas of everyday life? To investigate this, Bailleul-LeSuer draws on a number of categories that are deliberately taken from contemporary discourse on the role and the rights of animals: companion animals, animals raised for utilitarian purposes, animals used for entertainment, and animals associated with sacred animal cults. This approach makes one thing clear above all: there was no such thing as a coherent animal ethic in ancient Egypt. Rather, animals were sometimes treated in diametrically opposite ways and their treatment was conditioned by context. Even for the ancient Egyptians, it was possible to treat animals like family members. On the other hand, this did not prevent them from resorting to factory farming for certain purposes, which degraded animals to mere disposable objects.

Under the category "animal companions," Bailleul-LeSuer cites as a characteristic example the instructions of a ruler of the Old Kingdom who orders that his dog be buried like a high-ranking statesman. Below this level of companionship, animals were typically part of the human life world, what we would call farm animals. They served as a food source, as pack animals, or as sacrifices within the cult. Bailleul-LeSuer highlights the domestication of geese as one particularly important achievement of Egyptian culture. Even though there could be personal attachments to these animals, they are treated as material possessions that could be sold, rented, or otherwise used. Jumping ahead, one might ask if, in Egypt, the rights of domesticated animals were also understood as a model for rights among humans, as was the case in Mesopotamia and Israel. In Israel, for example, both people and animals were valued economically (see the contribution by Saul Olyan) and therefore, socially classified. In this way, animals also contributed to the—admittedly, hierarchical—definition of personhood. In contrast to farm animals, which were closely integrated into everyday life in agricultural societies, exotic and wild animals were mainly used for the entertainment of the elite, especially the king. Hunting scenes or depictions of non-native animals in zoolike environments are well documented, especially in tombs.

A bizarre but nevertheless astonishing parallel to today's conditions is to be found in the evidence for factory farming in ancient Egypt. Apparently, millions of animals were bred in temples. Unlike in modern times, however, this was not done to produce food. Rather, the aim was to mummify animals en masse and then to perform the mouth-opening ritual on them in order to turn them into divine beings. As such, they functioned as intermediaries between humans and gods, capable of acting on behalf of humans as they made their transition from this world to the next. Interestingly, this did not lead to a particularly caring treatment of animals. On the contrary, these animals were apparently kept under harsh conditions. Their purpose was not to live but to become mummies. Even if the comparison may seem far-fetched, the Egyptian practice reifies and depersonalizes animals for human purposes and has parallels in today's food industry.

In a concluding reflection, Bailleul-LeSuer turns to the question of whether and to what extent people in ancient Egypt perceived animals only in relation to themselves, or whether they also recognized an intrinsic value in animal life. Bailleul-LeSuer affirms the latter by referring to texts such as the fable "The Lion in Search of Man," which, albeit in a fictional way, depicts animals as beings capable of perception and suffering. In the Hebrew Bible, one might think of the story of Balaam, which does something similar by transforming the donkey of the foreign seer Balaam from a pure pack animal into a sensitive being that suffers from the blows of its rider and that even acts much more responsibly than Balaam by saving him from certain death.

Against the background of this broad consideration of animals and society, the contributions of Seth Richardson and Saul Olyan turn to questions of animal rights in the narrower sense. This topic has two aspects. On the one hand, it is about the extent to which animals were objects of law, that is—as also presented by Bailleul-LeSuer—legally available possessions. More interesting and, in some ways, more difficult to answer is the question of whether and to what extent animals were perceived as legal subjects. Do animals possess independent rights and responsibilities, as do human beings? It is above all this second aspect that Richardson and Olyan examine for Mesopotamia, on the one hand, and for biblical Israel, on the other.

Richardson explores the issue of animals as legal subjects from two perspectives. First, he investigates the extent to which animals have a "symbolic function" within Mesopotamian law. The term "symbolic" takes into account the fact that Mesopotamian law sometimes constructs "theoretical" cases that were not always relevant in practice. For example, Richardson considers the case of the goring ox that injures or even kills people, known in both Mesopotamia and the Hebrew Bible, as a constructed problem. At least, there is no evidence that concrete claims have ever been derived from such a scenario. This raises the question why such cases were constructed in the first place. Richardson examines this with regard to a specific group of legal texts that deal with accidents involving animals outside of civic space. The characteristic example of this is a lion mauling an ox in the steppe. The question arises as to whether the owner of the animal can claim any compensation, which is not the case. Again, the practical relevance of this scenario remains doubtful. If at all, such attacks were so rare that they hardly appeared in the purview of the law. Richardson argues that the casuistry should be understood symbolically: Animals in "liminal spaces" mark the boundaries of the area covered by state law. Whatever occurs beyond these limits cannot be the basis for a claim of legal protection. Animals are thus symbolically represented here as legal subjects in order to mark the boundaries of the legal system. In short, just as there are no damage claims for cattle mauled by a lion somewhere out there, so a person who is harmed outside of the sphere of state-controlled law cannot make such a claim. Animals can therefore be used to mark the limits of human rights.

With this admittedly very specific aspect of animals and the law in view, Richardson examines the extent to which animals—symbolically or nonsymbolically—were perceived as persons. From this examination, Richardson develops the concept of "partial personhood." The term may seem provocative from a modern perspective. Is it possible to be a person only to some extent? In Mesopotamia and also in Israel, this is the case insofar as different groups of people are treated differently, at least in terms of the law.

In order to illustrate this idea for Mesopotamia, Richardson first refers to the class society that slowly developed in Babylon and that distinguished between "free citizen," "commoner," and "slave." Notably, the boundaries between these groups were neither a historical given, nor did they reflect exactly actual societal conditions. However, these distinctions became relevant in the legal system, insofar as assignment to one of these groups decided, for example, the amount of compensation one might receive in the event of injuries or accidents. According to Richardson, the implementation of social hierarchies was based on the assumption that people were assigned to different levels of personhood.

Such a representation of ascending or descending degrees of personhood, however, required legitimization. The legal system achieved precisely this by including animals in the social ontology. In other words, including animals allowed the social hierarchy to claim to represent the natural order of things. In particular, domesticated animals (especially cattle) played an important role. Animals were "naturally" placed at the lowest level of the social scale, but at the same time, they provided the minimal standard of "partial personhood." Animals thus symbolized the social order. More important, however, animals also "naturalized" the social order and gave it the appearance of something objective and unquestionable. In this way, animals could also be used as a point of comparison where, in civil or criminal law, the proportional value of people or, in criminal law, of body parts, was at stake (e.g., in the context of the *ius talionis*). This "naturalization" is also evident in other cultural areas, such as omen literature, which uses animal bodies as a natural/objective medium for statements about social and political events. Perhaps with regard to Mesopotamia, one can say that it was expected of the social and political spheres that, although they were not always in harmony with the natural order of things, they had to contain at least analogous patterns. Comparing again the contribution of Bailleul-LeSuer, it seems that recourse to the "natural" as a way to legitimize social conditions was less pronounced in Egypt than it was in Mesopotamia. However, the notion of the "natural" might be a fruitful topic of further research across the different cultures of the ancient Near East.

Overall, Richardson leaves little doubt that animals played an important role within the (human) social order and with regard to its boundaries, but not outside this particular frame of reference. In other words, animals do not necessarily appear interesting for their own sake. There were undoubtedly people in Mesopotamia who regarded their pets as family members and thus as (almost) full persons. Outside this narrowly defined realm, however, the appreciation of animals was limited to their usefulness to people at various levels of social life.

The concepts of "partial personhood" and "proportional value" used by Richardson lead one naturally to consider the contribution of Saul Olyan, who deals with the role of animals in the legal corpora of the Hebrew Bible. In the Hebrew Bible, too, the question arises as to what degree of personhood animals are accorded in relation to humans and whether this is handled consistently or differently in different parts of the text. To investigate this, Olyan uses the distinction between symmetrical and asymmetrical relations. In many legal provisions of the Hebrew Bible, asymmetrical relations exist between men and women, free citizens and slaves, Israelites and foreigners. Frequently, adult male Israelites rank higher than all other legal subjects who have a lower (or, asymmetrical) status. On the other hand, there are areas in which this is not the case, and, instead, symmetry (one might also say equality) forms the basis for social relations. This is the case, for example, with regard to the regulations for the Passover, in which it is emphasized that the festival should be observed and celebrated in the same way by all members of a household.

From this perspective, Olyan poses the question of the extent to which domesticated animals are seen in symmetrical and/or asymmetrical relationships with humans. For this purpose, he refers to cultic texts and sacrificial laws. These specifications are relevant, insofar as Olyan (unlike Bailleul-LeSuer and to some extent Richardson) does not examine the role of animals in everyday life; rather, he is specifically interested in the comparison of humans and animals in the context of the cult. A broader question would be whether one could generalize the results that Olyan presents with regard to other segments of societal life in ancient Israel and Judah. However, texts that might be pertinent to this question are far fewer in number than in the case of the cult.

One would generally expect that animals and humans should be viewed asymmetrically. But this is not so, for instance, in a particularly drastic case: According to Lev 27:28–29, both human beings and animals can be equally destined for destruction (*ḥērem*); this presumably means, in this context, to be offered as a whole burnt offering. And neither the animal that is thus designated and "sanctified" nor the human male can be redeemed by a material or monetary substitute. This is, of course, interesting above all because here, in addition to animal sacrifice, human sacrifice is obviously also being considered without objection or restriction. The asymmetry consists at best in the fact that it is only humans who can designate a human or an animal for destruction in this way.

It is also striking that symmetrical and asymmetrical relationships are viewed differently in different legal corpora of the Hebrew Bible. Even for the exact same case there are different regulations. This is evident, for example, in regard to sacrifices of firstborn male children and animals. Exodus 34:19–20 states that a firstborn bull or a sheep is to be sacrificed. In the case of a donkey, the choice is either to kill it in a nonsacrificial manner or to replace it with a sheep. A firstborn human male, on the other hand, must not be sacrificed in any case. Asymmetry is thus evident here with regard to different living beings and also with regard to gender: the female firstborn is not sacrificially relevant at all in this text. Exodus 22:28b–29 treats the same case very differently. No differences are established here. All firstborn (female living beings are at least not explicitly excluded) are to be sacrificed on the eighth day to Yhwh. The possibility of redemption is not granted here, neither for the human nor for the animal firstborn.

The overall picture of symmetries and asymmetries is therefore neither uniform nor following any recognizable patterns. Nevertheless, the examples cited by Olyan show that animals—at least with regard to the sacrificial cult—are not treated as asymmetrically with respect to humans as one might expect. This is supported by the fact that animals can be used as substitutes for humans, which at least suggests a certain form of equivalence. Of course, these ritual regulations alone say little about actual practice. Here one can ask with Richardson how literally or how symbolically these regulations are intended to be understood. This applies especially to the regulations about sacrificing humans. Was this really ever official practice? Or are we rather dealing here with theoretical considerations of the scribal schools behind these texts? That human sacrifice (despite the claims of Exod 22:28b–29 and Lev 27:28–29) was probably a theoretical option rather than a common practice may be assumed, because there is no evidence in the narrative texts of the Hebrew Bible for the lawful performance of such sacrifices. Foreign and apostate kings are said to embrace such practices, which biblical writers view as evidence of their religious ignorance or disloyalty. Yet the circumcision of male offspring on the eighth day after birth (Gen 17:12, paralleled by Exod 22:29) and the narrative of Isaac's "sacrifice" (Gen 22:1–19) prove that humans, too, were subject to Yhwh's claim of ownership.

Olyan's reflections on symmetry and asymmetry could easily be extended from the legal corpora to the narrative texts of the Hebrew Bible. Possibly, connections between legal and narrative traditions could be established. For example, the Primeval History (Gen 1–11) thematizes whether and to what extent animals are living beings equal to humans. This is partly denied (in both creation accounts, animals are very clearly subordinated to humans), but partly affirmed. Genesis 7:15–16 states that animals, like humans, carry the "breath of life" within them and that animals, like humans, are gendered beings (in Gen 1:27b, the distinction male/female is reserved for humans, while animals are only commanded to reproduce according to their "kind"). Finally, the non-Priestly flood narrative even goes so far as to say that God—unlike before the flood—no longer accepts the death of animals as collateral damage for human offenses (Gen 8:20–22). The symmetries and asymmetries are by no means always consistent, even in the narrative and mythological texts. Precisely this indicates that they were an important topic, as Olyan shows for the legal corpora.

Miira Tuominen's contribution on Porphyry's rejection of animal sacrifices focuses on the role of animals in the cult but approaches this topic from a different angle than does Olyan. As we have seen, the Hebrew Bible and other materials from the ancient Near East are concerned with using animals to establish criteria for economic valuations, which are then applied analogously to the social world of humans. This can be viewed critically, because animals are always placed at the lower end of the social ontology. However, animals are granted the status of persons with legal capacity (albeit with restrictions). Porphyry, at least at first glance, ascribes to animals a higher status than they receive in ancient Near Eastern materials because he categorically rejects animal sacrifice. Thus, the power of humans to dispose of animals as they wish is limited at a crucial point. Tuominen examines why Porphyry takes such a position and how he justifies it. In general, one can say that Porphyry, in good Socratic fashion, questions common patterns of thought and action. Animal sacrifice is a traditional part of the culture of his time. But is this a practice that stands up to standards of justice, based on reason? Porphyry seeks to refute the notion that it does. Interestingly, however, his argumentation is not a strong plea for animal rights. Porphyry assumes that animals are perceptive beings that feel pain. He also attributes a certain degree of intelligence to them. In Tuominen's reading, however, these two criteria are not decisive for Porphyry's rejection of animal sacrifices.

In order to capture Porphyry's reasoning, one must understand that he argues on two levels. On the one hand, he turns to the "common man." Here Porphyry makes an ethical argument: Sacrificing an animal is an act that corresponds to the crime of theft. To take a life is to steal it from another. It remains an open question, however, whether Porphyry assumes that animals own their own lives, because only then could one argue that taking their lives represents the crime of theft. The second level of Porphyry's argument is more clearly developed. This is about the ideals of the philosopher, whose quest should be to become like God. Whatever this might mean in detail, animal sacrifices do not direct the human being striving to live a philosophical life toward God, but rather toward phenomena of the material world. Animal sacrifices, therefore, work against the ideal of life that is actually to be pursued. Or to put it another way: Animal sacrifice prevents one from becoming what one is actually meant to be. The bloody materiality of animal sacrifice is opposed to the ideal of silent meditation, which is the only meaningful sacrifice. Thus, the true philosopher should not sacrifice animals and should eat only vegetarian food. According to Tuominen, not interfering with animal lives in any fashion serves primarily the self-perfection of humans. The welfare of animals is of subordinate importance in Porphyry's line of argumentation. Nevertheless, Porphyry's position can also be understood to suggest that the purpose of animal life is not to satisfy human needs, whether spiritual or material.

Different as Bailleul-LeSuer's, Richardson's, Olyan's, and Tuominen's contributions are in terms of the cultural areas that come into view, there are nevertheless some continuities. First of all, in the world of antiquity, there are no "animal rights" that are the equivalent of "human rights." With respect to rights, the ancient world was no different than the modern, although there are at least some signs in our time that suggest that this could change. Since 2003, the Swiss Civil Code has stipulated that "animals" are not "things." The same is true of the French *Code civil*, where animals are described as sentient beings. Numerous countries are strengthening regulations concerning animal protection, and this may represent a preliminary move adumbrating the establishment of animal rights. In the ancient world, the degree of proximity or distance between humans and animals, on the one hand, and the material usability of animals, on the other, determined whether and to what extent animals were legally protected. Of course, we are dealing here primarily with agricultural societies in which the salutary treatment of animals genuinely served human interests. Granting animals a legal status was a matter of care and also a matter of one's own economic interests. As part of the human world, animals were subject to the provisions of civil and criminal law, and in this respect they were granted at least partial personhood. The conspicuous exception to this general rule is Egyptian factory farming for the creation of mummies, which objectifies animals to such an extent that they are no longer granted any protection or rights whatsoever.

The legal texts under consideration here are mainly concerned with how animals are to be located in the human environment. What must animals be like and what must they do in order to be endowed with certain rights, especially the right to life? There is also the emotional side. The four contributions discussed here show that people have at all times formed emotional bonds with animals, which elevates them to the level of quasi-human persons. At the same time, humans never hesitated to treat animals as mere possessions whose right to exist depended on human needs. This once again raises the question posed at the beginning of this essay: How meaningful is it to talk of "animals"? In any case, "animals" are beings with whom humans maintain the most varied relationships of proximity and distance. And, of course, one can ask whether this is true only in relation to animals, or whether animals symbolically stand in for relationships among human beings, as Richardson suggests.

A question that goes beyond the subject matter of this volume, but one that might be worth exploring, would be the following: Did people in ancient times ever reverse their perspective and consider that, outside their cultured worlds, they belonged to the world of animals? Is there an awareness in these cultures that there is such a thing as undomesticated nature that humans do not control—and should not control? In Richardson's contribution, this topic is alluded to insofar as it deals with "liminal spaces" that mark the boundaries of human culture. Looking at the Hebrew Bible, there are in fact texts that include such a broader perspective. One might think of Psalm 104 or the famous speeches of God in the book of Job (Job 38–41). These texts present themselves in the overall context of the Hebrew Bible as a corrective to the idea that the world belongs to humans or is tailored to their particular needs. Thus, God asks Job,

> Is it by your wisdom that the hawk soars,
>   and spreads its wings toward the south?
> Is it at your command that the eagle mounts up
>   and makes its nest on high?
> It lives on the rock and makes its home
>   in the fastness of the rocky crag.
> From there it spies the prey;
>   its eyes see it from far away.
> Its young ones suck up blood;
>   and where the slain are, there it is. (Job 39:26–30 NRSV)

Response to McGowan, Naiden, Rosenblum, and Ullucci

BETH BERKOWITZ
Barnard College

Ancient Law and Its Afterlives

On Christmas day in 1990, at a family gathering in New Jersey, a dog named Taro jumped up and bit the lip of his owners' ten-year-old niece. The series of events that unfolded led to Taro's celebrity as "the death-row dog."[1] Hospital officials notified the police, Taro was quarantined, and a panel ordered Taro to be killed under New Jersey's vicious-dog law. Taro's owners appealed the ruling, claiming that their niece had provoked the attack and lied about it. The appeal garnered support from Brigitte Bardot and other animal activists. *People* magazine did a feature on Taro in the Bergen County Jail, where Taro waited while his case worked its way through the courts.[2] Governor Christine Todd Whitman, on her twelfth day in office, delivered on her campaign promise to save Taro's life and issued an executive order to free him, on the condition that he live in exile outside of New Jersey. Taro was moved to an undisclosed site in Westchester, where he appears to have lived out his days.

The story of Taro's near-execution and exile, mentioned by Fred Naiden in his contribution to this volume, captures key themes in the essays by Naiden, Jordan Rosenblum, Andrew McGowan, and Daniel

---

1. For details of the case, see Robert Hanley, "For New Jersey Dog, 1,000 Days on Death Row; Is Taro Vicious? Who Cares? By Now, Most of the State's Judicial System," *New York Times*, 14 October 1993, sec. New York; Jerry Gray, "Dog's Death Sentence Is Reduced to Exile," *New York Times*, 29 January 1994, sec. 1; Kate Stone Lombardi, "Pardoned in Jersey, Taro Incognito," *New York Times*, 20 March 1994, sec. Westchester Weekly.

2. People Staff, "Ready for a Milk-Bone Last Meal?," *People*, 13 December 1993, https://people.com/archive/ready-for-a-milk-bone-last-meal-vol-40-no-24/.

Ullucci, to which this response is dedicated. The story points, first of all, to the intimate relationships between animals and people, to how closely bound up human lives are with animal ones, a central theme for each of these authors. The story of Taro points also to the intersection between political power, public opinion, and laws about animals, a concern in each of the four essays. The violence in the story, by animals and to them, is likewise picked up in all four essays, as is the sense of danger associated with animals. Other themes from Taro's story—the timing on Christmas Day; the preoccupation of the public and the press with the expense of Taro's upkeep and legal fees; the strenuous denial by Christine Todd Whitman that she had granted "clemency" to an animal—also find their way into these essays, as they address religion, economics, and the inferior social status of other species, respectively.[3] The story points, most of all, to the powerful afterlives of ancient laws in contemporary times for, as Naiden observes, Christine Todd Whitman's "pardon" of Taro was in fact a relict of Roman law's practice of noxal surrender. As William Faulkner said, the past isn't dead, and it's not even past; these essays show this to be the case for animals and the law. The ancient texts treated by Rosenblum, McGowan, Ullucci, and Naiden are often strange and foreign-seeming, but their thinking, for better or for worse, is still with us.

Jordan Rosenblum's "Dolphins are Humans of the Sea (b. Bek. 8a): Animals and Legal Categorization in Rabbinic Literature" reads rabbinic passages that associate non-Jews with animals to show that animality and humanity are moving targets in rabbinic law, with non-Jews often falling on the animal side of the split. The human is associated exclusively with the Jew in the texts that Rosenblum treats. Daniel Ullucci's "Banning Animal Sacrifice ad Infinitum: Cui Bono?" addresses the bans on animal sacrifice that proliferated in the late Roman Empire. Ullucci considers Constantine's stance on animal sacrifice, and several formulations of the ban in the Theodosian Code, to argue that a reframing of the ban on animal sacrifice is essential for understanding the expansion of Christianity. The equation of "pagan" with a position that is pro-animal-sacrifice and "Christian" with being anti-animal-sacrifice is, Ullucci argues, misleading.

Fred Naiden's "Animals in Greek and Roman Criminal Law" addresses two legal topics —animals' damage to human property and animals' harm to human bodies—in two legal traditions, Greek and Roman. Comparing

---

3. A spokesperson for the governor took pains to clarify that this was not a granting of clemency: "There is no clemency for anything other than a two-legged creature" (Gray, "Dog's Death Sentence Is Reduced to Exile"). Nevertheless, coverage of the case spun the story as the governor's pardon of a dog. Responsibility for the expense of legal work and Taro's upkeep, which ran to at least $100,000 according to the *New York Times*, became a subject of controversy; see Hanley, "For New Jersey Dog, 1,000 Days on Death Row."

the status of animals to that of slaves and objects, Naiden explores the religious beliefs and ontological assumptions that animated classical criminal law about animals. Andrew McGowan's "Animal Acts: Diet and Law in the Acts of the Apostles and Early Christian Practice" shifts focus away from dietary controversies in early Christianity—what people are permitted to eat—to questions of commensality—whom people are permitted to eat with. In two passages in the New Testament's Acts of the Apostles, McGowan shows that animals form the framework for defining Christian identity in relation to Mosaic tradition, and that the former does not reject the latter in the ways usually thought.

The wide range of the essays is apparent from the literatures their authors are reading. For Rosenblum, it is rabbinic literary corpora; for Ullucci, late Roman imperial codices; for Naiden, classical Athenian sources and Roman codes (Justinian's *Digest* and *Institutes*), with an assay into medieval Europe; for McGowan, juridical and legislative moments in the narrative of Acts. The legal topics also vary. Rosenblum treats animal slaughter, the prohibition on Sabbath labor, and restrictions on relationships between Jews and gentiles. Ullucci's topic is animal sacrifice. Naiden's is death, injury, and damage caused by animals to human beings. McGowan addresses consumption of animals and commensality. As the topics vary, so too does the character of the encounter between animal and human being: sacral, sexual, visual, gustatory. Many different species of animals populate these essays: dolphins, mice, donkeys, reptiles, birds, bulls, cows, oxen, horses, dogs, rabbits, pigs, bears, lions, insects, and fish. The scholars treat a wide variety of concepts in law, religion, and society: dehumanization and bestiality in Rosenblum; piety and superstition in Ullucci; substitution and pollution in Naiden; hospitality and commensality in McGowan.

In the following response I single out several themes that seem to me most revealing of the riches that await those who study animals and law in antiquity: (1) piety; (2) rationality and agency; (3) identity and ideology; and (4) anomaly, ambiguity, and contradiction. What sorts of piety and impiety do animals facilitate, and what relationships with God or the gods do they possess or mediate? How do animals define the parameters of rationality and agency? How do animals articulate human identities and ideologies and mark out human difference or sameness? What anomalies do animals pose to normative categories, and what contradictions and ambiguities do they create? I turn to these questions as they are raised by Rosenblum, Ullucci, Naiden, and McGowan and conclude by considering the contribution of these essays to the study of antiquity and to our thinking about animals and the law today.

Piety

Animals serve to distinguish piety from sacrilege in the ancient legal texts addressed by these four essays. The bans on animal sacrifice found in the Theodosian Code, shows Ullucci, transform a practice that had long been an expression of piety and civic pride into a source of shame and a cause for punishment. The Code associates animal sacrifice alternately with vanity, audacity, magic, sacrilege, treason, and evil. Missing from the bans, Ullucci notes, is any mention of Christianity. The problem with animal sacrifice was not, apparently, that it was un-Christian. After all, Ullucci points out, Christians offered animal sacrifices in honor of their ancestors, saints, and martyrs. The problem with animal sacrifice, according to the Theodosian Code, was that it was impious and depraved, if not just plain crazy.

Virtue is a concern also in Rosenblum's rabbinic texts, which contrast the animalistic sexual desire of the non-Jew with the chaste and species-appropriate sexual desire of the Jew. Mishnah Avod. Zar. 2:1 characterizes non-Jews by their desire to have sex with animals. The talmudic commentary (b. Avod. Zar. 22b) imagines a non-Jewish man, who, upon visiting a friend's wife in order to seek an adulterous liaison with her, is content to have sex with her animal if she happens not to be home. Rosenblum observes that the non-Jew in this depiction violates not only basic legal and moral sanctions against adultery but also the species boundary. The Talmud goes still further in claiming that the non-Jew prefers sex with a Jew's animal to sex with his own wife. Animalistic sexual desire is remarkably literal in this passage. The non-Jew is not only like an animal but also longs for an animal. Rosenblum proposes that the rabbis' portrait of the non-Jew is so deeply animalistic that the non-Jew's sexual activity with animals should no longer be called bestial. Bestiality implies a species crossing, but non-Jews are already, for this rabbinic passage, on the animal side.

Animals define piety also in the realm of ritual. In the rabbinic passages about animal slaughter and the Sabbath boundary that Rosenblum discusses (t. Eruv. 5:19), animals distinguish permitted from prohibited behaviors in the areas of diet and Sabbath observance. Dietary law is at stake also in the Epistle of Barnabas, discussed by McGowan, which reads the Torah's dietary laws as teaching not what kind of animals to eat, but what kind of people to be. In Barnabas's reading, when the Torah prohibits consumption of the pig, its inner meaning was to prohibit association with people who are like pigs. The status of actual pigs as food remains uncertain, however, in Barnabas and in Acts 10, a passage central to McGowan's discussion. Piety consists, counterintuitively, in the withdrawal of ritual in the bans on sacrifice that Ullucci treats, as he writes, "… the killing of animals had been transformed. It was radically dissociated from piety and Roman identity. It was also dissociated from its ritual context. In the newly evolving conception of religion in late antiquity, the killing and butchering of animals had nothing to do with religion." One might speak, finally, of another kind of ritual, that of the courts, found in Naiden's texts, which dictate proper judicial ritual for animals who had caused harm, whether it be animal trials and executions or "noxal surrender," when the owner of the animal would surrender the animal to the victim or victim's relatives.

Rationality and Agency

In the bans discussed by Ullucci, people who sacrifice animals are pronounced irrational. A formulation of the ban attributed to Constantius in 341 applies the fraught epithet *superstitio* to the practice, declaring it a form of madness. Naiden's texts, by contrast, raise the question of rationality for the animals themselves. Ancient Greek philosophers took a variety of positions on the question of whether animals possess rationality. Demosthenes writes that animals have no share of reason, while Pythagoreans stake out a position in favor of animal rationality and moral accountability and make human beings, in turn, accountable for their actions toward animals. Aristotle is closer to Demosthenes, saying that humans have nothing in common with horses or cattle, who merit no justice, but he seems to waver between the two positions when he says elsewhere that animals have volition.

Do ancient animal trials presume that animals are rational and have moral agency? Probably not, says Naiden. The ancient Greeks put murder weapons on trial too. In one case that Naiden describes, a statue that fell on a man and killed him was given a criminal trial (Pausanias *Descr.* 6.11.6–9). Roman law in the *Digest* and the *Institutes* is clear, says Naiden, that animals are incapable of manifest intent to kill and therefore of being guilty for homicide. Ulpian says outright: "… an animal is incapable of committing a legal wrong because it is devoid of reasoning powers" (*Digest* 9.1.1.3). The more urbanized animals became, the less the question even came up, points out Naiden, since urban animals tended to be restrained in ways that countryside animals were not: "Roman law envisioned increasing control over animals as well as decreasing criminalization."

The Greek and Roman texts do nevertheless attribute some degree of agency to animals, suggests Naiden, who turns to religious ideas in order to make sense of the legal practices. Greeks and Romans would have seen animals as capable of housing divine, demonic, or human spirits, and of possessing the agency of nature. Noxal surrender and animal trials start to make sense when interpreted in this light, proposes

Naiden. Passages from the Roman codes that rule out noxal surrender for what they describe as predictable animal behavior—"if a horse kicks because pain upsets it" (*Digest* 9.1.1.6–7)—also presume some degree of animal agency and intentionality.

Agency is a theme also in the rabbinic texts discussed by Rosenblum. In a passage in which the animal slaughtered by a non-Jew is considered *nəbēlâ* ("carcass," i.e., an animal who had died a natural death; m. Hul. 1:1), it is as though the animal had not been slaughtered at all. The non-Jew is regarded as a non-entity. In a related passage, slaughter by a non-Jew is compared to slaughter by an ape (t. Hul. 1:1). All Jews, whether good or bad, possess potential legal efficacy, while non-Jews and non-humans possess none, as Rosenblum writes: "In limiting agency, the non-Jew regularly is equated with a nonhuman animal."

Identity and Ideology

The essays show that in ancient law animals define a variety of identities and ideologies. A case in point is Constantine's bans on animal sacrifice, which were likely motivated by a number of ideological factors, according to Ullucci. Constantine would have wished, first, to sound like a typical Roman intellectual turning his nose up at sacrifice; second, not to repeat the failure of previous Roman emperors to rally the public around the practice; third, to draw power away from the civic networks supported by animal sacrifice in favor of broader imperial bureaucratic structures; and, finally, to distinguish his empire from the neighboring Sasanian empire, where animal sacrifice played a significant role. Ullucci suggests, counter to the usual thinking, that Constantine may have been drawn to Nicene Christianity because of its opposition to animal sacrifice, not the other way around (i.e., Constantine was not drawn to oppose animal sacrifice because of his loyalty to Nicene Christianity). The aim of Constantine's ban was not to promote Christian over pagan—"pagan" as an identity did not really exist in this period, writes Ullucci—but to produce a new Roman imperial identity. Animals were central to the formation of *Romanitas* in Constantine's empire, as Ullucci writes, "Anyone, particularly any elite, living in a major city of the empire during the period from roughly 300 to 365 could not have failed to notice that animal sacrifice was very much in play in the cultural competition and discourse of their day."

Like Ullucci, McGowan considers the role of animals in the promotion of new identities. In the episode of Peter's vision in Acts, God tells Peter to kill and eat various animals (Acts 10:9–16). That vision is decoded later in the story, and by subsequent interpreters even more unambiguously, as a "zoomorphic" lesson (a term McGowan borrows from Patricia Cox Miller) in which "visionary animals turn out to be prosaic people." The instruction not to discriminate among the animals is in fact an instruction not to discriminate between Jews and gentiles (Acts 10:28). The dreamed animals, what McGowan calls "virtual animals" or "animals-as-people," mark a new Christian identity in which gentiles and Jews join together in community. In the second episode McGowan treats, that of the Jerusalem Council, James asks gentiles to abstain "from strangled things and from blood" (Acts 15:20). Here, the new Christian community is based on practices that revolve around real animals in the flesh, not virtual ones. McGowan argues that the concern in Acts for real animals often gets missed.

Animals stand in for people also in Rosenblum's rabbinic texts. While in Acts animals are used to undermine difference between Jew and gentile, in Rosenblum's texts, animals accentuate it. Rabbinic texts liken the non-Jew to the ape (t. Hul. 1:1), imagine the non-Jew's courtyard as a cattle-pen (t. Eruv.5:19), attribute bestial desires to non-Jews (m. Avod. Zar. 2:1), and compare non-Jewish women and non-Jewish slaves to donkeys (y. Ber. 9:2, 13b–c; b. Nid. 17a). These recurring associations of the non-Jew with the animal create a robust and bounded Jewishness firmly set apart from non-Jewishness.

Naiden's texts also create an identification between animal and person. When an animal harmed a person, the logic of restitution in Greek and Roman law was that "the animal served as a substitute for its master." The substitution of animal for person is illustrated most clearly in the practice of noxal surrender, in which the animal responsible for harm is turned over to the victim's family; the owner does this rather than pay restitution. While the animal's master is technically considered responsible, the animal pays the consequences. The animal is fellow creature enough to serve as substitute, but not such a fellow creature that turning them over to slaughter created discomfort. In certain circumstances the animal was paired with his or her master for punishment rather than serving as a substitute for the master, such as in the case Naiden mentions of the man whose ox overturned a sacred boundary stone. The man and his ox were together executed.

Anomaly, Ambiguity, and Contradiction

Animals sometimes appear in the ancient texts to be in harmony with other creatures and things that inhabit the universe. The sightings of a beautiful person, an animal, or a plant would all require the same blessing, according to one of the rabbinic passages Rosenblum discusses (y. Ber. 9:2, 13b–c). In Peter's vision in Acts, the assortment of animals that are mentioned—"all kinds of quadrupeds and reptiles of the earth and birds of the air"—are meant to reflect the full order of creation, says McGowan. Yet more often, animals seemed to the ancients to constitute a challenge to their taxonomic systems. In a talmudic passage discussed by Rosenblum (b. Bek. 8a), the dolphin is, according to one textual tradition, a hybrid creature of human and fish and, according to another, a creature who reproduces just as humans do. Hybrid human-animal identities emerge also from Naiden's classical texts, where animals are what Naiden calls "a parasocial quiddity," subhuman in some ways, but quasi-human in others. In the worldview of the Greeks and Romans, "the categories of the superhuman, the human, and the bestial overlapped." Greek and Roman legal discourse, as well as rabbinic discourse, is riddled with ambiguities regarding the categorization of animals.

Ullucci's work shows animals also to be generating legal contradictions. One Roman emperor (Decius, then Diocletian) requires everyone to sacrifice, while the next (Constantine and his sons) bans it, the next (Julian) requires it again, and then the next (Julian's successors) bans it again. It must have been awfully confusing to be a resident of the late Roman Empire! Moreover, Ullucci says, it was a point of disagreement even in antiquity whether Constantine did in fact ban sacrifice. According to Eusebius, Constantine banned animal sacrifice; according to Libanius and the triumphal arch in Rome depicting Constantine himself performing sacrifice, Constantine did not. The Theodosian Code has twenty laws banning sacrifice, Ullucci writes, each one offering a somewhat different formulation and focus. Ullucci's essay points to abundant ambiguity and contradiction, as well as repetition and evolution, in this area of law relating to animals.

Ambiguity surrounds the passages also in McGowan's discussion. The zoomorphic reading of Peter's vision leaves the laws of eating real animals "frustratingly vague," says McGowan. McGowan speaks of the ambiguity also within James's request that gentiles abstain "from the pollutions of idols and from immorality and from strangled things and from blood" (Acts 15:20). Later in the narrative, this request turns into a formal resolution (Acts 15:28–29). But what precisely is being asked of the gentiles? McGowan says that the textual tradition displays confusion on this question, especially the prohibition on eating strangled animals, which seems to have puzzled transmitters of the tradition. One textual tradition, the Western D tradition, substitutes the golden rule for the prohibition on strangled animals and implies that the prohibition on blood relates to shedding it rather than eating it, thereby eliminating animals altogether from the legislation. But the dominant textual tradition, the B, or Byzantine tradition, retains the flesh and blood of the animal bodies that appear to have been intended by the legislation, if one reads it, as McGowan does, as a resolution to the legal and dietary questions posed in the earlier episode of Acts 10.

Rethinking Antiquity

These essays together show that animals were essential in ancient law for promoting certain forms of piety over others, for determining who possessed agency and rationality and who did not, for delineating a variety of identities and ideologies, and for testing the taxonomic systems that reigned supreme. These essays at the same time represent a radical rethinking of major questions in their fields. How did the rabbis shape Jewishness? Why did early Christianity expand? How did early Christians relate to the Torah? What assumptions about reality did ancient Greeks and Romans hold? Rosenblum, Ullucci, McGowan, and Naiden are addressing problems at the very heart of the ancient Mediterranean experience. This volume may as well have been called "Rethinking Antiquity." The essays illustrate that animals are not a boutique subfield or special interest inquiry but are fundamental to the study of antiquity.

The essential ingredient in the work is thick contextualization or, to put it otherwise, the avoidance of anachronism. The work is "synchronistic," self-consciously so. Ullucci cautions against a view of the ancient bans on animal sacrifice as constituting anything like a proto-animal rights position. Bans on animal sacrifice rechanneled violence against animals; they did not oppose it. McGowan's approach to Acts is similarly sensitive to the problem of retrojection, which in McGowan's case would entail the reading of later battles between Judaism and Christianity back into the formative period. All four authors are highly sensitive to problems of translation and terminology. Naiden observes that Greek had no equivalent to the English word "animal": *zōon* means "living thing," *empsychon* means "living and breathing," while *thēr* means "beast of prey." Jacques Derrida's critique of the homogenizing term "animal" does not then apply to the ancient Greeks.[4] Naiden points also to the many distinctions among animals made by the Roman codes, which speak of quadrupeds, of wild versus domesticated animals, and of native versus foreign ones. Rosenblum argues that the language used by rabbinic texts for sex with an animal, *rəbîʻâ*, should not be translated as bestiality when it applies to gentiles, since gentiles are themselves grouped with animals by the rabbinic texts. All four essays toggle between the past and the present, clearing out the brush of modern perspectives that obscures our view of the ancient ones.

---

4. Jacques Derrida, "The Animal That Therefore I Am (More to Follow)," trans. David Wills, *Critical Inquiry* 28.2 (1 January 2002): 369–418.

The algorithm in these texts involves multiple, overlapping binaries: Jew/gentile; Jew/Christian; Jew/pagan; pagan/Christian; Roman/non-Roman; rabbi/non-rabbi; free/slave; male/female; pious/impious; orthodox/heretic; rational/irrational; loyal/treasonous; elite/common. Chief among these is the human/animal binary, which these essays show to be critical to the making and linking of all the others. These authors also show that animals shape the meaning of key human activities as the ancients understood them: eating, killing, having sex, traveling, reading, worshiping, sacrificing, blessing.

Animals emerge as a major feature of ancient law not only as a subject of law and as subject to the law, but also as essential to law's buy-in. There are prescriptions that have nothing to do with animals but that rely on them for their persuasiveness and imaginative power, as McGowan shows in his reading of Peter's vision of "virtual animals," and as Rosenblum shows in the rabbinic laws of Sabbath boundaries that compare the quarters of gentiles to those of animals. The animals that appear in these ancient legal texts remind us that law cannot just compel; it must be compelling. Indeed, the extent to which the regulations described in these ancient texts were observed or enforced may have been minimal. Ullucci writes that there is "no direct evidence that anyone in the fourth century was actually prosecuted for defying these laws"; rabbinic law's relationship to social reality is notoriously messy; and McGowan tells us that the legislation of Acts 15 regarding animal food prohibitions faded into obscurity.

There is a spatiality evident in these ancient imaginings about animals. Animals determine which spaces one should enter, for what purpose, and with whom. In the passages from Acts treated by McGowan, animals are the means by which the Lord reveals that Peter may host the gentile envoys of the centurion Cornelius, and that Peter may be hosted by Cornelius with Cornelius's friends and relatives. In the Avodah Zarah text discussed by Rosenblum, animals are the reason Jews should avoid gentile inns. In the sacrifice bans addressed by Ullucci, animals reshape the spatial networks of the empire. Animals are often what lies beneath, literally and figuratively. The Christian and pagan elites described by Ullucci saw animal sacrifice as beneath them, appropriate only for lower gods, if at all. In a talmudic story noted by Rosenblum, a rabbi riding a donkey is surprised to suddenly find a woman underneath him instead (b. Sanh. 67b), and gentiles are portrayed by the Mishnah as inclined to "mount" animals. Animals also mark the dark underbelly of "religion," a category that Ullucci describes as developing in the period of our discussion. The association of animals with magic and divination in classical biblical, rabbinic, and Christian texts makes them suspect in the context of worship and divine service. Animals, in sum, generate anxiety in the realms that matter most: social status, sex, religion. The flip side of that anxiety is allure: the allure of the dolphin for the rabbis, for example, or the shared table for Acts.

Animals seem to have a distinctive relationship to the yuck factor, however, if the ancient texts discussed by our authors are any indication. The passage in Acts 15 at the center of McGowan's discussion imbues dead animal bodies with disgust, loosely drawing upon Leviticus 17–18. The talmudic passage discussed by Rosenblum that imagines gentiles having sex with animals is lurid; so too the talmudic passage prohibiting Jews from having sex in front of other living creatures. Even the sober Codex Theodosianus is evocative in the perverseness it attributes to animal sacrificers. The "yuckiness" of animals and the people who relate to them in a taboo manner is undoubtedly related to ambivalence about human embodiment, and the mortality and vulnerability that are entailed in it, as well as the desires for food, sex, or blood. Peter's vision of animals in Acts 10, from McGowan's essay, begins with his being hungry (Acts 10:10). McGowan concludes that the story told by Acts, and the new law it decrees, is one "inscribed on the bodies of animals."

Conclusions: Was Antiquity Good for Animals?

The animals in ancient literature require us to read between the lines. Animals in these ancient texts are sometimes similes and metaphors, at other times "real," but their voices are not heard, even when their presence is keenly felt. Like the women, slaves, and many others whose perspectives are not directly captured in ancient literatures, the subjectivity of animals remains a mystery. If the ancient animals could speak, what would they tell us? What was it like to be an animal in antiquity? Was it better to be an animal then, or now?

Ullucci says up front that "[t]he 'end of animal sacrifice' and the laws mandating this end would, seemingly, represent the high point in the history of ancient animal rights. But of course, the laws were not about animal welfare at all, and it is not apparent that they had any impact on either animal husbandry or meat consumption." Naiden observes that "Greek and Roman law ignored cruelty toward or neglect of animals and also ignored blood sports. The Greeks and Romans reserved laws against cruelty and the like to free persons, especially citizens, and most especially heads of households." Legal texts may have been particularly inhospitable to animals, says Naiden: "On the whole, classical literature takes some interest in animal suffering ... philosophers did. The law did not." McGowan writes that his texts do not tell us very much about animals at all ("People ... are always the real point in these texts"). Nevertheless, we might pause to imagine the lived experience of the animal on the altar or butcher block, or stabled at an inn, or put on trial.

The plight of animals, both then and now, is no joke, but these essays have their fair share of wit. Ullucci observes that "[m]any American tourists have spent more time in Rome than Constantine ever did. He visited only three times in his life." Naiden closes his essay with comic drawings from an eighteenth-century English satire. McGowan wonders whether Peter would have eaten his new friend Cornelius's succulent fig-fed pork. Rosenblum's acknowledgments read: "I am the only human animal to whom any remaining errors should be attributed." Animals help preserve our sense of humor and inspire us to try on alternative perspectives. In discussing Emperor Julian's expansion of animal sacrifice, Ullucci describes the quip of a critic who declared that if Julian's excessive sacrifice program continued, no more white birds would be left in the Eastern Empire. Ullucci writes: "Fortunately for the birds, Julian did not get his way." Naiden similarly adopts the animal's perspective when he writes: "For lack of case law, this chapter has avoided the question of how animals responded to standing trial." Ullucci and Naiden here adopt the animal's perspective and point to the limits of their own.

These four case studies in law and animals in antiquity surely broaden our perspective, whatever might be its limits, and reveal to us the contingency of history. If the author of Acts 15 had had a greater impact, Christians today might be observing some form of kashrut, suggests McGowan's essay. If Nicene Christianity had not taken a strong stand against animal sacrifice, Christianity would look very different and might not exist at all, we could speculate based on Ullucci's arguments. The talmudic rabbis, in that case, might not have felt it necessary to dehumanize non-Jews to the extent that they do, as featured in Rosenblum's essay. And Taro the Akita in New Jersey might well have been put to death immediately if, long ago, the Romans had not developed the practice of forfeiture, the subject of Naiden's essay. These essays invite us not only to consider how the laws of the ancients continue to inform our own but also to wonder about the afterlives of our own animal laws when we, should our planet survive, someday become the ancients.

Index of Passages

Hebrew Bible/Old Testament

Genesis
Ref	Pages
1–11	184
1:18	10
1:24	107
1:26–28	7n21
1:26–27	7n21
1:27–28	70n4
1:27b	184
1:28	6, 6n18, 7, 7n21, 8, 8n23, 163, 164
1:29–30	7
2:19–20	12
2:21–23	70n4
2:23	12n33
3:9	70n4
3:13	70n4
3:16	70n4
6:20	107
7:15–16	184
8:20–22	184
9:2–3	7n21
9:3–4	7
9:8–17	7
17:12	183
22:1–19	183
22:13	74n19, 80
22:5	174, 175

Exodus
Ref	Pages
4:22	75n20
11:5	75n20
12:29	75n20
12:47	70
12:48–49	70, 80n34
13:11–13	75n21
13:12	74n15, 75, 79
13:13	11, 80
13:15	11, 79, 80
19:15	70n4
20:17	73n11
21:7	73n11
21:28–36	45n17
21:28	7
21:29	64, 64n101
21:33–36	46n22
22:1	45n13
22:4	45n13
22:9	45n13
22:18	175n52
22:28b–29	75, 79, 80, 80n34, 183
22:29	183
23:4	47n27
23:10–11	71n8, 81n38
23:12	7, 10, 11, 81n38
23:17	70, 70n5
27:28–29	79
34:19–20	74, 75, 75n21, 79n33, 80n34
34:19	75, 79
34:20	11, 80

Leviticus
Ref	Pages
1:3	78
1:10	78
4:3	78, 80n36
4:13–14	80n36
4:14	78
4:22–23	80n36
4:23	78
4:27–28	80n36
4:28	78
4:32	78
5:15	78
11	108
11:10	110n11
12:1–8	70
15:16–18	70
15:19–24	70
16:1–4	76n25
16:5	78
17–18	116, 197
17:1–9	116
17:10–17	116
18:6–23	116
20	63n93
21	76n26
21:6–8	77n26
21:9	77n26
21:17–23	77
21:17	76, 77
21:18–20	76n24
21:21	69, 73n13, 76, 77
21:22	76, 77
21:23	69, 76, 77
22:3	77n27
22:11–13	76n26
22:15	77n27
22:20–22	77n28, 77n29
22:22–23	76n24
22:23	77, 77n28, 77n29, 78n32
22:24	77n28, 77n29
22:25	76, 77, 77n28, 77n29
24:19–20	76n24
24:21	81
25:2–7	81n38
27:1–13	71, 72, 75
27:2	53n53
27:9	72

Index of Passages

Leviticus (cont.)		6:24	73n14	**New Testament**	
27:10	72n10	7:24	73n11		
27:12	72n10			Mark	
27:14–21	73n11	1 Samuel		5:1–13	6
27:14	72	15:4–35	73n11	7:2	109
27:21	73				
27:28–29	72, 75,	2 Samuel		Luke	
	80, 182, 183	5:8b	78n30	24:47	112
27:28	73n11				
		1 Kings		Acts	
Numbers		3:16–28	55n59	2	108
2:41	76n23	16:34	75n20	2:39	112
3:11–13	76n23			3:25–26	112
16:12–17	69n2	Job		8:27–39	112
17:5	69	38–41	186	10	105, 106, 117,
18:9–19	77n27	39:26–30	186		118, 190,
18:9–10	76n26				195, 197
18:11	76n26	Psalms		10:9–16	192
19:1–10	78	104	186	10:9b–16	107
				10:10	197
Deuteronomy		Isaiah		10:12	107
5:12–15	7, 81n38	66:3	7	10:14b	107
5:21–22	69			10:15	107, 108
7:2	173, 173n44	Jeremiah		10:28	108, 193
11:5	8n24	17:21–22	168n28	10:34–35	108
12	107n6	31:9	75n20	10:41	112
13:13–19	73n11			10:44	108
14:21	70, 80n34	Ezekiel		11:1–2	113
15:19	75, 79	4:14	107	15	106, 113, 117,
15:21–23	76n24				118, 196, 197,
15:21–22	77	Micah			198
15:21	76, 77,	6:6–7	80n37	15:6	113
	77n29	6:7	75n20	15:8–9	114
15:22	77n27			15:19–20	114
16:11	70n5	Malachi		15:20	193, 194
16:14	70n5	1:7	77, 78n31	15:22	114
16:16	70n5	1:8	76n24, 77	15:23	114
17:1	76, 76n24,	1:14	76, 77, 78n31	15:25a	114
	77, 77n29,			15:28–29	115, 194
	78n31				
21:15–17	75n20	**Apocrypha and**		Romans	
23:2	78n30	**Deuterocanonical Books**		14:14	109
23:10–12	70				
25:4	6, 7	1 Maccabees		1 Corinthians	
		1	109	9:9–10	6
Joshua					
6–7	73n11	Letter of Aristeas		Hebrews	
6:19	73n14	315	109	10:29	109

Index of Passages

Josephus
Antiquities of the Jews
16.163   114

Rabbinic Writings

Mishnah
m. Avodah Zarah
2:1   170, 190, 193

m. Bekhorot
1:2   163

m. Eruvin
6:1   168, 169

m. Hullin
1:1   166, 192

Babylonian Talmud
b. Avodah Zarah
22a–23a   170
22a   170n34
22b   171, 190

b. Bava Qamma
80a–b   8n26
80b   8

b. Bekhorot
7b–8a   163
8a   161, 164n11, 164n14, 188, 194

b. Berakhot
20a–b   173n46
58a   174n47
40a   8

b. Eruvin
61b–62b   169n31
62b   169n29

b. Ketubboth
65a   175n53

b. Niddah
16b–17a   174

17a   174, 193

b. Pesahim
49a–b   172n42

b. Sanhedrin
67b   174n47, 196

b. Yevamot
62a   175

Palestinian Talmud
y. Avodah Zarah
1:9   173n46
1:40a–b   173n46

y. Berakhot
3:4, 6c   175n52
9:2, 13b–c   173, 193

y. Eruvin
6:1   169n29, 169n31
6:23a–b   169n31
6:23b   169n29

Tosephta
t. Bekhorot
1:10–11   163
1:11   163
6:4   173

t. Eruvin
5:19   169, 190, 193

t. Hullin
1:1   167, 192, 193

Old Babylonian Sources
Altbabylonische Briefe
I 37   42n3
I 56   60n79
I 114   49n32
II 83   44n11
II 86   49n32
II 177   42n3
III 11   42n3, 49n35, 60n79

III 36   42n3
III 38   42n3
III 39   42n3
III 46   49n35
III 54   42n3
IV 131   60n79
IV 146   42n3
IV 150   49n33
V 151   42n3, 44
V 160   44n11
V 218   42n3
V 230   42n3
VI 9   49n32
VI 10   49n32
VI 66   49n35
VI 179   42n3
VII 47   49n33
VII 49   49n33
VII 50   49n33
VII 139   49n32
VII 143   42n3
VIII 7   49n35
VIII 12   60n79
VIII 84   49n32
IX 30   60n79
IX 37   42n3
IX 39   44n11
IX 48   42n3
IX 59   42n3
IX 67   49n35
IX 71   49
IX 83   49n33
IX 107   42n3
IX 185   42n3
IX 195   60n79
IX 243   60n79
IX 256   42n3
X 7   49n32
X 11   44n11
X 15   49n35
X 20   49n35
X 41   49n35
X 96   49n35
X 121   42n4
X 186   42n4
XI 7   49
XI 27   49n35
XI 57   44n11

Index of Passages

Altbabylonische Briefe (cont.)		6.1.28	66n105	106	59	
				107	59	
XI 58	49n34	Instructions of Šuruppak		112	59	
XI 102	60n79	94	46n18	114	55n57	
XI 132	49n35			116	55n58, 55n60	
XI 160	49n35	Iraq Museum		119	55n58	
XII 9	42n3	67692	50n41	120	59	
XII 52	60n79			121	58n76	
XII 54	60n79	Laws of Ešnunna		124	59	
XII 58	60n79	1–2	60n84	126	59	
XII 165	42n3	3	45n12, 45n13	127	59	
XII 172	49n34	3ff.	60n85	137	59	
XII 177	49	10	45n12, 45n13	138	61n90	
XII 190	42n3	12	59	141	61n90	
XIII 23	60n79	22	55n57	142	62n93	
XIII 41	49n32	23	55n58, 59n78	143	63n93	
XIII 70	44n11	25	59	158–84	62	
XIII 104	60n79	40	45n12, 45n13	160–61	59	
XIV 54	49n35	42–48	56n62	170–71	61n90	
XIV 55	49n35	42–47	56	176a–b	59	
XIV 62	49n32	49	55n58	181–82	59	
XIV 74	60n79	50	45n12, 45n15, 46n47, 47, 47n28, 51n47	191	59	
XIV 91	42n3			192	62	
XIV 94	49n45, 49n35			193	62	
		53–57	45n12, 45n15, 56n64	196f.	56	
XIV 105	49n35			198	56n63	
XIV 111	46n20	53	57	199	56n63, 59	
XIV 132	49n33	54	64	201	56n63	
XIV 140	60n79	54/55	56	203–4	56n63	
XIV 142	42n3	55	55n58	205	62n92, 65	
XIV 146	49n32	56/57	56	207–9	56, 56n63	
XIV 164	49n35	56	44	213–14	56n63	
XIV 174	49n35	57	55n58	214	55n58	
				217	55n58	
Cuneiform Texts in the British Museum		Laws of Hammurabi		219–20	54	
		5	59	220	55n58, 59	
39 25	50n43	7–8	45n12	223	55n58	
		8	45n13, 59	224–25	45n12, 45n15, 56n64	
Cornell University Studies in Assyriology and Sumerology		17	47, 47n24			
		23–24	51n45	225	57n67, 57n70, 59	
		29	59	228	58n76	
36 61	51n45	35	45n12, 45n13	231	55n57	
36 130	51n45	46	59	238	59	
		56–58	58n76	241–54	45n12	
Electronic Text Corpus of Sumerian Literature		57–58	45n12, 45n13	241	45n13	
		63	58n76	242/243	45n13	
1.8.1.4	64n99	64	59	244	46n22, 47n24, 47n25, 50n44, 51	
5.6.1	50n42	101	59			

Index of Passages

245–48	56n64	34–38	45n12, 45n15	21–24	56n62
245–46	57n66, 57n72	34–37	45n14, 56n64,	24	55, 55n57
246	46n22		57n67, 59	A III 135f.	60n87
247	46n22, 54,	34	46n22, 56,		
	57n69, 59		57n68, 59	University of	
248	46n22, 57n67,	35	46n22, 57n69, 59	Pennsylvania,	
	57n70, 59	36	46n22, 56	Babylonia Section	
249	49n36	37	46n22	8/2 196	46n21
250	47n27	38	45n14, 45n15,		
251–52	56n64		46n22	Sumerian Laws	
251	64	a	45n12, 45n13,	Exercise Tablet	
253	57n74		60n85	3'	59
254	56n64, 57n73, 59	d	56, 63n93	4'	55n57
255	45n13, 58n76	e	63n93	9'–10'	45n12, 45n15,
256	45n12, 45n13	f	56		47n27
258	45n12, 45n13			9'	46n22, 47n25,
261–71	45n12	Laws about Rented			50n44
261	45n13	Oxen		10'	51n47, 56n64,
262	45n14, 45n15	1–9	45n12, 45n15		57n66, 57n72
263	47n27, 51n47,	1–6	56n64		
	56n64, 57n66,	1	46n22, 57n69, 59	Sumerian Laws	
	57n72	2	46n22, 57n68, 59	Handbook of Forms	
264–65	45n13	3	46n22, 57n67, 59	ii 26	59
265	59	4	46n22, 57n70	iii 10	59
266–67	45n15, 57n66	5	45n14, 45n15,	iii 13–15	45n12, 45n13
266	47, 47n25,		46n22, 57n67, 59	iii 13	59
	50n44	6	46n22, 47n23,	v 12	59
267	47		51n46, 57n71	v 45	45n12, 45n14
268–71	45n13	7–8	57n66	vi 1	45n15
273–74	60n85	7	47n25, 50n44,	vi 3	46n22
278	55n57		57n72	vi 11	45n12, 56n64,
281	55n57	8	46n22, 47n25,		57n67, 59
282	62n92, 65		50n44, 57n72	vi 16	45n12, 45n15,
		9	47n23, 51n46,		46n22, 47n26,
Laws of Lipit-Ištar			56n64, 57n70		51, 56n64,
Prologue ii 25–26	60n86				57n72
7	59	Laws of Ur-Namma		vi 23	45n12, 46n22,
12	55n58	Prologue A iv 162f.	53		47n23, 51n46,
13	55n57	5	55n58		56n64, 57n66,
14	55n58, 59	6	56		57n72
15–16	61n88	9	56	vi 32	45n12, 45n15,
24	61n90	10	56		46n22, 47n25,
26	55n58, 61n90	15	59		50n44, 56n64,
27	61n90	18–22	56n65		57n66, 57n72
28	61n90	18	56	viii 11–15	55n57
29	59	19	56	viii 16	59
30	61n90	20	56	viii 22	55

Index of Passages

Sumerian Proverb
Collection
2.154   46n18
28.8   66n105

Textes cunéiformes.
Musée du Louvre
1 4   46n20

Egyptian Sources

Book of the Dead
125   33

Chicago Hawara
Papyrus
2, 1–2   31n76

Instruction of
'Onchsheshonqy
9/8   21
20/15   21

Instructions of
Merikare
E 132–133   16

Leiden Demotic Papyrus
I 384   33

O. DeM
118 rt.   31n78

P. Ashm.
1984.77.2/8–9   29, 29n70

P. Berlin
3130   32, 33
23757 A line 25   29

P. Cairo
57058   31
58057   31n80

P. Lansing
2.6–8   10, 38

P. Turin
1976   31n79

Tale of the Two Brothers
1,5–7   21
5,9   21

Greek and Latin Classical Sources

Aelian
De natura animalium
11.4   93n19

Aeschylus
Agamemnon
1297   93n19

Apicius
De re coquinaria
7   113n20

Apollonius
Mirabilia
13   93n19

Aristotle
Athenaion politeia
54.7   85n5
Ethica nicomachae
1111a–b   94n21
1132a   93n17
1161b   94n21
De Anima
413a   177
De mirabilibus auscultationibus
844b no. 137   93n19
Physica
7.2.244b8–245a1   121n3
Politica
1256b   94n21

Codex Theodosianus
1.1.5   154n38
9.16   157n48
9.16.7   155
16.1–7   158
16.2.5   158n49
16.10   157n48
16.10.1   155
16.10.2   151n24, 155
16.10.4   155
16.10.5   155
16.10.7   156
16.10.9   156

Cicero
Tusculanae disputationes
5.27.78   29

Demosthenes
In Aristocratem
23:80   85n5

Digest/Digesta
2.21.4   90n12
2.21.42   90n12
9.1.1.pr   87
9.1.1.3   191
9.1.1.3 (Ulpian)   88
9.1.1.4   90n12
9.1.1.6–7   89, 192
9.1.2   87
9.1.3   87
48.7.1.3   87n8

Diodorus Siculus
Biblioteca historica
1.83.8–9   29

Diogenes Laertius
Vitae/Lives
9.36   96
10.16–21   129n23

Empedocles
131 B 127–20   94n21

Gaius
Institutes
2.14a–16   90
4.8.2   89

Herodotus
Historiae/Histories
2.65   29
2.66–67   17

Index of Passages   205

Julian		Pliny the Elder		2	138, 139, 140
Misopogon		Naturalis historia		2.2.1	126
361b	159	8.17.64	91n13	2.2.2	125n16
		32.17	93n19	2.3.1	131, 138n42
Libanius				2.4.1–2	125n17
Orations		Plotinus		2.5–6	129
1.27	150n22	Enneads		2.12.2	125
1.201	159n54	2.3.8.1–9	132n31	2.12.3–4	124
14.41	159n54	2.3.8.2–5	132n31	2.12.4	125, 125n16
24.36	159n54	3.2.15	94	2.12–13	121n3, 122,
30	159n54	4.4.[28]	136		124n14
30.6	150n22	5.1.[10].6	136n39	2.13	122n8
30.7	156–57	5.1.[10].6.11–16	136	2.18.3	129n22
		5.8.[31].9	136n39	2.33	126
Life of Plotinus		6.9.[9].3.33–39	135	2.33.1	125, 126, 133
4.8–13	123			2.34	135, 135n34
11	123	Plutarch		2.34.2	135, 135n35
		De sollertia animalium		2.34.3	136
Livy		965b	94n21	2.36	135n34
History of Rome		De esu carnium		2.36.3	137, 137n40
9.1–10	88n9	99e	94n21	2.36.4	137
		Lucullus		2.36.5	137
Inscriptiones Creticae		24.7	93n19	2.37	135n34
1.1.18	88n9	Pelopidas		2.38–43	135, 137
		22	93n19	2.38	137
Marcus Diaconus		Quaestionum convivialum		2.40	137
Vita Porphyrii		729e	94n21	2.40.3	137
26	146n8	Solon		2.43.2	125
		22.4	88n11	2.44.1	125n17
Paulus				2.45.3	132n31
Sententiae		Porphyry		2.47.1	123
5.23	87n8	De abstinentia ab esu		2.58.2	137
		animalium		2.61.6	126, 134
Pausanias		1.1.1	123	2.61.7	132n29, 132n30
Graeciae descriptio		1.1.3	123	3	123, 130
5.27.10	86	1.2.3	126, 128	3.3.3	126
6.11.6–9	86, 191	1.5.3	126, 129	3.19.2	124
		1.7–12	129	3.26	122
		1.7–9	129	3.26.9	121
Philostratus		1.11	129	3.26.10	125
Heroicus		1.12	129	3.26.12	121n3, 122n8,
294	93n19	1.12.6	129		124n14
329	93n19	1.16	122n4	3.26.13	123n9
		1.18	124	3.27.2	124n14
Plato		1.28.3	131	3.29.9	125
Leges		1.28.4	126, 130	3:55–56	122n6
9.873e	85	1.38.2	123	4.15.2	132n29
9.936d–e	88n11	1.56.4	130n25	4.18.5	131

Porphyry
De abstinentia (cont.)
4.18.7	131, 132
4.18.8	131, 132
4.18.9	139
4.22	122
4.22.2	128
4.22.7	128, 129

Stobaeus
Florilegium
2.1.13	95

Zosimus
New History
1.13–16	152n29
2.19.5	151n25

Early and Medieval Christian Sources

Ambrosiaster
Ad Galatas
2.2.4	116

Letter of Barnabas
10.1–5	110

Eusebius of Caesarea
Preparatio evangelica
4.10.7	135n35

Vita Constantini
2.44–45	150n21
3.1.5	150n21
3.15	152n29
4.10	152n29
4.23	150n21
4.25	150n21

Origen
Homilies on Leviticus
7.4.1	110
7.4.7	110
7.7.1	110n12

Thomas Aquinas
Summa theologica
II 2, q. 90, art. 3	88n10

Index of Subjects

On Abstinence from Killing Animals (Porphyry), 121–25, 138
Acts of the Apostles, textual tradition, 115, 116, 117, 194. *See also* Jerusalem Council (Acts 15); Peter and Cornelius story (Acts 10)
age, as basis of monetary value of humans and animals, 72, 75
agency
  of animals, among Romans and Greeks, 88, 89, 191, 195
  divine, diabolical, and natural, 94
  of non-Jews and nonhumans, 192
Ambrosiaster, interpretation of ruling at Jerusalem Council, 116
anachronism, and study of animals in antiquity, 195
analogy, reasoning by, in Babylonian law collections, 46–52
ancient laws and customs
  and contemporary discussion of animal rights, 9–11, 188
  on harming animals, 128–30, 138
  nonspecialists/specialists engagement with, 6–9
  use in arguments about animal rights, 1
animal(s)
  as actors in mythological reenactments, 35
  as agents of a god's will, 93, 94
  association with cult, 26–29, 179
  being harmed, in Old Babylonian law collections, 45
  capable of perception and suffering, 94, 124, 180 (*see also* sentience, of animals)
  close relationship with people, 186, 188
  cognitively complex, rights of, 4, 4n7, 5
  combined with object, in murder trial, 86, 87
  commodified bodies of, 63
  conceptual distinctions among, 64
  corralled for hunting, in ancient Egypt, 23, 24, 25
  criminal liability, 95, 96
  with defects, legal treatment of, 76, 77, 78; proscription from being sacrificed, 77, 77nn28, 29; 78
  distinguished from possessions in estate divisions, 63
  domesticated, treatment in biblical law, 71, 182
  as economic resource, 20–23
  in Egyptian legal system, 30–32
  as fundamental to study of antiquity, 195
  Greek and Latin words for, 102, 103, 103n33, 195
  as household members, 42, 42n3, 43
  with human souls by metempsychosis, 95
  and humans, comparable value for sacrifice, 80, 81
  in iconographic material from Egypt, 13
  injured, absence from Roman and Greek legal texts, 92
  interaction with humans, in ancient world, 16
  Jewish, superior to gentile women, 172, 172n40
  killing of, for wrongdoing, 95

208   *Index of Subjects*

animal(s) (*cont.*)
　lack of moral agency, 64, 65
　as lacking reasoning powers, among Romans and Greeks, 88, 89
　and legal reasoning about limits of jurisdiction, 66
　legal status, 177, 178, 180; in ancient Egypt, 13–39
　as living symbols of important concepts, 35, 180
　as manifestations of the deity in ancient Egypt, 27, 28
　and masters, paired for punishment, 193
　mistreatment of, in ancient society, 9, 36, 37
　as mute and dangerous in Akkadian literature, 43
　as naturalizing the social order, 181
　neglect of, ignored in Roman and Greek law, 91, 92, 197
　with personal names, 63
　as personal property, 15, 30, 37, 179
　and personhood (limited, partial), 65–67, 96, 181, 186, 193, 196; in rabbinic categorization, 164, 165
　in Peter's vision (Cornelius story), 107, 108
　in proportional social order, 63
　protection in national constitutions, 2, 3
　as rational agents, 94, 95
　representing people, 106–11, 117
　and rights of children and adults lacking cognition, 3, 4
　serving as substitutes for owners, 85
　in social order, 63, 64
　sociality of, 44
　symbolic function in Mesopotamian law, 180
　symbolic of limits of human rights, 181
　symbolism of, in unregulated spaces, 48, 49, 180
　symbolizing the social order, 181
　treatment on farms and in cities, 91
　as unable to commit *parricidium* or *homicidium*, 87
　as unable to obey laws, 126
　used for entertainment, 9, 23–26, 179
　useful, 20–23, 179
　view of rabbinic authorities, 8
animal cruelty
　in ancient Egypt, 33–37
　animals voicing mistreatment, 33, 34
　depictions of suffering animals in ancient Egypt, 34
　ignored in Roman and Greek law, 91, 92, 197
　violence toward and neglect of animals, 9
animal cults, in ancient Egypt, 26–29
Animal Law
　categories of concern, 15
　courses in law schools, 2
　current international trends, 2, 3
　definition and objectives, 14–16
　See also animal rights
Animal Law Conference, 2
Animal Legal Defense Fund, 2, 14
animal rights, 2, 2n3, 3, 4, 5, 7n20, 7n21, 185
　ancient texts and contemporary discussion of, 9–11
　in ancient world, 185
　domesticated animals, as models for rights among humans, 179
　in France's *Code civil*, 2, 2n2, 15, 185
　in Germany and Switzerland, 3n4
　in Hebrew Bible, 7, 8, 182
　lack of, 3; in ancient philosophers, 96
　lacking in ancient law, 99
animal sacrifice, 132, 134
　ban on, in Codex Theodosianus, 143
　ban on, in Roman Empire, 188
　by Christians, 190
　comparable value of animals and humans for, 80, 81
　contradictory laws on, 144–47
　as floating signifier, 144, 144n2
　and Greek ritual traditions, 129

Index of Subjects   209

as irrational, 191
laws about, and Roman imperial identity, 146
laws against, 11, 125–28, 128n21
laws requiring, 127, 128
and legitimation of power of Roman elites, 158
and maleficent *daimones*, 137
negative position on, in Roman and Greek intellectual history, 151, 152
proof of performance, 144, 144n3
purpose, in ancient Egypt, 36
and religious practices of Roman population, 159
and Roman piety, 148, 190, 191
as working against the life of the philosopher, 185
and Zoroastrian identity, 153
animal trials, 95, 96, 98, 100–103
in ancient Greece, 85, 86
and combining categories of animal and object, 86, 87
for homicide, 86, 92
in medieval England, 92, 93,
and noxal surrender, 97, 98, 191, 192
and personhood, 10, 11
religious explanation for, 96
response to being on trial, 100
animals and slaves, 11, 95, 96, 99, 189
and commission of crimes, 84
legal status, 84
as victims of crimes, in Greek and Roman law, 91
See also slaves
animal/human distinction, as anthropocentric, 177
animality, use of, to dehumanize humans, 65n104
animate beings, as including plants, 121n3
Apis bull, cult of, 27
Aristotle
on animals acting voluntarily, 95
attribution of souls to plants, 121n3
classification of living beings, 177
on lack of reasoning in animals, 95
on retribution for wrongdoing, 93

Asociación de Funcionarios y Abogados por los Derechos de los Animales (Argentina), 2
awīlum, free citizen, 52, 53, 61

B tradition of Acts, concern with commensality, 116, 117, 118
baboons
connection with divine world, 26, 27
mistreatment of, 29
Barnabas, Letter of, on dietary laws, 110, 111, 190
barter system, animals used in, 31
battery, by animals, Greek and Roman law on, 88, 90
bestiality
Jews engaging in, 175, 175n53
and non-Jews, 170–72, 190, 195, 196
sexual activity between human animal and nonhuman animal, 173–75
biblical texts, and status of animals, 6, 7, 8, 69, 71–79
birds
enclosure of, in ancient Egypt, 22
use in ancient Egypt, 20
blood, abstention from, 114–18, 194
blood sports, ignored in Roman and Greek law, 91, 92
Book of the Dead, 34
Book of the Dead of Hunefer, 34
boundaries, legal, marked by symbolism of animals in unregulated spaces, 181
boundary stone, upset by plow animals, in Roman law, 91, 193
burials, of companion animals, 18, 19, 179
butchery, as distinctly Jewish practice, 167

carcass, as improperly slaughtered animal, 166, 166n21
categorization, rabbinic, 162–65
cats and dogs, death of, in ancient Egypt, 17, 18, 19

cattle, use in ancient Egypt, 20, 31, 32
children, rights of, and animals, 3, 4, 44, 67, 71
Christian(s)
   and paganism, 147, 148; position on animal sacrifice, 188
   sacrificial offerings of, 149, 149n50, 150, 159, 160
Christianity
   absence from mention of, in laws banning animal sacrifice in Codex Theodosianus, 158, 158n49
   antisacrificial discourse, and Roman identity, 160
   rise and spread of, and end of animal sacrifice, 145, 159, 160
circumcision, of gentile converts to Christianity, 113, 114
class identity, proportional, 42
class structure, in Mesopotamia, and different levels of personhood, 52, 53, 181
class system, and social proportionality, 60, 61
clean and unclean animals
   and law of firstborn, 74, 75
   sanctified/unsanctified status of, 72
Codex Theodosianus
   and ban on animal sacrifice, 143, 145, 146, 151n24, 154–60, 188, 190
   transformation of meaning of animal sacrifice, 190
Coke, Lord, on legal status of animals in English law and Roman law of noxal surrender, 83, 97
commensality, and eating animals, 111–19, 189
common sense, and animals as akin to humans, 96, 96n23, 97
companion animals, 9, 15, 17–20, 37, 179
   types of, in ancient Egypt, 18
Constantine
   Christianity of, 151
   depicted as performing sacrifice, 151, 194
   dynastic imperial identity of, 152, 152n31, 153, 192
   position on animal sacrifice, 145–47, 150–54, 188, 194
   and religious policies of predecessors, 152
   and Sasanian Empire, 153
   vision of Roman identity, and banning of sacrifice, 158
Contendings of Horus and Seth, 35
corporations
   and animals, in American law, 99
   as legal persons, 98, 99
courtyards, of Jews and non-Jews, legal opinions regarding, 168–70
cows, in Egyptian sales agreements, 32
creation of animals, in Egyptian cosmogony, 26
Critical Animal Studies, 161, 161n1, 162; and rabbinic literature, 161n2
cruelty, to animals. *See* animal cruelty
cultic status, of animals and humans, 80, 81

daimones, beneficent and maleficent, and sacrifice, 134n33, 135, 137, 137n41
damage, by animals, to humans and property, Greek and Roman tradition on, 90, 188
death, animal, and creation of divine beings, 28, 179
Decius, decree on animal sacrifice, 128, 128n21, 144–48, 194; and Roman identity, 148
defect (*mûm*), legal treatment of priests and animals with, 76–78
dehumanization
   and male homoerotic intercourse, 171n36
   of non-Jews, 165–72, 190
   of slaves, 174, 175
Democritus, on killing of animals for wrongdoing, 95
deodand, in American and English law, 97, 98

depraved persons, and ban on animal sacrifice, 155, 157
Derrida, Jacques, on the category "animal," 12, 177, 195
desert, argument of, 125, 140
dietary law, 106–19, 190, 194
Diocletian, and animal sacrifice, 144
divination, association with animals, 156, 157, 196
divine law
   animal sacrifice as violation of, 132
   as morality, 130–33
   as superior to natural law of cities, 130, 131, 132, 133
divine malfeasance, and lack of animal rights, 99
divinities, and demigods, 134, 134n34, 135, 136, 137, 138
dog(s)
   in Mesopotamian literature, 44
   with name inscribed on coffin, 18, 19
   treatment similar to slaves in Greek law, 88
   vicious, noxal surrender of, 88
dolphins, reproducing like humans, 163, 164, 194
domesticated animals
   in ancient texts, 11
   rights of, as model for human rights, 179
   treatment of, 71, 72, 182
donkeys, use in ancient Egypt, 20
Drakon code, and harming animals, 128, 129
ducks, sacrifice of, 35, 36
duty, absence from Porphyry's sense of morality, 133, 139

eating, and propriety of association with persons, 111–19
eating animals, 105, 111, 112, 113, 131, 132
   and community identity, 105, 106
   laws against, 126, 127
Empedocles, on the suffering of animals, 94

'*erub*, rabbinic law concerning, 168, 169
estate, division of, and proportionality, 61, 62
Eusebius, on Constantine and sacrifice, 146, 150, 151, 194
euthanasia, of animals, 98
factory farms, 9, 10, 179
   and sacred animal cult, 27, 28, 179
farm animals, 15
   as personal property, 9, 30, 31, 37
   relation to humans in ancient Egypt, 21, 22
   value in ancient Egypt, 21, 179
Farm Animal Welfare Committee (UK), 15
firstborn, law of
   symmetrical/asymmetrical treatment of humans and animals, 74, 75, 79, 79n33, 183
   treatment of clean and unclean animals, 74
firstborn females, 75, 75n20
firstborn sons, ransoming of, 74
fish, use in ancient Egypt, 20
Five Freedoms, for farm animals, 15
foods, common and/or unclean, 106–9
forced feeding, of birds and cattle, 10, 22, 37
forfeiture, in American law, 98
Fourteenth Amendment, and protection of artificial persons, 99
funerary inscription, for guard dog, 18

Gamaliel, Rabban, blessing on a non-Jewish woman, reason for, 173, 174, 193
geese, in ancient Egypt, 23, 179
gender
   as basis of monetary value of humans and animals, 72, 75
   inequality, 70, 70n4, 78, 81
   and law of firstborn, 74, 75
   and sacrificial animals, 78, 79, 81
Genesis, influence on Common Law of England, 83

gentile, inclusion in Christian community, 113 (*see also* non-Jews)
Global Animal Law Project (Switzerland), 2
god(s)
  and animal trials, 100
  assimilation to, as highest goal in life, 121, 121n2
  highest and lower-level, and animal sacrifice, 152
  metamorphosed into animals, 100
golden rule, 116, 194
good citizens, and the divine/natural law, 131–33

habeas corpus petitions, and legal rights of animals, 3, 3n5
harmful creatures, allowable to control, 122, 122n4
haruspices, 155, 156
heads of households, in Roman and Greek law, 84
ḥērem
  and status of animals and humans, 80, 183
  and symmetrical treatment of humans and animals, 72, 73, 73nn11,12; 74, 79, 182, 183
  and treatment of nonliving things, 73
heretic, slaughter by, as idolatrous, 167
Hermarchus, on lack of reason in animals, 129
Hesiod, on justice/injustice toward animals, 129
homicide
  due to animals, Greek and Roman law on, 90
  trials of animals for, 85
homicidium, in Roman law, 87
hospitality, in Acts, 111–13
household, beings included in, 44, 44n10
household animals, 63, 64
human animal/human beings
  as capable of agency, 165
  dehumanizing, 65n104, 162, 165–72, 174, 175, 190

speaking of and for animals, 12
  and struggle for personhood, 5
  symmetrical treatment with animals, 11, 72–75, 79, 79n33, 182, 183
  treatment in biblical law, 71
human sacrifice, 183
human–dolphin intercourse, 164, 164nn12, 13; 194
hunting
  in ancient Egypt, 23, 24, 25, 179
  as elite/royal activity, 9, 179
hunting parks, in ancient Egypt, 24, 25
hybrid animals, in rabbinic legal tradition, 162, 163, 194
hybris, committed against slave, 92

idol offerings, 115, 116, 118, 194
impiety, link with animal sacrifice, 157, 190, 191
interbreeding, and gestational periods, 163

James (apostle), ruling at Jerusalem Council, 114, 115
Jerusalem Council (Acts 15), 106, 113–17
Jew, as normative human animal, 168, 169, 170, 190
Julian (Roman emperor), program of animal sacrifice, 145
jurisdiction
  legal, and nonurban areas, 50, 51
  and spatial location of animals in Old Babylonian law collections, 47, 48, 49

knowledge, natural and divine, and depiction of animals, 43

language of animals, 126, 127
Lavery (NY State Appeals Court case), 4
law, animal. *See* animal law
laws
  divine and natural, distinction between, 130
  divine and natural, on harming animals and animal sacrifice, 126, 130–33, 139

Index of Subjects 213

limited reach in unregulated spaces, 51, 52
law collections/legal traditions
  biblical, equal/unequal treatment of classes of persons, 70, 71, 182
  biblical, privileged constituencies, 69
  biblical, symmetrical/asymmetrical treatment of humans and animals, 79, 80, 182
  Egyptian, animals in, 30–32
  Egyptian, sources, 30
  Mesopotamian, and animals in space liminal to state power, 42
  Mesopotamian, animals in, 44, 45
  Old Babylonian, social animals in, 45, 45n13
  Old Babylonian, symbolic potential of animals in, 46, 47, 180
  Roman, as moralizing ideology, 154, 154n39
legal animals
  in Mesopotamia, 44–46
  and proportional personhood, 52–66, 181
legal personality, of animals, 98, 99
legal things, animals as, 15, 38, 39
Leviticus, influence on Common Law of England, 83
Lewis & Clark Law School, Center for Animal Studies, 2
Libanius, on Constantine and sacrifice, 150, 150n22, 151, 156, 194
Lion in Search of Man, 33, 39, 180
lions
  hunting of, in ancient Egypt, 23
  metaphorical relationship to lawless people, 50
  in Old Babylonian literary texts, 50

magic, association with animals, 155, 157, 159, 190, 196
males
  as constituting the people of Israel, 70n4
  privileging of, in biblical legal material, 70
mammals, domestic (cattle, ovicaprids), in ancient Egypt, 20

market value, as basis of damages for animal injury, 57
master, responsible for conduct of animal, 87, 91, 193
metempsychosis, 95, 96
mirabilia, done by animals, 93, 94
monetary compensation, for crimes of slaves, 89, 90
monetary valuation, of humans and animals, 71, 72, 80, 80n36
morality, as superior to legislation, 131, 132, 133
mummies
  of companion animals, 19, 179
  and sacred animal cult, 27, 28
muškēnum, commoner, 52, 53, 61
Myth of the Eye of the Sun, 33

natural law, relation to divine law, 130
nocturnal rituals/sacrifice, 155, 156, 157
Nonhuman Rights Project (USA), 2, 3, 4
non-Jews
  as animalistic, 171, 190, 193
  animalization of, 188
  dehumanization of, 162, 165–76
  as lacking self-restraint, 171, 172, 190
  See also Jerusalem Council (Acts 15); Peter and Cornelius story (Acts 10)
normality, criterion of, and noxal surrender, 89
noxal surrender, 96, 193
  as alternative to compensation, 88, 193
  and natural/unnatural behavior of animals, 89
  Roman law of, 83
  and trials of animals, 92, 92n16
numbers, as expressive of divine names, 66n82

offerings
  to divinities and demigods, 135, 136, 137, 137n41, 138, 139
  immaterial, as appropriate for divinities proper, 135–40

Index of Subjects

offerings (*cont.*)
  sacrificial, by Christians, 149, 149n50, 150, 159, 160
omens, interpreting, and banning of animal sacrifice, 155, 156
One Voice (France), 2
Opening of the Mouth ceremony, 28, 35, 179
Origen of Alexandria, zoomorphic hermeneutics of, 109, 110, 111
Orpheus, negative position on animal sacrifice, 152
oxen
  goring, in Old Babylonian law collections, 45, 45n16, 46
  as ideal symbols for limiting discourse about social life, 66
  in proportional social order, 62

paganism, understanding of, 147, 148
parricidium, in Roman law, 87
Paulinus of Nola, on Christian animal sacrifice, 149
pauperies, in Roman law, 87, 90
Pausanias
  combining animal with object in murder trial, 86, 87
  on legal proceedings against animals, 86
personal property, animals as, 9, 15, 30, 31, 37, 179
personhood
  of animals, 4, 5, 10, 11, 52–67, 96, 181, 186, 193, 196
  complete/incomplete, 58
  proportional, of people and animals, 42
Peter and Cornelius story (Acts 10), 105–13
pets, 178
Philip the Arab, dislike of sacrifice, 152n29
philosophers
  abstention from meat, 121
  and animal sacrifice, 125, 126
  and the divine law, 131, 132, 133
  and following natural laws, 133
  guidelines for ritual practices, 134–39, 141

  offerings to offspring of the supreme god, 136, 137, 139
  participation in rituals of a city, 137
  and quest to become like the supreme god, 185
  refraining from harming animals, 121
physical condition, and valuation of animals, 75
physical wholeness, and inequality, 81
piety
  and ancient legal texts about animals, 190
  role of animals in defining, 190, 191, 195
  in Roman legal system, 148
pilgrimages, as obligation for males only, 70
Piye (Nubian king), anger at neglected horses, 19, 20
plants
  harming, 124, 124n14
  incapacity to feel pain, 124
  justice extended to, 122
Plato, on trials of animals for homicide, 85
Plotinus
  on the suffering of animals, 94
  on two kinds of prayer, 136
pollution, in homicidal law in Greece, 85, 86
Porphyry
  on accepting or changing natural laws, 133, 134, 139
  on ancestral laws and customs on animals, 126, 128, 129, 130, 138
  on animal language, 126, 127
  and animal rationality, 123, 124
  guidelines for ritual practices of philosophers, 134–39, 141
  on intrinsic injustice of harming creatures, 124, 125
  on justice for all nonhuman animals and plants, 123, 124, 125, 140
  life of, 123
  on refraining from harming animate beings, 121
  and rejection of animal sacrifice, 10, 152, 184

on requirements of the divine/
natural law, 130, 131, 132
on the suffering of animals, 94
and traditional sacrificial cult, 134,
137, 138
on vegetarianism, 122, 185
prayer
appropriate and illicit, 156, 157
kinds of, in Plotinus, 136
priesthood, male-only, 70, 70n4
priestly privilege, 69
priests, with defects
legal treatment of, 76, 77, 78
sanctified status of, 77
proportionality
and bodily punishment, 62
and commercial value of animals,
53, 54, 55
in family life, 61, 62
beyond juridical literature, 58, 60
of liability for damages to or by
animals, 56, 57
in Old Babylonian laws, 53, 54, 55
of punitive damages to infraction, 56
social, 60, 61
punitive damages, class basis for, 56
pure silence, in Porphyry, 136
pure thought, in Porphyry, 135, 136
purity status, and valuation of animals,
75
Pythagoras
on animals and people becoming
vegetarians, 95
on animals committing murder, 94,
95
on animals with human souls, 95, 96
negative position on animal
sacrifice, 152

rabbinic Other, 162, 165n17, 171
rabbinic texts, animalizing gentiles,
11, 188 (see also under dehumanization)
Rashi, on procreative sex of dolphins,
164
rationality, of animals, 123, 124,
191, 195; Greek philosophers'
position on, 191

reason
animals lacking, 95
animals with, 10
religion, understanding of, in ancient
Mediterranean world, 147,
147n11, 148
resident aliens, treatment in biblical
legal material, 70, 79
rights, animal. *See* animal rights
rituals, and standing as legal persons,
100
Roman identity, and end of animal
sacrifice, 148, 153, 154, 192

Sabbath rest, for animals, 7, 10
sacred animals, mistreatment and
killing of, 29
sacrifice, animal. *See* animal sacrifice
sacrilege, 190
sales contracts, animals in, in ancient
Egypt, 32
Santería, 160
scapegoats, animals as, 93
self-defence, against animals, as
allowable, 121, 122n4, 129
sentience, of animals, 15, 124, 124n13,
140, 185
as criterion for justice, 124, 124n13,
140
in Porphyry, 184
in Sumerian literature, 43
sexual intercourse
with a dolphin, 164, 164nn12, 13;
194
with a female slave, 175, 175n52
in front of a living creature, 174
silence and pure thought, as appropriate offering to supreme god,
135, 135n35, 136, 139, 140, 185
slaughter, of animals
by an ape, 167
by a gentile, 165–68
valid rabbinic, requirements for,
165–67
slavery, American, 54
slaves
association with donkeys, 174,
174n51, 175

216 Index of Subjects

slaves (*cont.*)
   dehumanization of, 174, 175
   noxal surrender of, 87, 89
   and proportional class identity, 42
   and proportionality in Old Babylonian laws, 54, 55, 56
   See also animals and slaves
social beings, as commercially valuable, 44
social status, and commercial valuation, 56
sociality, of animals, 44
space
   nonurban, and laws about animals, 42
   unregulated, laws about animals in, 46–52
spatiality, and ancient imaginings about animals, 196
Stoics, and animal rationality, 123, 124, 127
strangled things, abstention from, 114–16, 118, 194
strangulation, of animals, prohibition of, 116, 117
substitution and subordination, and status of animals, 96, 97
suffering, of animals, 5, 15, 94, 180, 197
   in classical literature, 92
Sumerian literature, talking animals in, 43
superstitio, and banning of animal sacrifice, 155, 156, 157, 159, 191
symbolism
   of animals in bordering spaces, 48, 49, 180
   of people in unregulated areas, 51
symmetry/asymmetry, in treatment of persons and animals, 11, 72–75, 79, 79n33, 182, 183
   in biblical narrative texts, 184

talking animals, 63, 66, 92; in Sumerian literature, 43
Taro, "the death-row dog," 187, 188
Theodosian Code. *See* Codex Theodosianus

Theodosius II, 143, 154
Theophrastus
   on illegality of sacrificing animals, 125
   on intrinsic injustice of harming creatures, 124
   negative position on animal sacrifice, 152
The Trial of Farmer Carter's Dog Porter, for Murder, 100–103
trials, of animals. *See* animal trials
Triptolemus, on not harming animals, 128

Ulpian
   on animals as devoid of reasoning, 88
   on *pauperies* in Roman law, 87
value, sacrificial, of animals and humans, 80, 81
vegetarianism, 122, 159
vegetarians, animals and people as, 95
virtual animals, 193, 196
virtue, and requirements for following divine/natural law, 131, 132

wardum, slave, 52, 61
whole/defective distinction, and symmetrical/asymmetrical treatment of animals and humans, 78
wild animals
   tethering and beating of, in ancient Egypt, 25, 26
   treatment in Roman law, 90, 91
wild bulls, hunting of, in ancient Egypt, 23, 24
women
   gentile, Jewish animal superior to, 172, 172n40
   Rabban Gamaliel's blessing on a non-Jewish, 173, 174, 193
   secondary social status, 70, 70n4

zoomorphism, 109, 110, 111, 192, 193

www.ingramcontent.com/pod-product-compliance
Lightning Source LLC
Chambersburg PA
CBHW031356230426
43670CB00006B/557